Philip Hale

A Doctrinal Exposition of Galatians:

A Sermonic Commentary for Laymen

Originally Recorded as Audio in 15 hours
October 2014
for
KNNA 95.7 The Cross
Good Shepherd Lutheran Church, Lincoln, Nebraska

PUBLISHED BY MERCINATOR PRESS

MERCINATORPRESS@GMAIL.COM

14205 Ida St.
Omaha NE 68142

Cover Illustration: "Law and Gospel" by Lucas Cranach

Philip Hale.
    A Doctrinal Exposition of Galatians: A Sermonic Commentary for Laymen

    Mercinator Press
    Includes bibliographical references.
    ISBN: 978-0-9975197-3-0

Contents

Translation of Cover Verses

(based on NKJV)

Top Front:

Is. 7:14 – *The Lord Himself will give you a sign: Behold, the virgin shall conceive and bear a Son*

Top Back:

Rom. 1:18 – *The wrath of God is revealed from heaven against all ungodliness and unrighteousness of men*

Bottom: (starting from the Law on left of the back cover moving to the Gospel on the front cover)

Rom. 3:23 – *All have sinned and fall short of the glory of God*

1 Cor. 15:56 – *The sting of death is sin, and the strength of sin is the law*

Rom. 4:15 – *The law brings wrath*

Rom. 3:20 – *Through the law is the knowledge of sin*

Mt. 11:13 – *All the prophets and the law prophesied until John*

Gal. 5:6 – *In Christ Jesus neither circumcision nor uncircumcision avails anything, but faith working through love*

Jn. 1:6 – *Behold! The Lamb of God who takes away the sin of the world!*

1 Pet. 1:2 – *Through sanctification of the Spirit, for obedience and sprinkling of the blood of Jesus Christ*

1 Cor. 15:54-55, 57 – *Death is swallowed up in victory; "O Death, where is your sting? O Hades, where is your victory?" But thanks be to God, who gives us the victory through our Lord Jesus Christ*

Introduction

Galatians is different from the other epistles of Paul; it is the most passionate and intense of his letters. While it addresses a historical situation, the assumption here is that it is just as relevant and applicable to the people of this day. But the addressees of this letter and their situation do affect the tone and language of this Word of God. While it would be interesting to figure out the specifics of their historical situation, the simple fact is that the Spirit who authored Scripture gave us all that we need to know for salvation—though not enough to satisfy our curiosity. Therefore, we will stick to the words we have been given and not attempt to go behind, around, or under them. The actual scriptural words must be the starting point and foundation for a faithful reading of the text.

The Word of God is timeless. We do not have to put ourselves in the place of the ancient Galatians to understand this letter from Paul. The Word of God gives salvation, so it is also addressed to you and all people. So this commentary will not interpret Galatians as a historical document that has to be made relevant, but as the always contemporary Word of God—addressing *your* problems, issues, and world. This method is not popular among scholars today, but it is what the Scriptures themselves do. This interpretation will stick closely to the words (and their meanings) which comprise this bold and fiery letter on the center of Christianity and the Gospel.

This commentary is meant to lead into the text, not out of it. It aims to address what the text actually says, not what scholars or curious people wish it would have said. Unlike modern scholarly commentaries, this is not a strictly exegetical work. It desires to pay careful attention to the original Greek text to explain, apply, sermonize, and provide doctrinal and devotional meat—all at a layman's level. It tries to leave aside issues which the text does not make clear or actually address. Instead, the words of Scripture itself are the guide to how we are to think and do theology. Therefore, this commentary is really meant to be a positive companion and help to an actual study of the text. This commentary requires the biblical text to be open, side-by-side, with it. Since it was originally recorded for a radio program, it is somewhat informal and meant to be easily understood, though theologically meaty enough to challenge.

This commentary is organized by verse numbers, with each new verse expected to be read indicated in the text by the bolded verse number, "[v1]," for example. This bolded indicator starts the discussion on a new verse. The header on each page has the last chapter and verse discussed on that page for easy reference. Verses quoted from a translation are italicized. Translation of phrases in quotes are my own. Passages cited from an English translation are from the ESV, unless otherwise noted, but any fairly literal translation of Galatians can be used with this guide.

Bible Abbreviations

ESV – English Standard Version

KJ21 – 21st Century King James Version

KJV – King James Version

MRINT – Mounce Reverse-Interlinear New Testament

NIV – New International Version (2011)

NKJV – New King James Version

OJB – Orthodox Jewish Bible

YLT – Young's Literal Translation

Chapter 1

Unlike most letters today, this epistle starts with its author, in this case, Paul. [v1] Next, in v2, we are given the addressees: the people of Galatia, a region which had become part of the Roman Empire. These Greek speaking people—this letter of Paul was written in Greek—are mentioned several times in Acts. In fact, Paul founded these churches. But false doctrine had entered immediately after he left. Satan hates the pure doctrine and continually attacks those who rest their hearts on Christ's death and resurrection. All the scriptural epistles warn of this danger and speak of the diligence needed to remain in the true faith, which the Spirit works through the Word of Christ. So, Paul is not engaging in an intellectual discussion, but is saving souls from hell—from teaching which turns one away from the true God. In the parable of the seed, we read that where the Word of God goes out, there Satan is, ready to pounce and disrupt God's work. *When anyone hears the word of the kingdom and does not understand it, the evil one comes and snatches away what has been sown in his heart. This is what was sown along the path* (Mt. 13:19).

While the author is normally the first word of an epistle like this one, the second word in v1 immediately starts the main content. No words are wasted with a generic greeting. Paul might sound a little self-centered, since he talks about himself. But it will become clear that he is establishing his divine office and calling from Christ, since he was being challenged by false teachers. In fact, most of the first two chapters are a self-defense of Paul's apostleship.

Compare this greeting to Paul's other epistles. Some read, "Paul, an apostle by the will of God," as in Ephesians. That greeting is quite short and to the point. Others, like Philippians, read only "Paul, [a] servant" (along with Timothy who is also an "author," because he acts as Paul's secretary). 1 and 2 Thess. only have simple greetings, with no defense of Paul's apostleship. In Philemon, Paul calls himself only a "prisoner," which also reveals the subject of the letter—the escaped slave Onesimus.

Romans 1 has a strong defense of his calling by God, but it is not as defensive as here in Galatians ("not from man"):

> *Paul, a servant* [same Greek word for slave] *of Christ Jesus, called to be an apostle, set apart for the gospel of God, which he promised beforehand through his prophets in the holy Scriptures, concerning his Son, who was descended from David according to the flesh and was declared to be the Son of God in power according to the Spirit of holiness by his resurrection from the dead, Jesus Christ our Lord, through whom we have received grace and apostleship to bring about the obedience of faith for the sake of his name among all the nations, including you who are called to belong to Jesus Christ, To all those in Rome who are loved by God and called to be saints.*

The contrast Paul makes in Galatians is unique. He pits all men against Christ. Since Paul is an apostle not from man or though man, he is including himself. He did not chose himself to be a preacher—it was a duty laid upon him by Christ. We read about his calling in Acts 9:

> *But Saul, still breathing threats and murder against the disciples of the Lord, went to the high priest and asked him for letters to the synagogues at Damascus, so that if he found any belonging to the Way, men or women, he might bring them bound to Jerusalem. Now as he went on his way, he approached Damascus, and suddenly a light from heaven shone around him. And falling to the ground he heard a voice saying to him, "Saul, Saul, why are you persecuting me?" And he said, "Who are you, Lord?" And he said, "I am Jesus, whom you are persecuting."*

Ananias, a Christian in Damascus—Paul's destination when Christ confronted him on the road—was told to go to Paul, despite his unsavory reputation. It says in Acts 9: *Go, for he is a chosen instrument of mine to carry my name before the Gentiles and kings and the children of Israel. For I will show him how much he must suffer for the sake of my name.* Paul preaches because God told him to preach. The Lord called him to this special office. It is too lofty of calling for him to do it on his own; it must be God's will. *For if I preach the gospel, that gives me no ground for boasting. For necessity is laid upon me. Woe to me if I do not preach the gospel!* (1 Cor. 9:16).

What is this office? The pastoral office which Paul was put into is basically the same one God supplies to His church today. The major difference is that pastors are not chosen directly by God as they were in apostolic times—either by Jesus Himself in His state of humiliation (the 12 disciples) or by the ascended Christ (Paul). Rom. 1:1 says that Paul was *called to be an apostle, set apart for the gospel of God,* which means he was marked and separated from other men by the Lord. "Not from men nor through man," speaks of the divinity of the call. Paul's call is from God directly, not even through the Church or Christians. God works today, though, through the means of people—the Church.

To be in the preaching office still requires a divine call, but God does it through the congregation. Feeling a call in the heart or desiring one internally is not the same as the public call from God that all can point to and know that it is sure and certain. For example, Paul in Tit. 1:5 directs Titus, a pastor, to chose qualified men: *This is why I left you in Crete, so that you might put what remained into order, and appoint elders in every town as I directed you.* An "elder" here is not what we call a layman "elder" today, but an overseer or pastor, called by God. All pastors today are called through men, unlike Paul, to shepherd God's flock. Even this mediated call is divine, since it is a holy office designed by God. No one should preach because they want to or like it, but because they are commanded by God. In the words of one theologian: "If there is no divine call, preaching is a fiendish temptation for those who preach and those who hear" [Maurer, 192].

The special office of preaching, the public ministry of the Word, is setup by Christ. This troubles many Christians today who believe rightly that all people are saved by faith and have the same inheritance from God. Paul does not claim any special status before God, but only before men in his duty of preaching. He defends his apostleship because of the words he must speak. The office makes the proclaimed Word necessary to be honored and less easily dismissed. This is nothing like priests in the Old Testament, who mediated between the people and God. Christ is the true and only priest for us, who offered Himself as the eternal sacrifice for trespasses, earning freedom for all from the slavery

5

of sin.

Paul declares himself an apostle. The word "apostle" means "one who is sent." The sender here is the holy God. He mentions Christ, but also the Father, since they are together with the Spirit one God. What Paul does is not self-chosen; it is not a hobby or something he can give up. He was commissioned by God to this role of proclaiming Christ. So the Word he proclaims cannot be dismissed, since he is God's ambassador. To ignore his preaching would be to dismiss the call of the holy Christ. This is why Paul clings so strongly to his special call to be an apostle, because Christ knows how Satan hates to see His Word going out.

The term "apostles" generally refers to the ones Christ chose after His ascension. Before then they were called disciples (learners), who actually did not do much. The apostles are generally considered the twelve minus Judas, plus Matthias and Paul. Paul is the most special case.

In 1 Cor. 15:3–9, Paul relates that he was a witness to the resurrection of Christ from the dead, just not in the same way as the other apostles. Thus, he could testify as a firsthand witness. That account lists all the witnesses of this historical event, which proves that Christ's sacrifice was accepted, and the world was absolved from sin.

> For I delivered to you as of first importance what I also received: that Christ died for our sins in accordance with the Scriptures, that [Jesus] was buried, that he was raised on the third day in accordance with the Scriptures, and that he appeared to Kephas, then to the twelve. Then he appeared to more than five hundred brothers at one time, most of whom are still alive, though some have fallen asleep. Then he appeared to James, then to all the apostles. Last of all, as to one untimely born, he appeared also to me. For I am the least of the apostles, unworthy to be called an apostle, because I persecuted the church of God.

Though humanly speaking, Paul is the least of the apostles, from the very first verse of Galatians he puts himself on the same level as the other apostles, which is shown to be a major theme of this letter. However, it is the teaching we have in the Holy Scriptures that matters. Paul is proving his authority to speak on the risen Christ's behalf. Paul is not a fly-by-night people-pleaser. The Father who raised Jesus from the dead, God the Father, authorized Paul's words and office. That is the ultimate claim: "Listen up, hear well these words, they are from God and I speak on His behalf. If you hear me, you hear God." God wants us to be sure of the teaching we hear and believe, so He gives the Church called servants as a special comfort, to impress upon us the importance of His Word. There can be no higher earthly calling. The one who has the power of life and death and accepted the sacrifice of Christ stands behind this persecuted and unimpressive Paul.

Paul recounts his calling and conversion to King Agrippa near the end of his ministry in Acts 26:

> *In this connection I journeyed to Damascus with the author-*
> *ity and commission of the chief priests. At midday, O king,*
> *I saw on the way a light from heaven, brighter than the sun,*
> *that shone around me and those who journeyed with me. And*
> *when we had all fallen to the ground, I heard a voice saying*
> *to me in the Hebrew language, "Saul, Saul, why are you*
> *persecuting me? It is hard for you to kick against the goads."*
> *And I said, "Who are you, Lord?" And the Lord said, "I am*
> *Jesus whom you are persecuting. But rise and stand upon*
> *your feet, for I have appeared to you for this purpose, to*
> *appoint you as a servant and witness to the things in which*
> *you have seen me and to those in which I will appear to you,*
> *delivering you from your people and from the Gentiles—to*
> *whom I am sending you to open their eyes, so that they may*
> *turn from darkness to light and from the power of Satan to*
> *God, that they may receive forgiveness of sins and a place*
> *among those who are sanctified by faith in me."*

Why all the fuss about Paul's direct call to teach Christ? Because the false teachers did not have it. They were infiltrating the very churches Paul founded and undoing his work. They evidently made special claims about their authority and experience, so Paul blasts them right from the beginning of this letter and demolishes their arguments. A similar defense of Paul's authority is made in 2 Cor. 12:11: *For I was not at all inferior to these super-apostles, even though I am nothing.* But the false teachers sent themselves; they were not called by God. It is not enough to know Christian doctrine and want the office, God Himself must place the man there. This is how God desires to work among us still today. Paul boasts of his immediate calling from God the Father and Christ Jesus. Without this teaching of the call, who would dare to speak for God and wage war against Satan? It is a weighty office, so God gives His ministers the comfort of the divine call.

A boast in the call is a boast in God's own work. *Pay careful attention to yourselves and to all the flock, in which the Holy Spirit has made you overseers, to care for the church of God, which he obtained with his own blood* (Acts 20:28). There are no apostles today—that time has long since passed. Now God does not call immediately or directly. Still, God saves by the Word. He chooses men to speak His Word and feed His sheep.

What separates an apostle from a pastor today who also has the preaching office? Eph. 2:20–21 speaks of Christians who are *built on the foundation of the apostles and prophets, Christ Jesus himself being the cornerstone, in whom the whole structure, being joined together, grows into a holy temple in the Lord.*

In a real way, the apostles established the Church, by preaching to the people who may have heard Jesus originally, but heard differently after the giving of the Holy Spirit at Pentecost. Then Paul was sent to the Gentiles. Several of the apostles in this first generation (after Jesus ascended in power to fill all things) also wrote what we have today as the New Testament (the Gospels and the Epistles). They recorded what they knew and saw of the God who became man for us in words the Spirit gave. Jesus could easily come to us like He did to Paul, but He instead directs us to His Word, proclaimed by sinful men who were called by Him to preach this saving Gospel.

If the defense of Paul's apostleship is omitted, the opening greeting reads: *Paul . . . and all the brothers who are with me . . . to the churches of Galatia.* [v2] This is quite an interesting phrase: *and all the brothers who are with me.* Paul is including all his "brothers" with him as authors and witnesses, as if they are backing him and writing this letter with him. This is the only epistle in which he does this. Paul's passion for the truth and his anger at the false teaching in Galatia will become even more evident. He is not writing his personal opinion, but confessing the truth with the support of the whole Church, on behalf of God Himself. Ultimately these words are speaking to us as well.

Unlike other epistles of Paul, this letter is written to multiple churches or congregations in the specific region of Galatia. Timothy, who later becomes a prominent associate of Paul, is actually from this area. He is from the area of Derbe, Lystra, and Iconium—which we take as churches of Galatia, to whom Paul is writing. How many others and how far it was distributed, we are not told.

When we hear the word "church," we may think of a building or a synod or a denomination. But in the New Testament, "church" is the assembly of believers united in doctrine in an area who gather together around God's Word. There is one true Church, the invisible Church which consists of all believers in Christ. Yet, there are many churches or congregations, so-called because of the believers that exist there (though there are also hypocrites, who we leave to God to weed out). Paul speaks of expelling the unrepentant, public sinner from the congregation in 1 Cor. 5. But Paul assumes that those in the congregation not denying their confessed faith by their actions are saints—that is, holy in the risen Christ, by virtue of His Word. Despite various doctrinal problems, Paul calls his addressees "saints"—that is, part of the true Church—at the beginning of his epistles to the Romans, Corinthians, and Ephesians. But here in Galatians he is not so forward. He does not use the term "saints," though he does still call them "churches."

There could have been a delegation or letter from Galatia sent to Paul to ask him to resolve this conflict, though the text does not say how he came to know of the problems in the Galatian churches. He does speak with some knowledge of the false teachers' doctrine, methods, and motives.

Evidently, the error was not isolated to a single congregation, but spread throughout the whole region. Like yeast or an infection, false doctrine spreads rapidly. True doctrine takes years of patient teaching, but it can be undone in short order. *Do you not know that a little leaven leavens the whole lump?* That saying, from 1 Cor. 5:6, is also found in this letter (5:9). A small impurity in doctrine infects the whole thing, that is, it goes everywhere else. If unchecked, it harms others in the fellowship and it also infects all other doctrines.

Though the Galatians have been led astray, they are still called "churches," because some undoubtedly still believe. They have heard the true word of God, even if it is under attack at the time Paul is writing. Indeed, the truth must be persecuted: *for there must be factions among you in order that those who are genuine among you may be recognized* (1 Cor. 11:19).

[v3] After the author and recipients are named, there is a greeting in vv3–5, which is typical of Greco-Roman letters, excepting Paul's

defense of his divine calling.

He does not praise the Galatians like he does congregations in most of his other epistles. His displeasure is evident.

Grace and Peace—these are the goal of Paul's epistle. He wants them to be sure of what they have—God's favor, that is, that He loves and holds nothing against His people. This is not because of anything we have done, but because of Jesus' loving self-sacrifice unto death. *Through him we have also obtained access by faith into this grace in which we stand, and we rejoice in hope of the glory of God* (Rom. 5:2).

The peace Paul offers here is in Christ—to know that God the Father is not our enemy. Our sins are not seen or considered. He does not hold anything bad you have done against you, but offers you His love. This peace is with God Himself. It is not inside you or worldly—in your dealings with other people. We are not told we will have no problems, but that God's Spirit will support us in our temptation. The angel's song in Lk. 2, right after the birth of Christ, describes this peace we have in Him: *Glory to God in the highest, and on earth peace among those with whom he is pleased!* To have God pleased with you and be certain of it is the highest gift one can have. It trumps comfortable days and great riches.

Christians are promised more troubles than unbelievers. *Through many tribulations we must enter the kingdom of God* (Acts 14:22). But if we are at peace with God, all is able to be endured, even the worst situations on earth. We have already been delivered from the present evil age. The Word rescues and Baptism bestows God's righteousness and favor upon us. Faith is being sure of this new status before the Father in Christ, and only because of Christ. This is the Gospel Paul defends in this letter to the Galatians.

As with the testimony to Christ's resurrection in v1, here we see the content and truth of the Gospel put forth. If Christ did not rise, our faith is useless, all preaching is vain, and this letter would be lies (1 Cor. 15). No one would believe in a dead Christ, but only in one who is alive and is true God. He is Lord, a proper title expressing Jesus' divinity. A confession that this man is God is foundational in Scripture. *If you confess with your mouth that Jesus is Lord and believe in your heart that God raised him from the dead, you will be saved* (Rom. 10:9). Our Lord's resurrection, which Paul already laid out in v1, leads to this confession of faith, which connects the Christ who was born and lived in this present evil age with the eternal God. Our God is not an anonymous man upstairs or unfeeling power. He has been through suffering and knows your temptations and fears. He truly gave Himself for your sins, to save you—all of you.

[**v4**] Here it speaks of Jesus Christ, *who gave himself for our sins to deliver us from the present evil age.* The necessity of Jesus' death is due to sin. Not sin in the abstract, but our sin, that is, also your sin. What is sin? Rebelling against God and failing to love Him. No matter how hard we try to be good and obey the commandments (written on our heart), we do not live up to God's standard. We are unrighteous and deserving of eternal punishment. The Gospel which saves gives Jesus' righteousness. He gave Himself willingly for us.

Right away, Christ's righteousness is contrasted to man's sins, because of which there is no true righteousness in us. Our sins are great. This teaching of sin is necessary to preserve the value of Christ's death. If there is something good in us, we do not need the Savior's blood to cover us entirely. The guilt of our sin drives us to Christ Jesus, who is the answer to every transgression against the divine Law. *If we confess our sins, he is faithful and just to forgive us our sins and to cleanse us from all unrighteousness* (1 Jn. 1:9).

Sins are not just those of believers—though we are to see our sins as dead, because they rested on the man of sin, Christ—the sins of all the world are atoned for. But those who do not trust in Christ for forgiveness are rejecting what He earned for them. They remain outside of Jesus. There is nothing we have to do for this righteousness. All that is needed is this Word, which tells us that we are rescued and that our sins are of no consequence to the Father.

Why did Jesus do this? *To deliver us from the present evil age.* The Greek word translated as "deliver" is stronger than the English suggests. It can mean "to tear out" or "remove" in the active sense. It can even mean "choose" or "pick out of." We were plucked out of the way of life leading only to destruction—we had nothing to do with it, it was all Christ.

With this phrase God dismisses everything about this age or era. The Greek word for age ("aion") is equivalent to our word "aeon." It means a definite period of time.

By talking of a present evil aeon or age, Paul limits corruption and sin. All the filth in the world and in our flesh will not last that long. A blessed eternity has been promised. Those in Christ cannot die. He said: *everyone who lives and believes in me shall never die* (Jn. 11:26).

The word for "evil" here can also mean "wicked," "useless," "unprofitable," or "unserviceable." All of man's work is fruitless by itself. That is why Christ came to give His life. Without God's intervention, all man's actions, no matter how good they seem, end in death. Even our most careless words and thoughts condemn us. *The good person out of his good treasure brings forth good, and the evil person out of his evil treasure brings forth evil. I tell you, on the day of judgment people will give account for every careless word they speak, for by your words you will be justified, and by your words you will be condemned* (Mt. 12).

There is only one way of escape from the frustration of this fallen age: Christ, who rose from the dead. That author of evil, Satan, is called the evil one. In the Lord's Prayer, "deliver us from evil" could be translated "And deliver us from the evil one," meaning Satan. He is the original cause of sin and the one who still afflicts our world and attacks faith in Christ.

Christ did not pray for us to leave this sinful world, but to be protected and remain in Him until we are taken home: *I have given them your word, and the world has hated them because they are not of the world, just as I am not of the world. I do not ask that you take them out of the world, but that you keep them from the evil one* (Jn. 17:11–15). In Him we have overcome all sin.

One of the strongest statements of Satan's power and rule is in 2 Cor. 4:4, where he is called *the god of this world*. His influence here is established, but our citizenship is not in the world. We reside here, but belong to Christ.

The same word used in the plural (ages or aeons) is used for eternity in Scripture. In 1 Timothy 1:17, we have a little doxology: *To the King of the ages, immortal, invisible, the only God, be honor and glory forever and ever. Amen.* It is a different way to express that God encompass all times. In English we have the word "eternity," which expresses an abstract concept we cannot really comprehend.

Whatever we suffer now is temporary. We should not be surprised at difficulty or suffering. Jesus gave Himself not to improve our lot in this world just a little bit, but to completely rescue us from this evil world. He gives us much better than we could ever expect in this Gospel. *The world is passing away along with its desires, but whoever does the will of God abides forever* (1 Jn. 2:17). Our attention is drawn from the fading cares of this world to a better inheritance. We reside in this promise and have this forgiveness now, which is salvation. Apart from this Gospel there is nothing but evil, no matter how glittery and bright it looks.

Salvation is not merely leaving this world or only something in the future. Christ has already given Himself. Your redemption is a past action—it is final and completed. This gives complete certainty now. The Father is pleased with us, since our sins are dead, having been nailed to the cross of Christ.

All this is *according to the will of our God and Father*. This is not from our will, which can only sin and lead away from the holy God. God's loving will took definite action to remedy our evil situation and deeds. This is not just factual information, but the bedrock of our hope.

Paul concludes the introduction with a small doxology: [**v5**] "Forever and ever" in Greek is "into ages and ages" or "into aeons and aeons." There is no end to His glory. God is above time, but the Son graciously entered time to save us. He sends out the Gospel in our time, so we may hear and believe. This plan of redemption naturally leads to a plan of choosing people out of this world to know Him. Therefore, we can be certain that the calling of the Gospel is real and can be relied upon.

What is God's will? That can be a satanic question. We want to know what God is doing or what we should do in very specific situations, but we usually ask it about things God does not reveal to us in Scripture. Trying to guess or divine God's hidden thoughts is most dangerous. He does not want us to ask "why," but to trust in His gracious will, so that we know His will is good. He sent Jesus to die in our place, to deliver us *according to the will of our God and Father*. If we hear this will of God and trust it, we need nothing else. Our biggest questions are answered in Christ. We can certainly trust Him in day-to-day trials, because now we know God as Father through His Son's self-giving. Sin is no more to the Father, or for us in faith.

"Amen" comes from the Hebrew, like "hallelujah." It is not a translation, but a transliteration, so that it remains in the Hebrew language.

The root of this Hebrew word means "true" or "faithful." It can be a formula of acquiescence. That is exactly how we use it today: to assent to, assert, and concur with a prayer or positive statement of faith. It used to be common to sing "Amen" after hymns which declare the grand scriptural doctrine. It expresses belief and confidence in the truth stated. It is not just a throw-away word, but a statement of faith that casts out all doubt. Amen means, "So be it, since it is true."

When speaking of our Lord, Paul does not dissect the Gospel, but praises the author of it. This doxology, or word of praise, conveys the nature of God as the only One to be called upon in faith and praised. He is truly our Father who art in heaven.

After this introduction and heavenly praise, which also gives the content of the Gospel and the basis for eternal hope, the matter at hand is addressed. [v6] The Galatians are the subject of this harsh letter. Paul minces no words—he expresses shock and disappointment at what is going on amongst them. By changing the eternal Gospel, they were deserting the true Christ.

The first word in the original text is "Amazed." The occasion for this letter is no minor issue. There is no question, but only a bold statement. In effect, Paul says, "what have you done?" They are *deserting him who called you*. They did not leave Paul—he merely spoke the words of Christ. They are leaving Christ and, therefore, eternal life. What can be worse? They are changing their loyalty to someone or something else.

Not only are they deserting the Author of Life, they are doing so rapidly. It seems that Paul had left them not too long ago. Right away everything went wrong. It is easy to find fault in congregations and church leaders, but Satan infects everything in this world. Thankfully, the Gospel does not depend on Christians, but Christ. We are to close our eyes and hear God speak, even if our congregation seems full of complete sinners—and it is. It should be Christ's righteousness that is offered, not the holiness of people who truly need the gift of righteousness.

Paul is speaking as a father to a rebellious child. He is displeased, but he cannot fix the problem for them. He seeks to win the various Galatian churches over with his words. He wants to win them to his side, not just force them to obey his dictates, so that they have faith in Christ. Since he had first preached the Gospel and laid the foundation of faith, he acts and talks as a spiritual father. He says to the Corinthians:

For though you have countless guides in Christ, you do not have many fathers. For I became your father in Christ Jesus through the gospel (1 Cor. 4:15). He describes himself as a mother in birthing pains later in Galatians (4:19).

What is the Gospel? We call the four books at the beginning of the New Testament the Gospels: Matthew, Mark, Luke, and John. They give historical accounts of Jesus' earthly life, along with varying amounts of interpretation. All four are inspired accounts from different vantage points of the same time period and person (Jesus), so they agree. "Gospel" in Mk. 1:1 is used in a wider sense—not just what saves, but the actions and teaching of Jesus, even when he condemned: *The beginning of the gospel of Jesus Christ, the Son of God.* Paul is using Gospel in a much narrower sense here.

By "Gospel," Paul means the teaching that applies Christ's righteousness and changes our status before God. It is this basic teaching and power which saves. There is only one. The "Gospels" (the biblical books) include not just that justifying teaching which forgives sins and rescues from hell, but also the miracles and words of Jesus' teaching. One can know those facts and not believe them. "Gospel" for Paul means what translates into God's Kingdom, in contrast to the power of the Law. The Law is revealed by God, but does not strictly save, though it has a rightful place in every Christian church. Paul, on the other hand, has in mind with his definition of Gospel that which creates faith in Christ and reveals and apprehends God's good will and eternal salvation. Rom. 1:16 definitively states: *For I am not ashamed of the gospel, for it is the power of God for salvation to everyone who believes, to the Jew first and also to the Greek.* "Gospel" for Paul gives salvation and is itself salvation for the believer. It is the specific power of God to remove sins in heaven, causing the sinner to be clean in faith.

While moderns often use the Gospel (narrow sense) iconoclastically against other aspects of Scripture, such as morality, the commands of God, and historical details, that is a misuse of it. Those things are scriptural and given by God for our comfort and strength. But without the Gospel, which brings Christ and eternal life, they are worthless to us. With Christ in the Gospel, they give us a fuller understanding, and do not harm faith or Christian living, but promote them.

The Old Testament ceremonies and civil laws do not apply to us, but having them and knowing how they relate to Christ is very valuable, as long as they are not used against Christ. This is not the situation in Galatia. Paul speaks very harshly against those who make circumcision necessary for salvation, but in Rom. 3, where the saving Gospel is not under attack, he speaks of its positive value: *Then what advantage has the Jew? Or what is the value of circumcision? Much in every way. To begin with, the Jews were entrusted with the oracles of God. What if some were unfaithful? Does their faithlessness nullify the faithfulness of God? By no means! Let God be true though every one were a liar, as it is written.* Every word that comes from God (even seemingly obscure historical facts) is useful and given by the Spirit. In no way should the Gospel be pitted against other revelations of the one, true God.

For Christ did not send me to baptize but to preach the gospel, and not with words of eloquent wisdom, lest the cross of Christ be emptied of its power (1 Cor. 1:17). Paul's definition of "Gospel" leads to faith, not mere intellectual knowledge. What can be known without changing the heart or creating faith is not the Gospel proper. 1 Thess. 1:5 reads, *our gospel came to you not only in word, but also in power and in the Holy Spirit and with full conviction.* All of Scripture can be studied, known, and memorized by unbelievers. That is not why the Scriptures were given, though. As the apostle John wrote in chapter 20 of his Gospel, or account, of Jesus, *Now Jesus did many other signs in the presence of the disciples, which are not written in this book; but these are written so that you may believe that Jesus is the Christ, the Son of God, and that by believing you may have life in his name.*

The Gospel is more than information, a call to action, or a plea to dedicate yourself to God: in it, God calls you into His kingdom and actually brings you into it. He gives the Spirit, who changes our hearts of stone, so we may trust in Christ and find our righteousness in Him. That is why Paul does not spend time attacking the Galatians with moral virtues—they cannot save no matter how diligent we are in keeping them. He does not focus just on the problem (our sins), but on the solution, the Gospel.

To listen to a different gospel is to leave Christ. The pure doctrine must be defended and error resisted, because only the one Gospel of Christ delivers from sins here in time. To be careless about the Gospel and desert it is to leave Christ. It is to turn your back on God Himself.

This rebellion is certain death, as stated in v6.

"A different or another Gospel"—what devastating words. While they sound neutral, Paul is making the point there can be no other, so they are leaving the true Christ and turning to a false god. Since they are deserting the one who calls in grace, they are leaving Christ and turning to falsehood.

"Deserting" here means changing one's state and turning from Christ. The Galatians were still religious, outwardly faithful, and thought they still were fine Christians. But outward works do not make the believer, only the Word of Christ can. So Paul blasts them and starts out this passionate defense of the Gospel with this: "You are turning your back on Christ." They have reached a crossroads and Paul is imploring them with heavenly wisdom to remain faithful to Christ by rejecting this false Galatian gospel.

Paul uses the present tense, "you are turning or deserting." They are leaving Christ, yet they have not left Him completely. They can still put down their error and return to what they were first taught. This is hard for the world to hear, which knows only of progress and improvement. To go back to where we started and repent is an admission that we have sinned against God. As Luther said in the 95 Theses: "the Christian life is one of repentance." It is a continual turning from our sin to Christ who gave Himself on behalf of our sins.

Paul is a great teacher and pastor. He is not just a nice guy who tells people what they want to hear. He says in his first letter to the Corinthians: *What do you wish? Shall I come to you with a rod, or with love in a spirit of gentleness?* (4:21). Paul gives his parishioners exactly what they need. In the words of the Early Church theologian Chrysostom: "For always to address one's disciples with mildness, even when they need severity is not the part of a teacher but it would be the part of a corrupter and enemy. Wherefore our Lord too, though He generally spoke gently to His disciples, here and there uses sterner language, and at one time pronounces a blessing, at another a rebuke."

We need to have our sin exposed, so it can be forgiven. Sin must be resisted and churches must have discipline, just like families. Paul shows how much he cares by rebuking the Galatians and calling them back to Christ. He does not enjoy this correction, but it is necessary. In 4:20 he expresses it like this: *I wish I could be present with you now and change my tone, for I am perplexed about you.* Like removing a splinter, the pain of hearing harsh words can lead to healing and greater health in the long term. At other times, though, we are broken in spirit and hearing the Law would cause despair. Paul is a careful surgeon, not a reckless writer.

A biblical parallel is the account of the golden calf. God was giving the tablets of stone engraved by His hand to Moses, but at the same time the people talked Aaron into turning their jewelry into an idol. The timing could not have been more striking. At the very moment God revealed His holy law, Israel displays their rebellion. But remember that the Law is not given to save us, but to reveal our sin and need for the Christ.

While it is easy to dismiss the Galatians as messed up and immature, the reality is that, without the Spirit, we can believe nothing. We are no stronger spiritually than the deserting Galatians. *Therefore let anyone who thinks that he stands take heed lest he fall* (1 Cor. 10:12). There is only one Gospel and one Christ for us, too. We must be vigilant and never think that the Gospel cannot be lost or taken for granted. It can never be less than the whole truth that saves. While moral issues, such as abortion, homosexuality, and divorce confront us in the world, just saying something is wrong does not save anyone. The Gospel must be the main word of the Church, but to preserve the Gospel sin must be called sin, in order that sinners may repent.

Right off the bat, the tone of this letter is set. Paul is not going to merely encourage them and tell them what they want to hear, he calls them to repentance and to the one Gospel he first preached to them. He is heartbroken over them, but has not given up hope. He means to win them over by this epistle, through giving the true Gospel in contrast to other gospel(s) that they were hearing. He shows his concern for them and his firm pastoral care.

"Gospel" is a special word. It is used in several different senses in Scripture. The simplest definition is "good news or message," but here Paul uses it in a technical sense. It refers to the content of the saving message of Christ, not just the outward form or words. The correct message, which gives the fruit of Christ's redemption, is the Gospel of life. Paul received this Gospel directly from Christ.

All parts of Scripture are important, but they are not all Gospel.

The Gospel is separated here from the Law and other God-given things that do not save in and of themselves. To believe this Gospel is to have Christ. That is why Paul puts so much stress on the Gospel. There can be only one.

Satanic teaching is just not outside churches, the worst demonic message is spoken by respected men in churches. No one is deceived by outward wickedness or by strong association with unbelievers—we are to watch out for the wolves in sheep's clothing. False teachers look good, like sheep. *Beware of false prophets, who come to you in sheep's clothing but inwardly are ravenous wolves* (Mt. 7:15). They say the words "Christ" and "faith" and "grace," but lead away from the true God. We cannot merely judge by appearances. *The spiritual man judges all things* (1 Cor. 2:15). We are to know who has the Gospel and who does not.

Satan does not lay his traps in plain view. He is smart and knows Scripture well. In Mt. 4, he tempted Jesus with a comprehensive knowledge of Scripture. The Devil is no fool. C.S. Lewis does a great job of showing how Satan works in his book *The Screwtape Letters*. He waits for an opportune time to attack and uses our sinful nature against us, so that evil seems to be good and good evil. Isn't that what happened to Eve in the Garden of Eden? Nothing looked better than the fruit, and Satan didn't come off as contradicting God's Word: *Now the serpent was more crafty than any other beast of the field that the Lord God had made. He said to the woman, "Did God actually say, 'You shall not eat of any tree in the garden'?" . . . "You will not surely die. For God knows that when you eat of it your eyes will be opened, and you will be like God, knowing good and evil."*

[v7] A "gospel" which does not deliver Christ and His forgiveness is fake. It can sound very spiritual, but does not bring people into God's grace. This attention to doctrine is not in our nature, so we are warned also by the holy words to be careful what "gospel" we are hearing. Though we may be very astute and wise in human matters, no one can resist Satan on his own or choose Christ. We are sheep who are always going astray. Hence, there is always the need to hear true preaching and receive the Supper of the Lord for the strengthening of our faith. The strong in faith know they are weak and only live by grace, not by anything in themselves. It is God who calls us in Christ. He must do it.

19

Newness is a problem in doctrine. Our world worships what is new. "New and improved" go together like peanut butter and jelly. However, God is eternal, king of the aeons. He is the same yesterday and today and forever (Heb. 13:8). What is new is false. Since God does not change, neither does His teaching. While fashion and ideas change from decade to decade and technology rapidly evolves, the Gospel is never out of date. A computer 20 years old is obsolete, but a Gospel 20 years old is false. The true Gospel must go back to creation and before. In Gen. 3, God first spoke to the serpent of his undoing after the fall into sin: *I will put enmity between you and the woman, and between your offspring and her offspring; he shall bruise your head, and you shall bruise his heel.*

This verse mentions those teaching a false gospel, yet Paul does not try win them over. This letter is addressed to the Galatians he first taught, the saints in the churches there. Others are distorting it, that is, changing it into something God did not give and which does not save. Not every mention of Jesus is saving. Christ Himself warns: *Not everyone who says to me, 'Lord, Lord,' will enter the kingdom of heaven, but the one who does the will of my Father who is in heaven* (Mt. 7:21).

Just as he does in Romans, Paul distinguishes between false teachers and ignorant hearers. The misunderstanding and erring should be loved and patiently taught, but wolves are to be beat away and not accepted. *I appeal to you, brothers, to watch out for those who cause divisions and create obstacles contrary to the doctrine that you have been taught; avoid them. For such persons do not serve our Lord Christ, but their own appetites, and by smooth talk and flattery they deceive the hearts of the naive* (Rom. 16:17).

The false teachers are harassing and disturbing the Christians in Galatia. The word "trouble" means literally "to shake or stir up." God's Word does not lead to uproar and controversy, but quiet confidence and trust that Christ will prevail over every enemy, including death itself.

Can false teachers be well meaning? Yes, most are. But like a bad doctor who wants to help you, good intentions can still kill. Think of preaching and pastoral care as spiritual surgery. The Word of God can be misused to kill and drive out faith. Heb. 4:12 reads: *For the word of God is living and active, sharper than any two-edged sword, piercing to the division of soul and of spirit, of joints and of marrow, and discerning the thoughts and intentions of the heart.* No one would sign up to go to a careless surgeon, but pastors are thought to be good if they are nice and talk well. How little we listen to their teaching, their "gospel," and compare it to Scripture, as did the Bereans in Acts 17:11: *Now these Jews were more noble than those in Thessalonica; they received the word with all eagerness, examining the Scriptures daily to see if these things were so.* We are to judge doctrine, and not the messenger's personality, to make sure God Himself is actually speaking, since there is nothing more important than to hear God's pure voice.

The true Gospel cannot be changed—it is the divine vehicle of salvation. Some tell Christians to physically go to the foot of the cross, but that is foolish. The cross is lost and probably disintegrated. Even if it did exist, it would do nothing for you. Those who witnessed Christ's death and touched Him on the cross were not automatically saved. Seeing the crucifixion with your own eyes would not save you. Rather, it is the Word of God we hear that delivers the fruit of Christ's death. We are to hold this in our heart and let it create faith in us.

Sinful man is addicted to change. We want an improved version of everything. We should not be surprised that false teachers are prevalent and popular. The same old Gospel will not be exciting to people sold on the idea that newer is better. Christ promises persecution, not acceptance, for His believers: *Blessed are you when others revile you and persecute you and utter all kinds of evil against you falsely on my account. Rejoice and be glad, for your reward is great in heaven, for so they persecuted the prophets who were before you* (Mt. 5:11–12).

The Judaizers using Christ's name are not blessed, though. [v8] They are cursed, since they are frustrating God's work. Paul curses them. The word for "accursed" here in Greek is "anathema," which has also been taken into English. Today, it means "a curse of divine punishment; or a person or thing accursed or consigned to damnation or destruction" [Dictionary.com]. It is not a personal wish, as when people curse objects because they are mad. Only people are judged, and God Himself will do it. This anathema simply echoes God's end of time judgment in time.

For emphasis, Paul repeats himself. [v9] There can be no mistaking his position. In the words of Martin Luther: "Here Paul is breathing fire. His zeal is so fervent that he almost begins to curse the angels themselves"

[*Galatians* (1535), 55]. To leave the true Gospel is to be outside of Christ and have a false faith. Then, sins are not forgiven, and that person is truly under judgment. Christians certainly pray for the repentance of Christ's enemies, but their judgment, their condemnation, is still valid. This is not yet damnation, or eternal judgment, but without repentance this state of unbelief will lead to it. Condemnation is a present state, not the final verdict. It is to be outside of God's grace and under His just anger for sin.

Is Paul being too harsh? Our culture is quite a bit softer than the biblical way of speaking. But consider that these false teachers are claiming to speak for God, yet driving sinners away from Christ and making His suffering and death small matters. Even Jesus, our Lord, said: *Woe to you, scribes and Pharisees, hypocrites! For you travel across sea and land to make a single proselyte, and when he becomes a proselyte, you make him twice as much a child of hell as yourselves* (Mt. 23:15).

A parallel is the imprecatory psalms, the ones which curse the opponents and enemies of God. "Imprecate" means "to pray evil against" or "to invoke curse upon," which is exactly what Paul is doing. These are not mere human emotions he is expressing. He is relaying God's righteous anger against the injustice and the evil that is happening. We, too, see sin in the world that cannot be excused: murder, abuse, heinous wickedness. This evil cannot be overlooked, but must be cursed, because that is God's judgment. How much more do false teachers, who drive away from Christ in Christ's own name, deserve judgment?

An example of an imprecatory psalm is Ps. 5: *Make them bear their guilt, O God; let them fall by their own counsels; because of the abundance of their transgressions cast them out, for they have rebelled against you.* These statements are really prayers. They express confidence that God will prevail, and evil will be abolished in the coming age. Those who persecute believers (often those who have God's Word) and blaspheme against the Lord deserve such curses. *For without cause they hid their net for me; without cause they dug a pit for my life. Let destruction come upon him when he does not know it! And let the net that he hid ensnare him; let him fall into it—to his destruction!* (Ps. 35:7–8).

Suffering for Christ's name does lead to a holy hatred of evil and those who stand against the righteous God. It is not personal or human emotion, but a confession of faith in the ultimate vindication the believer will receive at Judgment Day. God is a consuming fire who hates and punishes sin.

Salvation, though, is an unimpressive thing. Paul speaks in other places that he writes boldly, but does not speak as well. An angel preaching a different gospel would be more welcome than a weak sinner preaching God's Word, but Christ directs people to His Word, hidden and coming from the lowly form of humble servants. It was said to the rich man who was suffering eternally, *If they do not hear Moses and the Prophets, neither will they be convinced if someone should rise from the dead* (Lk. 16:31).

The authority of the Gospel does not rest with the speaker. Even if Paul himself teaches a different gospel, he says that he would be cursed. He actually says "we," including his associates and fellow preachers. An angel talking to us would certainly be impressive, but that is nothing compared to the Gospel, which frees from all sins and joins to Christ by faith. No one on earth has an angel, a spiritual being created by God, for a pastor. So no one, no matter how honored their earthly position is, can be the authority for the Gospel—it must be Christ's own Word that establishes it, or else we are in danger of trusting in a sinful man, not the One who gave Himself for our sins. The authority for our faith cannot be a person, no matter how holy or how important he seems; it must be the Word of God. Faith is nothing more than having the right God who loves, forgives, and is revealed in Christ. It is blasphemy to believe that something is divine just because a man spoke it. God uses men to speak, but the authority must be the Word of God, God Himself speaking to us.

A gospel contrary to the one we preached—literally, it says "besides the one which we preached." The verb for "preach" here is the verbal form of "evangel," meaning "good news." The closest English word is "evangelize," but it has a very different informal meaning today— denoting personal witnessing, and often intruding into someone's private space. "Evangelical" originally meant "about the Gospel," not a political view or a few narrow moral beliefs.

The teaching of the young is emphasized in Scripture, because we are to remain in the teaching we first heard. *Whoever receives one such child in my name receives me, but whoever causes one of these little ones who believe in me to sin, it would be better for him to have a great millstone fastened around his neck and to be drowned in the depth of the sea* (Mt. 18:6). Even if we heard it decades ago and it is unpopular now, the truth should be used to critique and question everything that is new. We are not to depart from the truth we have learned, succumbing to a changing and corrupt world.

To shipwreck someone's soul in the name of Christ is surely the worst sin. To say someone is wrong and cursed for what they sincerely hold is the worst "sin" today, though. But without the rejection of error there is no truth. It is not enough for a church to know what they believe, they must know what they do not believe. In the same way, we should condemn viewpoints and opinions contrary to Christ and His Gospel with gentleness, but also firmness. We simply speak what God speaks. To not do so is to put man's opinion above God's Word. As Paul states in 2 Cor. 10:5–6: *We destroy arguments and every lofty opinion raised against the knowledge of God, and take every thought captive to obey Christ, being ready to punish every disobedience, when your obedience is complete.* No one is strong enough to not fall away. We cling to Christ only by God's mercy—faith is in no way a work we can take credit for.

The possibility of absolute truth is not something instilled is us by our culture. We do not grow up thinking in those terms, that doctrine is either true or false, but if the Gospel is not absolute, offering salvation to all condemned sinners, it is really no Gospel at all. Then we fall into the same error as the Galatians. We should not take pride in being right, but be sad that others are rejecting the truth. Paul expresses such feeling for his own people, the Jews, in Rom. 9:

> *I am speaking the truth in Christ—I am not lying; my conscience bears me witness in the Holy Spirit—that I have great sorrow and unceasing anguish in my heart. For I could wish that I myself were accursed and cut off from Christ for the sake of my brothers, my kinsmen according to the flesh. They are Israelites, and to them belong the adoption, the glory, the covenants, the giving of the Law, the worship, and the promises.*

However, we must love God more than we hate those who reject Christ. It is the love of Christ that drives this curse of Paul. Forgiveness in His blood is something so precious that to make it small is blasphemy and the worst hatred of God. Paul speaks as strongly as possible, to shake us up, along with the Galatians. This Gospel is one of the most despised things in this world. How many think that just being a decent citizen and trying to be good to others makes one a Christian? Or doing a few visible works and looking religious makes one right before God? That is ignoring Christ and His holy suffering. Paul makes a big fuss, not about morals or our works, but about the Son of God's actions, which redeemed the entire world. Only this message gives life and brings us peace from God. Nothing can be allowed to compromise this truth, no matter how acceptable it is in the world.

Paul does not make this controversy about people. It is about the Holy God, who humbled Himself to be born for us. He cares only about His doctrine. No teacher or king holds a candle to Jesus' authority. Verse 9 could be read as "if anyone, anything 'gospelizes' you besides that [Gospel] which you have received, he is cursed."

Notice Paul's certainty and confidence in what he first preached to the Galatians. He is not modifying his message, adapting it to suit a new situation, but showing that what bought them to Christ is still the way to Christ. In the same way, the truth is the same today as when this letter was written—it should be preached and believed with the same confidence. After all, it is only Christ's Gospel which relieves guilt and opens heaven to us.

[**v10**] Here Paul returns to his call and rests in God's charge given directly to him. Clearly, Paul is not seeking approval from anyone. If he did not have the truth of God, he would be considered a madman. But he asks the rhetorical question and shows there are only two choices: to follow man or the true Father who sent His Son to be put to death in our place.

Paul was likely being attacked for neglecting the finer points of religion: ceremonial works. The same thing happens today when human morality is added to the Gospel and made necessary to be Christian. The Jewish Sabbath and use of alcohol are two examples where this happens today. The Sabbath is something Paul deals with later, but Christians still struggle with it, despite the clear statements of the New Testament. Some make Sunday the new Sabbath holy day, whereas our true rest is from the burden of guilt and the Law, which display God's wrath against our unrighteousness. This rest is found only in Christ, who forgives sin. Among some Christians, alcohol is made to be more

25

sinful than Scripture makes it. It is drunkenness that is forbidden and immoral. Jesus turned water into wine at Cana. His Supper gives His body and blood for Christians to eat and drink for forgiveness in bread and wine. It is easy to critique something that is misused by many (Paul mentions drunkenness as a work of the flesh later), but a right and godly use often escapes us. Ps. 104 does exactly that: *You* [God] *cause the grass to grow for the livestock and plants for man to cultivate, that he may bring forth food from the earth and wine to gladden the heart of man.* Sin starts in the heart and is rebellion against God. It is possible to use God's created gifts, even alcohol, out of love for him, that is, trusting Christ's redemption and forgiveness. Without faith, though, it is impossible to please God (Heb. 11:6).

The phrase translated "seeking the approval of" is one verb in Greek. Its normal meaning is "to persuade or convince," which does not fit here. The KJV has: *For do I now persuade men or God?* But God is not persuaded. "Please" fits better. The same Greek word is used with that meaning in Acts 12:20, where it could be "win over" or even "bribe." This verb is also used to describe the relationship of sheep to their pastors in Heb. 13:17: *Obey* [Follow attentively] *your leaders and submit to them, for they are keeping watch over your souls, as those who will have to give an account. Let them do this with joy and not with groaning, for that would be of no advantage to you.* This seems be the closest parallel to the use here, where Paul is saying: "do I obey or follow closely men or God?"

If these questions are answered in the positive, if Paul is a follower or pleaser of men, then he is not a servant of Christ. Again, the word for "servant" is also the word for "slave." The point is that Paul can obey only one master: God Himself who called him. If he is to be faithful, there is only one Gospel to relay. If he preaches differently, then he has not pleased God or honored the call he boasted about at the beginning of this epistle. 2 Cor. 5:10–11 reads: *For we must all appear before the judgment seat of Christ, so that each one may receive what is due for what he has done in the body, whether good or evil. Therefore, knowing the fear of the Lord, we persuade others. But what we are is known to God, and I hope it is known also to your conscience.* Paul puts himself under the same standard his opponents in Galatia are under: if he changes his message of salvation, he is cursed and false.

Just as he stated the curse on any false gospelizers twice, Paul asks his readers to discover his objective twice: *Or am I trying to please man?* The second verb is more straightforward than the first. It means "to have or seek favor; to please." Even today, being a people-pleaser with no conviction is shameful. Sinners, which all people are, do not want the truth, so they must be disappointed.

Paul boasts not about his success evangelizing, though there was some reception of the Gospel due to the Spirit, but of his persecution. This is exactly how Paul ends Galatians. He writes, starting at the end of 2 Cor. 11:

> *Are they servants of Christ? I am a better one—I am talking like a madman—with far greater labors, far more imprisonments, with countless beatings, and often near death. Five times I received at the hands of the Jews the forty lashes less one. Three times I was beaten with rods. Once I was stoned. Three times I was shipwrecked; a night and a day I was adrift at sea; on frequent journeys, in danger from rivers, danger from robbers, danger from my own people, danger from Gentiles, danger in the city, danger in the wilderness, danger at sea, danger from false brothers; in toil and hardship, through many a sleepless night, in hunger and thirst, often without food, in cold and exposure. And, apart from other things, there is the daily pressure on me of my anxiety for all the churches. Who is weak, and I am not weak? Who is made to fall, and I am not indignant? If I must boast, I will boast of the things that show my weakness. The God and Father of the Lord Jesus, he who is blessed forever, knows that I am not lying. At Damascus, the governor under King Aretas was guarding the city of Damascus in order to seize me, but I was let down in a basket through a window in the wall and escaped his hands.*

Rejection by the world is the proof of the truth that he teaches. He does not change the Gospel to please men, even if it angers the world and the Galatian leaders.

The world says we should bend and sway to get along, and in matters of love we should. But in the true doctrine which saves, there can be no compromise, unless man is put in God's place and God in man's. That would be to deny everything about God and have a false god. Chrysostom summarizes it nicely: "Is my account to be rendered to you [the Galatians]? Shall I be judged by men? My account is to God, and all my acts are with a view to that inquisition, nor am I so miserably abandoned as to pervert my doctrine, seeing that I am to justify what I preach before the Lord of all." It is a dangerous thing to judge God's Word by human standards of consistency. Whereas evil men see contradictions in God's Word, we should see only contradictions and guilt in ourselves, because all have sinned and fall short of the glory of God. Satan resists the truth in this world, his domain.

False teaching and divisions show the truth is near, because the world cannot stand it. In the words of Luther: "By contrast the false apostles teach human doctrine, that is, what is pleasant and reasonable. And they do this so that they can live a life of ease and earn the favor and plaudits of the people. Those who look for this find it, for they are praised and exalted by everyone" [*Galatians*, 60]. Beware of the successful and popular preacher—no one can serve two masters or outdo the Lord Jesus.

Suffering and persecution reveal our master and whether or not we are on the right path, the narrow one. While this is not pleasant, we cannot follow our own hearts, because Jesus calls them evil. So we are put in the most difficult circumstances to test our faith, to refine us by fire. Christ's disciples follow in the same path He walked, through suffering, to the cross. We are called to pick up our crosses and die. Where the true Gospel is, there the cross will follow. Suffering must occur in your own life, not because it is self-chosen or deserved, but for faithfulness to the one Gospel. Suffering is a sign of divine love, signaling that you are a child of God.

In contrast, false teachers and moralists act and teach for man's praise, not God's. *Thus, when you give to the needy, sound no trumpet before you, as the hypocrites do in the synagogues and in the streets, that they may be praised by others. Truly, I say to you, they have received their reward* (Mt. 6:2). In faith we are called to wait for Judgment Day and receive our reward. From the same chapter: *Do not lay up for yourselves treasures on earth, where moth and rust destroy and where thieves break in and steal, but lay up for yourselves treasures in heaven, where neither moth nor rust destroys and where thieves do not break in and steal. For where your treasure is, there your heart will be also.* Paul can only teach what he has been given by Christ—the Gospel. In other words, at the beginning of this letter he authorizes the content of what he teaches with God's approval. He is claiming: "thus saith the Lord."

Verse 11 marks a division in thought. [**v11**] Instead of steadily building up to to his thesis and making his case mathematically, he defends his calling from the very start. After doing that, he asks the rhetorical question about whose slave/servant he is. He then plainly states the facts and gives the holy evidence in the main body of the letter.

Paul makes known the clear facts of the case about the origin of this Gospel. If it is not from Christ, it must be from men. So we too must be sure of our teaching. If we cannot trace it to the Scriptures, we are unsure and may be relying on men. But only God's Word is to be believed absolutely, and is therefore above every human opinion.

Despite the evident problems, Paul still calls the Galatians "brothers." Fellowship has not been broken, though he warns about that conclusion, because an error in the Gospel cannot be blessed. It must be cursed. But at this time he gives them the benefit of the doubt and expects them to receive the truth through his defense and rebuke.

The Gospel which I have preached—both of these words ("Gospel" and "preached") have the same root in Greek, but English does not, so that connection is not as clear in translation. Literally it reads: "the evangel that I have evangelized," or "the Gospel that I have gospelized." The Gospel is not a treasure to be stored and locked away. It must be proclaimed and defended against false doctrine, or else it is lost. It is a message to be relied upon against all sin and doubt. It is not an intellectual list of facts that can be memorized and then laid aside. The Gospel is something to live in and by. *The righteous shall live by his faith* (Hab. 2:4).

This Gospel is singular: "the Gospel." Greek does not often have the article (it is not needed as in English), so when it is used it is often significant. Paul preaches **the** Gospel. He is the means God uses to speak, but unlike any of us, he did not receive it from man. The preposition used in "according to man" denotes relationship.

The Gospel "is not man's Gospel." It is even stronger in the Greek. It is not even a divine Gospel that he received or learned from a man. He received this directly from God, so it is divine in every way, even in the way he received it. He then details exactly how he received it to back up this claim. It is not in any way human. This echoes the words from v1: *Paul, an apostle—not from men nor through man, but through*

Jesus Christ and God the Father.

Paul is "making it known" to them, when it is clear they had already heard it from him. He is like a parent who has to answer the most basic question many times over.

Verse 12 is the central proposition according to Luther. Paul here describes the origin of the Gospel. [**v12**] This sets forth the basis for what he is teaching.

Revelation is an important concept in Scripture. It means "to disclose, uncover, or reveal." It denotes something that cannot be known, a divine mystery. No one could guess that God is love. Being well educated and knowing the news of our world is insufficient to understand the Gospel. All the study in the world could not show that God so loved the world that He sent His Son to die for us, to free us from our sins. Revealed knowledge must be told to us by a word of God. This is the opposite of natural knowledge, which everyone can know by their own observation and reason—namely, that there is a God, holy and powerful and eternal. He is judge and we have the basis for His judgment because we have the Law written on our hearts.

> *For when Gentiles, who do not have the law, by nature do what the law requires, they are a law to themselves, even though they do not have the law. They show that the work of the law is written on their hearts, while their conscience also bears witness, and their conflicting thoughts accuse or even excuse them on that day when, according to my gospel, God judges the secrets of men by Christ Jesus* (Rom. 2:14–16).

There are no valid excuses available to ignorant unbeleivers, even though salvation and God's goodness must be revealed.

This is why Christ sends ministers to send out the Gospel into all the world. Knowledge that God exists is not trust in the Father's goodness and reconciliation in His Son. He wants us to look to Him for all good and believe that we are His beloved children.

Luther speaks of the practical importance of the Gospel: "I know how I sometimes struggle in the hours of darkness. I know how suddenly I lose sight of the rays of the Gospel and of grace, which have been obscured for me by thick dark clouds" [*Galatians*, 63]. When we lose sight of Christ and His righteousness, given to us as a gift, we think of God as a tyrant and see only His anger and the punishment we rightly deserve. Without this knowledge of the one Gospel there can be nothing right in us or in all creation. Only this Gospel puts our hearts at rest and restores God's peace to us. When we rest on the promise of Christ, we are in Him and He is in us. This Gospel is the only way to Christ, who reveals God the Father to us. Without Him, God must remain a mystery.

Our world makes almost every internal problem into a psychological issue, that is, a physical or mental one, ignoring the spiritual. But the Scriptures do not speak like this. They recognize that man is a spiritual creature, created in God's own image. Without peace with Him, how can we be right with others or in ourselves?

The last book of the Bible is called in its entirety a "revelation" in its first verse: *The revelation of Jesus Christ, which God gave him to show to his servants the things that must soon take place.* A revelation of Jesus Christ is not just knowledge of a person. Paul, in Galatians, connects the full content of the Gospel to this revelation he received. We cannot separate doctrine or teaching from Christ. Jesus reveals Himself through the one Gospel. Paul makes it clear that this revelation is not just noetic—mere mental knowledge; to have it is to have Christ Himself and His own righteousness.

Notice how churches, that is, Christians and the man-made structures they create, are not an authority. It is Christ who is Lord and head of the Church. The Church is holy because of Him, not of herself. Scripture uses feminine language to speak of the one, true Church, because she is passive. She does not have any authority to make divine laws or change doctrine. Properly speaking, the Church is invisible—it consists of all believers—but today when most people think of a church they think of a human institution and its leaders. Yet, what does Paul say here in v12? Only the revealed Gospel makes the Church by forgiving sins. We can only speak what Christ has given us to say. He is still active now, so we, in the Church by faith, do not have to speak or take the place of an absent Christ.

The end of v12 does not have a verb, so it reads just, "but through revelation of Jesus Christ." Then Paul dives into His sordid past.

[**v13**] Paul points to the observable facts in vv13–14. He does not point to inner motivations or the deep feelings of his heart. We can know people by their fruit, and Saul's previous public actions spoke to his state of condemnation. Likewise, our public actions are telling and

can be judged by others.

Remember that Paul had two names, one Jewish, Saul of Tarsus, and one Greek, Paul. He is usually called Paul, but that may be because he was writing in Greek to Gentiles. Christ called him Saul at his conversion: *And falling to the ground he heard a voice saying to him, "Saul, Saul, why are you persecuting me?"* (Acts 9:4). But he was not given a new name, nor did he drop Saul. Ananias, the Christian in Damascus whom God told to find Paul, also called him Saul: *So Ananias departed and entered the house. And laying his hands on him he said, "Brother Saul, the Lord Jesus who appeared to you on the road by which you came has sent me so that you may regain your sight and be filled with the Holy Spirit" (Acts 9:17).* "Saul" is used a few more times early in Acts, but he seems to have gone mostly by Paul. This makes sense, considering His mission to the Gentiles. It would have been a more accessible Roman name. *I have become all things to all people, that by all means I might save some* (1 Cor. 9:22).

Paul does not hide his past, nor does he sugarcoat it. He persecuted the Church of God. Church here means "assembly," the gathering of God's people—not a single congregation or part of it, but the whole thing. The word "tried" is not in the Greek text. It literally says, "I persecuted the Church of God and destroyed it." The Greek word can also mean "devastate, attack, or kill." It is quite a strong word. It was used in Greek literature of sacking and pillaging cities. With this language Paul admits his sin. He did not succeed, but he wanted to stamp out this "heresy" and "sect" of Christianity.

Paul is repentant, not defensive, about his former way of life. It is unpopular and unseemly to admit one's guilt. We routinely gloss over mistakes and make our works seem better than they are. But there is no need to lift ourselves up in pride—God is the one who cleanses us. We did not save ourselves. Instead, we are to be humble and not forget our horrible sins against God. *If we say we have no sin, we deceive ourselves, and the truth is not in us. If we confess our sins, he is faithful and just to forgive us our sins and to cleanse us from all unrighteousness. If we say we have not sinned, we make him a liar, and his word is not in us* (1 Jn. 1:8-10). The purpose of Christ's Gospel is not to make us better than we appear, but to forgive all transgressions against God. *But if we walk in the light, as he is in the light, we have fellowship with one another, and the blood of Jesus his Son cleanses us from all sin* (1 Jn. 1:7).

What is confessed and forgiven before God can certainly be recounted to others, whose judgment is nothing. Only the Father's judgment counts, which Christ will make known on Judgment Day. Paul is uplifting Christ and His work by showing that He cannot do anything good himself—in fact, the opposite. He willingly opposed and "destroyed" the Church.

What the Galatians "heard," Paul makes a recorded fact. The beginning of Acts 7 details Paul's anti-Christian activities, which were truly against Christ Himself. After his confession, Stephen, a convert to Judaism—a Gentile by birth who takes up Jewish customs—was stoned for his teaching. *This man never ceases to speak words against this holy place and the law, for we have heard him say that this Jesus of Nazareth will destroy this place and will change the customs that Moses delivered to us." And gazing at him, all who sat in the council saw that his face was like the face of an angel. (Acts 6:13-15)*

Stephen confronted them with their own unsavory history: how they had always resisted the Holy Spirit and trusted in a Law which they did not keep.

> *Now when they heard these things they were enraged, and they ground their teeth at him. But he, full of the Holy Spirit, gazed into heaven and saw the glory of God, and Jesus standing at the right hand of God. And he said, "Behold, I see the heavens opened, and the Son of Man standing at the right hand of God." But they cried out with a loud voice and stopped their ears and rushed together at him. Then they cast him out of the city and stoned him. And the witnesses laid down their garments at the feet of a young man named Saul. And as they were stoning Stephen, he called out, "Lord Jesus, receive my spirit." And falling to his knees he cried out with a loud voice, "Lord, do not hold this sin against them." And when he had said this, he fell asleep (Acts 7:54-60).*

The next verse mentions, which begins a new chapter, Paul's complicit action and approval of this murder of one of Christ's sheep: *And Saul approved of his execution.* Notice the "and"—chapter and verse divisions are not inspired and came very late, so they are not to be relied upon for interpreting the text.

By human standards Saul (Paul) was an outstanding Jew. He was a Pharisee, a category Jesus often describes in the Gospels as hypocritical followers of an outward religion of works, concerned only about themselves. Mt. 23 contains a scathing sermon against the works righteousness of the Pharisees, Christ's most bitter opponents, who could not stand the idea of grace or that they were sinners in need of salvation. In it, Jesus says:

> *The scribes and the Pharisees sit on Moses' seat, so do and observe whatever they tell you, but not the works they do. For they preach, but do not practice. They tie up heavy burdens, hard to bear, and lay them on people's shoulders, but they themselves are not willing to move them with their finger. They do all their deeds to be seen by others. For they make their phylacteries broad and their fringes long, and they love the place of honor at feasts and the best seats in the synagogues and greetings in the marketplaces and being called rabbi by others. . . . But woe to you, scribes and Pharisees, hypocrites! For you shut the kingdom of heaven in people's faces. For you neither enter yourselves nor allow those who would enter to go in. . . . Woe to you, scribes and Pharisees, hypocrites! For you clean the outside of the cup and the plate, but inside they are full of greed and self-indulgence. You blind Pharisee! First clean the inside of the cup and the plate, that the outside also may be clean. . . . Woe to you, scribes and Pharisees, hypocrites! For you are like whitewashed tombs, which outwardly appear beautiful, but within are full of dead people's bones and all uncleanness. So you also outwardly appear righteous to others, but within you are full of hypocrisy and lawlessness (Mt. 23:2-28).*

According to Paul's own words in Philippians 3:4–7, *If anyone else thinks he has reason for confidence in the flesh, I have more: circumcised on the eighth day, of the people of Israel, of the tribe of Benjamin, a Hebrew of Hebrews; as to the law, a Pharisee; as to zeal, a persecutor of the church; as to righteousness under the law, blameless. But whatever gain I had, I counted as loss for the sake of Christ.* Saul rejected God's Son and trusted in his own works. God certainly used his education and training as a Pharisee, but it was all Christ's work and calling. Paul did not foresee his conversion and work for Christ. In fact, when Christ spoke to him on his way to Damascus, he was going there so *that if he found any belonging to the Way, men or women, he might bring them bound to Jerusalem.* He was going to take them by force to be punished in Jerusalem. Later, Paul was to face physical punishment for upsetting the tradition of the Jews by preaching Christ's death and resurrection for sins. *Five times I received at the hands of the Jews the forty lashes less one* (2 Cor. 11:24).

Paul did not just persecute, but did so "beyond measure." The NKJV has a nice translation of this verse: *For you have heard of my former conduct in Judaism, how I persecuted the church of God beyond measure and* tried to *destroy it.* ("Tried to" in the NKJV is in italics to indicate that it is not in the Greek, though proper English requires it.)

The adverb for "beyond measure" is one word in the Greek: "hyperbole." This word expresses an extraordinary degree; excess, great amount or quantity of something. In English, but not Greek, "hyperbole" means extreme exaggeration, but Paul is not exaggerating here. He is facing his guilt, which has now been forgiven in Christ. He does so as if talking about someone else. Because he lives in Christ by faith, he can talk as if he has not done anything wrong, even while condemning his former actions. So we, too, can be free in confessing our mistakes, since they have been nailed to the cross. We have died to our former way of life and live as new creations of God.

[v14] What Paul formerly took pride in was actually a rejection of the true God. This highlights his ongoing struggle in all his epistles to destroy trust in works, while making true good works pleasing to the Father and not optional for the Christian. The issue is always the heart, not just our external actions.

Paul was quite enthusiastic, or "zealous." He was not just a talker or boaster. But being excited and passionate in regards to the true religion is dangerous without true knowledge. As a Jew he had the promises of the Old Testament concerning the Messiah. Many Christians are full of missionary zeal, but do not know the distinction between Law and Gospel, so death (which the Law brings) and trust in oneself are taught, though quite enthusiastically.

We must also ask whether our supposed "progress" and "zeal" is not just self-trust and self-justification. Christ Himself, who is God over all, works all good through His Spirit. At times our zealous works can be impatience in waiting for God to act or even distrust in His promises. If we act because we think God will not or cannot do it without us, then we are acting "zealously," like Paul did as a Pharisee.

The only response to all our works should be repentance, confessing our sins to God and believing that in Christ we are whole and clean from all filth. Paul includes his former self when he speaks in Rom. 10:2: *For I bear them witness that they* [the Jews] *have a zeal for God, but not according to knowledge.* But zeal according to true knowledge and trust in Christ is very precious. Christians with the Spirit should not be lukewarm. Paul wrote in 2 Cor. 7:7: *Titus told us of your longing, your mourning, your zeal for me, so that I rejoiced still more.*

Later Paul addressed, in the Hebrew tongue, the people who were causing a disturbance at the temple in Jerusalem: *I am a Jew, born in Tarsus in Cilicia, but brought up in this city, educated at the feet of Gamaliel according to the strict manner of the law of our fathers, being zealous for God as all of you are this day* (Acts 22:3). All the zeal in the world without the revealed Gospel is death and hell. This is why Paul was so adamant that there can only be one Gospel.

Though Paul was surpassing his contemporaries, he was only surpassing them in works righteousness and unbelief—based on the assumption that he could enter the Kingdom of God by his own efforts. He says he had surpassing, abundant zeal. He was stirred by strong emotion and personal concern in his (wrong) convictions. But even if we are passionate about our religious views, the Law demands that we be motivated by love for the true God, not the desire to look good before men or surpass our contemporaries.

The fact that Paul had been much more insistent on Jewish observances and laws than the false teachers among the Galatians only emphasizes the revealed Gospel even more. Christ is the only way to salvation. Verse 14 makes it clear that we cannot follow our own hearts and strong religious convictions. Only the Word of God can light our way. There was no indication that Saul was a dissatisfied or lesser Jew in any respect, but God calls us according to grace, not according to what we are or have been.

Paul deals with tradition, still a sticking point within Christendom. Tradition in Greek literally means "handing over," in this case from generation to generation. We all have ingrained family traditions that are very significant to us. Congregations do, too. In and of themselves, traditional customs are neutral. The problem is that they can be held above God's Word, since they are familiar and we latch on to human ways of doing things much more readily than God's Word. We naturally think that if we do the same actions prior people have done, we are ok, and God will not fault us. But to trust in these works or comfortable ways of thinking is dangerous.

Tradition can be neutral (such as wearing one's Sunday best), agree with God's Word (such as the traditional idea that marriage is between a male and a female), or against God's Word, that is, it adds a command or obligation that God did not give. For example, Jesus' disciples broke Jewish customs without sinning: *Why do your disciples break the tradition of the elders? For they do not wash their hands when they eat* (Mt. 15:2).

This false elevating of tradition over the Word of Christ still happens today in regards to certain foods that are forbidden, even though Christ gave us freedom from ceremonial law. It also happens in the idea of an "age of accountability," which has no basis whatsoever in Scripture. It is natural to rest one's heart in tradition, but even the best customs must be evaluated and judged by the light of God's Word. To not do so is to trust in men against the clear Word of God. The Church is to be ever-reforming, by placing herself under the Word.

Man-made tradition can establish customs, but not an article of faith. Tradition, no matter how holy it looks, is nothing compared to God's Word. It is about man's works, not the Gospel that reveals Christ.

Jesus responded to the Pharisees about why his disciples did not wash their hands according to the received tradition: *Well did Isaiah prophesy of you hypocrites, as it is written, "This people honors me with their lips, but their heart is far from me; in vain do they worship me, teaching as doctrines the commandments of men." You leave the commandment of God and hold to the tradition of men* (Mk. 7:6–8). Paul was no less extreme in his works righteousness, but Christ revealed the Gospel to Him.

That salvation is of Christ is established clearly in vv15–16. **[v15]** Paul's choosing, as for all God's chosen, happened before we were born. In Christ, this election happened before the foundation of the world. Only the Lord can receive credit for our salvation—not the believer or the one relaying the message. Rom. 8:28–30 gives the divine logic:

> *And we know that for those who love God all things work together for good, for those who are called according to his purpose. For those whom he foreknew he also predestined to be conformed to the image of his Son, in order that he might*

*be the firstborn among many brothers. And those whom he
predestined he also called, and those whom he called he also
justified, and those whom he justified he also glorified.*

Predestination is without a doubt a scriptural teaching. However, it is
only to be used as a comfort for believers who have the Gospel. The idea
of double predestination (that God also elects to hell) is unscriptural.
Hell was prepared for the Devil and his angels (Mt. 25:41) and God
wants all to be saved and come to a knowledge of the truth (1 Tim.
2:4).

What are we to make of the fact that many are lost? God does
not prevent sin and rebellion, nor does he force people to believe as
if we are puppets. Scripture clearly says that all those who are saved
are saved solely by the Father, through Christ, in the Spirit. Yet the
reverse is unbiblical. Those who do not believe are guilty and deserving of
condemnation. We must stick to the scriptural mode of speaking and not
use our sinful reason to go beyond the Word of God we have been given.
We must not seek His hidden will, since God's loving will is accessible
and known only in Christ's Gospel. The doctrine of predestination is
a teaching that strengthens us and teaches us to rely on God's mercy,
since He cannot deny those He has chosen. *All that the Father gives
me will come to me, and whoever comes to me I will never cast out,* as
Jesus says in Jn. 6:37.

Here "set apart" means "to mark a boundary; to separate or to
appoint for a special purpose." God's goodwill is the cause of this separation, not anything in us. This makes the Gospel promise independent
of us. It is God's undeserved favor that is given through and in Christ.
The Father's love is shown and revealed in Christ, who is preached so
that we believe in the Spirit. *How then will they call on him in whom
they have not believed? And how are they to believe in him of whom they
have never heard? And how are they to hear without someone preaching?
And how are they to preach unless they are sent?* (Rom. 10:14–15).

When was Paul set apart? Not just "from birth," but from his
"mother's womb," that is, before his birth. Verse 16 in the NKJV
correctly translates it: *But when it pleased God, who separated me from
my mother's womb and called me through His grace.*

What makes a person? We can scientifically determine when certain
bodily functions start, but, ultimately, it is God who decides and gives

value to life. For we are made in His image and are valuable to Him even before we are conceived. This view of life from God's perspective, from eternity, is too wonderful to even comprehend.

A strong parallel is Jer. 1:5. The prophet Jeremiah was called to preach before he existed physically: *Before I formed you in the womb I knew you, and before you were born I consecrated you; I appointed you a prophet to the nations.* This calling strengthened Jeremiah as he spoke God's truth to a rebellious and ungrateful people.

Our predestination is made manifest in the call of the Gospel. It came to us through a person and words, but for Paul it was a direct revelation. No matter who brings the Gospel, it is the same Christ who is delivered in the forgiveness of sins. The call is in a specific promise to believe, not a vague sensation. It is to be a certainty. The Spirit in us *does* have an effect. Our emotions are real and effected by conversion, but the focus must remain on the One calling us.

Grace is God's favorable attitude. It is something in Him, not a recognition of qualities in us. It is entirely one-sided. It is only something God can have.

The verb "called" is past tense. It was a decision to love and save us out of our condemnation. In a world that speaks of falling in and out of love accidentally, we have here a witness to the perseverance and patience of true love.

For by grace you have been saved through faith. And this is not your own doing; it is the gift of God, not a result of works, so that no one may boast (Eph. 2:8-9). The Gospel is glorious because it gives a righteousness which we cannot attain. *Through him we have also obtained access by faith into this grace in which we stand, and we rejoice in hope of the glory of God* (Rom. 5:2). Grace is needed not only to first believe, it is always necessary to stand before God as righteous.

It is interesting to note that "Pharisee" means "separated one" (from sin by strictly keeping the Law), but here being separated is entirely God's work. Paul said he was set apart by God to be holy and a preacher of Christ from the womb. Some do not think unborn and little children can have faith, but if it is God's Word, who better to partake of His grace? *I thank you, Father, Lord of heaven and earth, that you have hidden these things from the wise and understanding and revealed them to little children* (Mt. 11:25). Trying to separate ourselves outwardly from sin only leads to hypocrisy, since the source of sin is our own fallen heart. Then we end up judging others around us and justifying ourselves by the Law. Righteousness must be God's work, if it is to be true. *Then the King will say to those on his right, "Come, you who are blessed by my Father, inherit the kingdom prepared for you from the foundation of the world"* (Mt. 25:34).

The main body of the letter to the Ephesians starts out with the sublime teaching of predestination:

> *Blessed be the God and Father of our Lord Jesus Christ, who has blessed us in Christ with every spiritual blessing in the heavenly places, even as he chose us in him before the foundation of the world, that we should be holy and blameless before him. In love he predestined us for adoption as sons through Jesus Christ, according to the purpose of his will, to the praise of his glorious grace, with which he has blessed us in the Beloved. In him we have redemption through his blood, the forgiveness of our trespasses, according to the riches of his grace, which he lavished upon us, in all wisdom and insight making known to us the mystery of his will, according to his purpose, which he set forth in Christ as a plan for the fullness of time, to unite all things in him, things in heaven and things on earth* (Eph. 1:3–10).

Notice how salvation is grounded in God's eternal will ("before the foundation of the world"), but revealed only in Christ. It is grasped in Him by faith in His forgiveness, which leads to being remade in His image.

What was the revelation? God's Son. The beginning of v16 goes with v15. [**v16**] Christ is called God's Son here, confessing Him equal to the Father. From Acts we know the call of Christ came to Paul on the road to Damascus. All believers are called by God. There is no faith apart from the Spirit's work in the Gospel. This is an internal calling. But Paul and approved ministers also have an external calling to preach the Gospel to others. This is not a spiritual estate that counts as something before God, but a public duty on behalf of the Church of Christ.

Paul was given the special task to preach to the Gentiles. Though a Jew by birth and training, he was set apart for this purpose. "Gentiles" is not a specific people, but designates non-Jews, that is, outsiders who have not always had God's Word.

The revelation was complete. Paul buttressed his point that he did not receive his Gospel from man, nor was he taught it. Flesh and blood was not consulted, ruling out all human authorities and intermediaries. The verb translated "consult" can also mean "to confer, contribute, or add to something." Not only did Paul's Gospel come from Christ directly, no one else added to it or filled it out. Paul received it in totality by revelation. Thus, he is an apostle equal to the twelve Jesus chose.

The phrase "to me" is not as definite as it seems in English. The Greek might be best translated "in me." The same phrase in the next chapter (2:20) is rendered in English: *I have been crucified with Christ. It is no longer I who live, but Christ who lives in [with] me.* In 4:19, Paul is in anguish, so that "Christ is formed in you [the Galatians]." Through faith we have the Son and He is *in* us.

How was the Son revealed in Paul? Through his message and life, others became aware of Jesus' work, which reveals God's great love. That Jesus is fully God is a large part of this message. This "gospeling" is still happening today (the "revelation of the Son in Paul") through these letters of Paul, which compromise about 1/3 of the New Testament. Together with the other inspired books, they are our divine authority and the gauge and fountain of all teaching. Paul tells Timothy: *But I received mercy for this reason, that in me, as the foremost, Jesus Christ might display his perfect patience as an example to those who were to believe in him for eternal life* (1 Tim. 1:16). Paul's great persecution of Christ shows that no one is too far gone to be forgiven. It is God who does the calling through His Word. Human circumstances and personal qualities do not make one more predisposed to believe. The Father elects from eternity in this Word, which we are bound to honor.

This defense of the originality and sufficiency of the Son revealed in Paul should have been quite convincing to the Galatians. The false teachers, both among the Galatians and in our day, can in no way refute the claim and authority of Paul. God used him in a unique way. Due to his previous manner of life, his ministry could not have been self-chosen. God Himself did it and could be the only one to call him. In faith, all believers are called by the Spirit in the Word and sacraments which give Christ's righteousness. It is always God's work. This stress on Paul's public task of revealing Christ is unequaled in the church and cannot

41

be duplicated today. Paul was at the first flowering of the Church after Christ's ascension and the giving of the Spirit. "God had appointed Paul as the last apostle" [Lenski, 59].

Next, Paul relates what he did after Christ revealed Himself, in the last part of v16. Paul did not consult with others. Who could modify or trump God's direct call? No man, no matter how important, could add to this Gospel. How about the apostles? Well, Paul was now an apostle, their equal.

As the Son was revealed in Paul, he now preached in, or among, the Gentiles. He was to be with them and became like them, so as to reveal Christ in the Gospel. He did this not through his deeds, but by his words which related Christ. In Paul's preaching Christ was communicated. Through his letters Jesus and all His righteousness, still come to us.

Saul did not go to Jerusalem, though it was a place of great religious importance. It was the capital of Judea and the site of the temple, where God formerly dwelt in a special way for His people before Christ's redemption was fulfilled in the temple of His body. One always went "up" to it. This is not merely referring to elevation. Jerusalem is often called the holy city in the Old Testament. But we are not to look for God's presence in a place now. That was God's way of allowing His grace to be known in the Old Testament, before Christ died. He bound His gracious presence to the temple and gave the Israelites many rites and ceremonies telling them how to approach the true God. Now we find God's grace fully in Christ, whom His Word reveals. The physical temple and divine ceremonies were merely pointers to, and shadows of, the Messiah. We are to hear and hold sacred the true preaching of Christ, because in it Christ comes to us to forgive and strengthen us.

[v17] Paul avoided the hub of activity (Jerusalem) around which Jesus taught, was condemned, rose, and last appeared. It was where the other apostles were based. Instead, he went to Arabia, which was not a place of importance to early Christianity. That is the point. He could not have been instructed there or learned any of this Gospel that Christ gave him. It is also an area of wilderness, where Israel had wondered for 40 years. The only other mention of this land (by this same name) in the New Testament is in this same letter: *Now Hagar is Mount Sinai in Arabia; she corresponds to the present Jerusalem, for she is in slavery with her children* (4:25). Mt. Sinai is the location where God gave His

holy Law to Israel through Moses.

What Paul did in Arabia is not stated in Scripture. It is quite likely that he preached Christ, since he already had the fullness of Christ in the Gospel. We know he preached Christ in Damascus. Right after Christ called Saul, he began proclaiming Jesus the Son of God in the synagogues in Damascus. The history is detailed in Acts 9:

> Now there was a disciple at Damascus named Ananias. The Lord said to him in a vision, "Ananias." And he said, "Here I am, Lord." And the Lord said to him, "Rise and go to the street called Straight, and at the house of Judas look for a man of Tarsus named Saul, for behold, he is praying, and he has seen in a vision a man named Ananias come in and lay his hands on him so that he might regain his sight." But Ananias answered, "Lord, I have heard from many about this man, how much evil he has done to your saints at Jerusalem. And here he has authority from the chief priests to bind all who call on your name." But the Lord said to him, "Go, for he is a chosen instrument of mine to carry my name before the Gentiles and kings and the children of Israel. For I will show him how much he must suffer for the sake of my name." So Ananias departed and entered the house. And laying his hands on him he said, "Brother Saul, the Lord Jesus who appeared to you on the road by which you came has sent me so that you may regain your sight and be filled with the Holy Spirit." And immediately something like scales fell from his eyes, and he regained his sight. Then he rose and was baptized; and taking food, he was strengthened. For some days he was with the disciples at Damascus. And immediately he proclaimed Jesus in the synagogues, saying, "He is the Son of God." And all who heard him were amazed and said, "Is not this the man who made havoc in Jerusalem of those who called upon this name? And has he not come here for this purpose, to bring them bound before the chief priests?" But Saul increased all the more in strength, and confounded the Jews who lived in Damascus by proving that Jesus was the Christ.

The revelation of Christ was in full. Paul was lacking nothing in regards to the Gospel.

[v18] Finally Paul goes to Jerusalem, three years after becoming an apostle. He meets with Peter to visit and become familiar with him. The implication is that Paul did not go there after three years of preaching to learn or be instructed.

The word for Peter here is "Kephas," or "Cephas," the Aramaic equivalent of "Petros" (Peter), the Greek name Christ gave him. This happened in Mt. 16:13–19:

> *He said to them, "But who do you say that I am?" Simon Peter replied, "You are the Christ, the Son of the living God." And Jesus answered him, "Blessed are you, Simon Bar-Jonah! For flesh and blood has not revealed this to you, but my Father who is in heaven. And I tell you, you are Peter, and on this rock I will build my church, and the gates of hell shall not prevail against it. I will give you the keys of the kingdom of heaven, and whatever you bind on earth shall be bound in heaven, and whatever you loose on earth shall be loosed in heaven."*

This passage has been much abused in the history of the Church. Peter is called "Petros," which literally means "a stone." However, when Christ says *on this rock I will build my church*, the word translated "rock" is not "petros" (Peter's new name) but "petra," a feminine noun. It occurs with the demonstrative adjective ("this") together in one clause. It refers not to Peter, the person, but what he had just confessed: *You are the Christ, the Son of the living God.* This could not come from flesh and blood, but was revealed by the Father to him. This confession of Christ, and the faith which produced it in Kephas, is the foundation of the Church, since Christ is the foundation. The word "petra" does not mean a detached stone (like "Petros," that is, Peter or Kephas), but a mass of rock. It is used in this teaching of Jesus: *Everyone then who hears these words of mine and does them will be like a wise man who built his house on the rock* [petra]. *And the rain fell, and the floods came, and the winds blew and beat on that house, but it did not fall, because it had been founded on the rock* [petra] (Mt. 7:25). Peter, the man, was not the rock, since he explicitly denied Christ three times and was the apostle most often sticking his foot in his mouth. But God used him to do His work. Paul by no means sets Peter up as a super-apostle.

[v19] Some argue that "brother" means "cousin" or "distant relative," rather than natural brother, but this is unnecessary to assume. Mary, Jesus' mother, was a virgin when Christ was born. After His birth, we can assume that she had a normal marriage to Joseph for as long as he lived. It was evidently not a long time, since Joseph is not present at the cross (some 33 years later) when Jesus gives John and Mary to each other as mother and son. Mt. 13:55 mentions James, who was a brother of Jesus, when the crowds questioned Jesus' authority: *Is not*

this the carpenter's son? Is not his mother called Mary? And are not his brothers James and Joseph and Simon and Judas? Of course, James could only be a brother through Mary, since Jesus was conceived by the Holy Spirit, leaving Joseph no part. But even being a half-blood relative of Jesus is nothing compared to knowing His Gospel and living by it: *For whoever does the will of my Father in heaven is my brother and sister and mother* (Mt. 12:50).

This James (in Hebrew, Jacob) is distinct from James, the brother of John, son of Zebedee. In Acts 12:2, Herod kills *James the brother of John with the sword,* but later in the same chapter Paul, after being released from prison, says: *Tell these things to James and to the brothers. Then he departed and went to another place.* James, the brother of the Lord, seems to have become an important leader of the early Church, though he was not at first, since he is not mentioned any earlier.

Paul does relate that Christ appeared after His resurrection from the dead to James: *Then he appeared to more than five hundred brothers at one time, most of whom are still alive, though some have fallen asleep. Then he appeared to James, then to all the apostles. Last of all, as to one untimely born, he appeared also to me* (1 Cor. 15:6–8). James, the brother of the Lord, was not one of the twelve or an apostle, but he was a minster of Christ and a leader of the church at Jerusalem.

While Peter, or Kephas, is central in the Gospels, he does not figure into the rest of the New Testament like Paul does. We only have two of his letters (1, 2 Pet.) in the Bible. Also, the book of Jude begins: *Jude, a servant of Jesus Christ and brother of James.* Paul being chosen last did not hinder him. He was given a different audience to preach to than the other apostles: the Gentiles.

Paul seals this history with an oath. [v20] These are not forbidden to Christians, but should not be done frivolously, like when people tell fish stories. Oaths can be made when it is good and loving for one's neighbor, such as testifying in court. The argument that Paul had learned his Gospel from flesh and blood and is therefore inferior to the other apostles is utterly destroyed. In the words of Luther: "why does Paul repeat so often, almost too often, that he did not learn his gospel from men or even from the apostles themselves? It is his purpose to persuade the churches of Galatia, which have been led astray by the false apostles, and to convince them beyond any doubt that his Gospel was the true Word of God" [*Galatians*, 76].

The same Gospel is attacked today, though in a slightly different way than it was among the Galatians. Still, we should have same confidence that the words Paul wrote are God's and confirm our status in Christ, in whom we have believed. No one, no matter how persuasive, can be put above these inspired words given through Paul, the apostle of the Lord. They must continue to remain the basis for all teaching in the Church, despite how the world rages against the Gospel of God's Son. Paul writes in the presence of God and confirms that he is not lying. This is a trustworthy word.

[**v21**] Syria and Cilicia were situated together northwest of Israel, along the Mediterranean. Paul's home of Tarsus was located in the region of Cilicia. It was the capital city, and Paul makes note of its importance at the temple: *I am a Jew, from Tarsus in Cilicia, a citizen of no obscure city* (Acts 21:39). Though Paul had no earthly reason to avoid the birthplace of the Church, he continues to exert his independence and differing mission (proclaiming the Gospel to Gentiles). Paul gives the facts and places of his first teaching activity on behalf of the Lord, boasting solely in the Lord's direct call.

[**v22**] Paul was unknown to the Judean Christians by his visage, meaning they did not know his face. The one invisible Church is located in specific spots, also called churches, which today we call congregations.

By reputation and his written words, the Judeans and all the churches did know Paul. [**vv23–24**] The "faith" here refers to the content of the faith, the doctrine of Christ. Our personal faith is created by the objective, saving doctrine that gives us the true Christ. It can be none other than God's own work. That is why they glorified God, not Paul.

Chapter 2

Chapter 2 does not mark a large break in Paul's letter. Remember that chapter divisions and verse divisions came long after the biblical books were written. You do not see Martin Luther or the early Reformers refer to verse numbers, because they came later—actually, after Luther's death. Our system of dividing the Scriptures into verses dates from 1551. Chapters in Scripture date back to the early 13th century, well over 1000 years after the New Testament was completed. The Bible's punctuation is also not in the early manuscripts we have. Basically, we just have letters. So any division, even of sentences, is really a matter of interpretation and translation, not God's inspiration. This is helpful to keep in mind as you read.

The text shows that this is not a major division, despite the start of a new chapter. [v1] The first word in Greek means "then," or "next." Again Paul goes to Jerusalem, though 14 years have intervened. Note that he has a fellow preacher of the Gospel, Barnabas, with him.

Barnabas is first mentioned at the end of Acts 4:

> And with great power the apostles were giving their testimony to the resurrection of the Lord Jesus, and great grace was upon them all. There was not a needy person among them, for as many as were owners of lands or houses sold them and brought the proceeds of what was sold and laid it at the apostles' feet, and it was distributed to each as any had need. Thus Joseph, who was also called by the apostles Barnabas (which means son of encouragement), a Levite, a native of Cyprus, sold a field that belonged to him and brought the money and laid it at the apostles' feet.

Barnabas was from Cyprus, the third largest island in the Mediterranean. It is still a predominantly Christian nation today, perhaps due in part to Paul's preaching. It is only about 50–60 miles south of the biblical

Cilicia (Paul's hometown Tarsus was its capital under Roman rule), and to the East 60–70 miles is Syria, right above Judea and Galilee. Syria includes Damascus, the city that plays a large part in Paul's conversion, and is the site of his first preaching activity.

When Paul came to Jerusalem the first time, Acts 9:26–28 describes Barnabas as the first to receive him.

> And when [Paul] had come to Jerusalem, he attempted to join the disciples. And they were all afraid of him, for they did not believe that he was a disciple. But Barnabas took him and brought him to the apostles and declared to them how on the road he had seen the Lord, who spoke to him, and how at Damascus he had preached boldly in the name of Jesus. So he went in and out among them at Jerusalem, preaching boldly in the name of the Lord.

Barnabas was sent to Antioch and enlisted Paul's help: *So Barnabas went to Tarsus to look for Saul, and when he had found him, he brought him to Antioch. For a whole year they met with the church and taught a great many people. And in Antioch the disciples were first called Christians* (Acts 11:25–26).

While at Antioch, *the Holy Spirit said, "Set apart for me Barnabas and Saul for the work to which I have called them." Then after fasting and praying they laid their hands on them and sent them off* (Acts 13:2). They began what is called Paul's first missionary journey together.

Titus is not with Paul in the same capacity as Barnabas; Barnabas was officially sent with Paul, while Titus seems to be a tagalong at this point. The word translated "taking with" is much how we would speak of taking a child along. Little children usually serve no practical purpose, though the experience can be good for them. Later, especially among the Corinthians, Titus worked on behalf of Paul as a full minister of the Gospel. Among several mentions of Titus in 2 Cor. is this one: *As for Titus, he is my partner and fellow worker for your benefit. And as for our brothers, they are messengers of the churches, the glory of Christ* (8:23). A book of the Bible is named for Titus. It is a letter written to him from Paul. In that epistle Paul calls Titus his true son in their common faith and details how he was left in Crete, the largest of the islands of Greece.

While vv1–2 seem very similar to the important council in Acts 15, in that it deals with circumcision and the Law of Moses, that was a very public event with an official response. Here in Galatians 2:2, a private encounter is described. [v2] It happened because of a revelation, which can only be a Word of God. The word for "private" is "idios" in Greek—where we get the word "idiot" from. The biblical word means doing things in a particular, private way. The English has a negative association today, but here it simply means that this conference was not a public matter (or at least Paul's part in it was not). We do not have enough information to say for sure that this was the same event Acts 15 describes.

In the Old Testament we often read that the Word of the Lord came to a prophet. The same happened to Paul—whether by means of another person or directly, we are not told. Regardless, it was God's Word he followed. It seems that Paul would not have gone otherwise, unless God had commanded him.

The length of time that had elapsed, 14 years, was great. Paul's work and reputation had been fully established. He had no need of anyone's approval in Jerusalem. He was no novice, but rather an experienced apostle who had suffered much for the sake of his Gospel.

Paul is not asking for approval—he is sure of what he teaches. He lays out *the gospel that I proclaim among the Gentiles.* The verb "preaching" or "proclaiming" is in present tense. It was an ongoing activity. He had not stopped. It had been 17 years since his conversion.

He speaks to *those who seemed influential.* The Greek does not have the word "influential." It says: "to those seeming [to be]." It means that he spoke to those who had a reputation, those regarded as something by others. It is an interesting phrase that shows that Paul does not cower before their supposed superiority. He has the Gospel from no man. It came directly from Christ Himself. Yet, he is not arrogantly teaching them either. He recognizes their legitimacy, but he is their equal. Why does he do this? *In order to make sure I was not running or had not run in vain.* He did not want his work in proclaiming the Gospel to be different than what he or they had received. Unity in doctrine is the basis for church fellowship. The content of what saves is the subject of this meeting, not internal, subjective feelings of the heart or public perception.

Paul loves the running analogy. The Christian life is a race. This illustration is natural to those who have run long distance races. It is easy to lead a long race at the beginning—to start well—but to finish a long race after starting fast is a challenge. Many runners fade, not having enough endurance. In the same way, believing in Jesus for a short time is not uncommon. Many fall away when the cares of the world take away the joy of fresh faith. After many years, the forgiveness of sins does not excite us, but seems to hold us back. In a race, the last portion is the hardest, but the entire effort is wasted if the runner stops before the finish line. This should encourage us to run and keep enduring hardship under Christ's name, looking forward to our reward. Our goal is the finish line of falling asleep in Christ. We aim to die to the flesh and leave the sinful nature, so we can be renewed completely and gain the object of our hope: eternal life with Christ. This race is a marathon, not a sprint.

In 1 Cor. 9:24–27 Paul expands on this comparison of the Christian life to a race:

> *Do you not know that in a race all the runners run, but only one receives the prize? So run that you may obtain it. Every athlete exercises self-control in all things. They do it to receive a perishable wreath, but we an imperishable. So I do not run aimlessly; I do not box as one beating the air. But I discipline my body and keep it under control, lest after preaching to others I myself should be disqualified.*

Paul is not saved by what he *does*, even though he has a divine calling. As a sinner (he calls himself the worst), he lives only by the forgiveness won by Christ's death.

Paul in 5:7 turns this analogy against the Galatians: *You were running well. Who hindered you from obeying the truth?* It is not Paul who ran in vain, but the Galatians who are stumbling. He does not intend for any false gospel to hinder them.

The idea of "once saved, always saved" is demolished here. Paul himself can lose faith and deny the Spirit, despite all he has done. Being God's special instrument to the Gentiles has nothing to do with Paul's life in Christ. No action of ours can ensure that faith will continue, since faith is simply reliance on the promise of God. Like Peter walking on the water, when we take our eye off Christ we sink. But, when the Spirit gives faith, He sustains us in Christ's Word. We suffer as weary runners. We are called to sacrifice our comfort in order to reach our goal.

If the focus of the Christian life shifts to our works, away from Christ, the race is lost. Paul exempts no one from the possibility of the sin of self-reliance and apostasy (falling away from Christ), even himself. If we stop running in Christ, all faith is vain. It is not enough to make it to the midpoint of a race—the goal is always the finish line.

"In vain" could be rendered here as "for an empty thing," that is, lest Paul had been running futilely and without purpose. It does no good to believe for 65 years and then indulge in the pleasures of the world, denying Christ. All would be for naught. Think of an Olympic runner who has sacrificed years of his life in training. He will not let up when the finish line is at hand. No, for that is what he has worked and sacrificed so much for. When he can see the finish line, he will ignore all pain and exhaustion, because the goal is at hand. He will sprint, running with everything he has left, because the goal is so close he can taste it. So also our desire for God's Word and thirst for Christ's forgiving righteousness should increase, as we are made aware of our sin and get closer to the day of Christ's return. The Scriptures exhort us to endure and persevere in our race of faith. We are called to finish what was started and not give up hope.

Paul's words should not be taken as an expression of doubt about his teaching. The phrase could be translated "if somehow I am running for nothing." The same phrase translated "if somehow" or "in order to make sure" is used in 2 Cor. 11:3: *But I fear lest by any means* [if somehow], *as the serpent beguiled Eve through his subtlety, so your minds should be corrupted from the simplicity that is in Christ* [KJ21]. In the same translation, our present verse reads: *And I went up by revelation, and communicated unto them that gospel which I preach among the Gentiles, but privately to them which were of reputation, lest by any means I should run, or had run, in vain.* There is no doubt at all in this Greek expression, despite what an English translation might imply.

The warning that Christ can be abandoned is necessary, especially for the Galatians, since they are being tempted by and latching on to a gospel which is not really a gospel at all. This false teaching does not rely on Christ, but on works of the Law. 2 Cor. 11:4 says exactly that: *For if someone comes and proclaims another Jesus than the one we proclaimed, or if you receive a different spirit from the one you received, or if you accept a different gospel from the one you accepted, you put up with it readily enough.* Faith does not change. Reliance on Christ and

His works is the start and end of our new life in the Lord. We are never deserving of salvation or qualified for it—it is a gift from beginning to end. Paul's race is also his work of proclamation among the Galatians (not just personal faith), as their spiritual father. He feels the weight of pastoral responsibility. He does not want them to make a shipwreck of their faith. *Do all things without grumbling or disputing, that you may be blameless and innocent, children of God without blemish in the midst of a crooked and twisted generation, among whom you shine as lights in the world, holding fast to the word of life, so that in the day of Christ I may be proud* [rejoice] *that I did not run in vain or labor in vain* (Phil. 2:14–18). Paul is not concerned about the temporal future of his congregations, with issues such as budgets or programs. He is looking forward to his teaching paying off at Christ's judgment of the world. He is concerned about their justification in Christ, which leads to the eternal verdict of righteousness. *Each of us will give an account of himself to God* (Rom. 14:12). Paul has an eternal perspective that allows him to suffer for the Gospel and patiently instruct in the mean time.

In v2, Paul asks an indirect question, like he often does, implying that the answer is no. Another way to put it is: "lest somehow I am running for nothing." He has not run in vain; rather it the Galatians who have put their race, their life in Christ, in danger. This is confirmed by the example of Titus.

[v3] Titus was a Greek who was not circumcised, since he was not raised as a practicing Jew. Due to the false contention that circumcision was necessary to please God, in no way could credence be given to the impression that the work of circumcision is needed in addition to Christ. Titus could not be circumcised under this pressure of false doctrine. At the end of this letter, Paul states that certain people were compelling or forcing the Galatians to be circumcised: *It is those who want to make a good showing in the flesh who would force you to be circumcised, and only in order that they may not be persecuted for the cross of Christ* (6:12). Both in Galatia and at the meeting in Jerusalem, circumcision was not just a personal preference or merely an issue of propriety or custom. This error invaded the heart of salvation: Christ and justification. Compromise would have led to a different gospel. The Gospel is not just a matter of saying the right words. If the Gospel is

denied or emasculated in practice, the preached words carry no power or truth. To circumcise at this critical juncture would be to give up Christ and heaven.

Unlike Timothy, another Greek who was circumcised as an adult in an entirely different context, this situation would not allow it for Titus. False doctrine was being perpetrated in this very issue. To give in would have been to deny the true Gospel. Whoever allows a practice or deed that contradicts the true teaching shows that he believes nothing.

Circumcision is nothing in itself. In technical terminology it is an *adiaphoron*, that is, it is indifferent to God. Paul says in 1 Cor. 7:19: *For neither circumcision counts for anything nor uncircumcision, but keeping the commandments of God.* In this very epistle he says the same: *For in Christ Jesus neither circumcision nor uncircumcision counts for anything, but only faith working through love* (5:6). *For neither circumcision counts for anything, nor uncircumcision, but a new creation* (6:15). But when the Gospel is under attack, to give any weight to that particular falsehood is to deny the Gospel of Christ. To compromise on the very point on which the truth of Christ hinges would be to despise the truth. This is why Paul is so adamant in this letter. Is circumcision necessary to be saved? No, because Christ's death and resurrection is sufficient. To require a work not commanded by God would be a total denial of the freedom our Lord won. The Gospel Paul preached (and set before the apostles in Jerusalem) dealt with Christ and the satisfaction for sins by His blood—not outward things like circumcision or food.

The key word in v3 is "forced." When someone adds to God's Word and says it *must* be done, no matter how minor it seems, it should not be done, lest the Gospel of Christ be nullified. Man's word cannot be put on the same level as God's Word, but when it is a matter of love (and not God's Word) we can by all means compromise on things which do not matter to God—things that are indifferent to the Lord, but not to the weak in faith. This was the case when Timothy was circumcised for the sake of his work among Jews. It was done in freedom, that the Gospel would not be hindered, not under the compulsion or dictates of a false gospel. The important point is to know the motivation.

This is also why circumcision in our context is completely free, and not a matter of the Gospel. It is often done out of tradition or custom by Christians today, not for salvation. But a Christian cannot be circumcised under the understanding that it is submission to the Jewish ceremonial law or that it has anything to do with salvation.

In Christ, we are free in these outward matters. Love must reign. Luther wisely says: "no one believes how dangerous traditions and ceremonies are, and yet we cannot do without them" [*Galatians*, 112]. Hearts naturally look to outward things, trust in works, and think that doing what others do is enough. But Christ's freedom is internal. It is not a matter of proper action or the judgment of others, it is the grace of God through Christ, which natural man, without the Spirit, cannot receive. Yet, God distributes it everywhere through the Gospel, the simple story of Jesus' suffering, death, and resurrection—all for you, to win you from death.

Even one action forced upon someone freed from sins, apart from a Word of God, becomes a total denial of the Gospel. This helps to understand seemingly contradictory statements by Paul. The context (what is at stake) gives us the reasons for radically different reactions. Clearly, circumcision in itself does not hold anyone back from Christ. It is free. Paul, of course, was circumcised according the Law. While we do not want to offend those who believe and understand weakly, the truth of God cannot be compromised without danger to our soul. *For this reason, when I could bear it no longer, I sent to learn about your faith, for fear that somehow the tempter had tempted you and our labor would be in vain* (1 Thess. 3:5).

Paul cuts to the heart of the issue. [**v4**] The Judaizers here are "false brothers" (one word in Greek). In 2 Cor. 11:26, Paul mentions "danger from false brothers" as one of his great burdens. They undid his work in forming Christ in his spiritual children. They outwardly claim to be followers of Christ and imitate what Christians do, but they do not have the Spirit or heed His Word. Jesus explains why hypocrites must exist in the midst of believers in Mt. 13:24–30:

> *He put another parable before them, saying, "The kingdom of heaven may be compared to a man who sowed good seed in his field, but while his men were sleeping, his enemy came and sowed weeds among the wheat and went away. So when the plants came up and bore grain, then the weeds appeared also. And the servants of the master of the house came and said to him, 'Master, did you not sow good seed in your*

> *field? How then does it have weeds?' He said to them, 'An enemy has done this.' So the servants said to him, 'Then do you want us to go and gather them?' But he said, 'No, lest in gathering the weeds you root up the wheat along with them. Let both grow together until the harvest, and at harvest time I will tell the reapers, "Gather the weeds first and bind them in bundles to be burned, but gather the wheat into my barn." ' "*

In the same way, we are not to root out false brothers by trying to peer into people's hearts. The righteousness of Christ cannot be seen by man. If they make themselves known (by teaching or practice), we should judge their doctrine and actions, but everyone who claims to be a Christian and does not directly contradict their confession by their action or words should be assumed to be a forgiven child of the Father. Putting the best construction on others' motivations is the loving thing to do. That is what the 8th commandment demands: "You shall not give false testimony against your neighbor."

The freedom of the Gospel is glorious—in Christ we are free from sins and all punishment. We live before the Father under His love in Christ's perfect righteousness. We depend on the grace given in Baptism and the Word. Free from the burden of the Law, we know God. To the world, this sounds very dangerous. Fleshly people need rules and laws to make them obey. They cannot understand people reborn and renewed by the Spirit, animated by the love of God. The natural man thinks only in fleshly terms. Moralists give rules and limit freedom, *so that they might bring us into slavery*, as Paul says.

Christianity is not a matter of right actions or following certain traditions. One cannot inherit this freedom as a birthright. The Spirit Himself must birth us into this glorious righteousness, which is given on account of Christ's suffering. It is peace with God and access to grace, as Paul previously detailed in this letter (1:3). It is a living hope in the future resurrection—we will enter physically into glory just as Christ rose from the dead. This is the confident trust and knowledge that Job expresses:

> *Oh that my words were written! Oh that they were inscribed in a book! Oh that with an iron pen and lead they were engraved in the rock forever! For I know that my Redeemer lives, and at the last he will stand upon the earth. And after my skin has been thus destroyed, yet in my flesh I shall see*

God, whom I shall see for myself, and my eyes shall behold,
and not another (Job 19:23–27).

This internal freedom (in Christ, not in the body) is to be declared free
from sin and death by God Himself, which He does through the Word.

Those who are not free cannot stand this Gospel freedom. It sounds
reckless and immoral to not be in bondage, that is, under the Law. The
unspiritual only know of a fleshly sort of freedom. Paul dealt with this
often.

> *What shall we say then? Are we to continue in sin that grace*
> *may abound? By no means! How can we who died to sin*
> *still live in it? Do you not know that all of us who have*
> *been baptized into Christ Jesus were baptized into his death?*
> *We were buried therefore with him by baptism into death, in*
> *order that, just as Christ was raised from the dead by the*
> *glory of the Father, we too might walk in newness of life*
> (Rom. 6:1–4).

The forgiveness of sins is the central theme of Christianity. It is the
only way to know God and love Him. But the world hears forgiveness as
excusing sin. They do not see the mercy in God's suffering on the cross,
nor His bleeding for our rebellious and angry thoughts and careless
hatred of others. The Gospel is not permission to sin. It will always
be misunderstood by sinners, who naturally trust in the Law to save.
Unbelievers are slaves to the Law and can only trust in and live by their
works. But Christ's love and freedom is not found in us, it must be
revealed. Paul deals with such slander against our delicious freedom:

> *But if our unrighteousness serves to show the righteousness*
> *of God, what shall we say? That God is unrighteous to inflict*
> *wrath on us? (I speak in a human way.) By no means! For*
> *then how could God judge the world? But if through my*
> *lie God's truth abounds to his glory, why am I still being*
> *condemned as a sinner? And why not do evil that good may*
> *come?—as some people slanderously charge us with saying.*
> *Their condemnation is just* (Rom. 3:5–8).

As Christ died for the world's sins, we are to die to sin and not let
the flesh rule us. The Spirit, given as a deposit, is to bear the fruit of
righteousness in us. Only when the tree is made good will it bear good
fruit. Hanging fruit on a dead tree will not make it alive. We must first
be made alive in Christ and live to God before any fruit can result.
This is the freedom Paul defends as the most important thing in all the
world.

Complete strangers have told me that I am not saved because I did not invite Jesus into my heart or say a certain prayer. But nothing is to be added to Christ's work. It is fully completed and finished. Trust in it alone. Whatever we do has nothing to do with our status before God. The sacraments are not works with which to buy God off; they are delivery vehicles of grace that connect us to Christ by forgiving our sins.

To be under the Law is to be subject to God's wrath, because we do not meet the righteous demands of the Law. That just anger in the Law is the opposite of the love of God in Christ. Paul in 2 Cor. 3 calls the Law *the ministry of death.* It cannot make us alive. It actually kills. *For the letter* [the Law] *kills, but the Spirit gives life* (2 Cor. 3:6). But it does serve the purpose of making us aware of our sin and helplessness.

Freedom or liberty is to be in Christ and have His Spirit within us, which makes us alive. *Now the Lord is the Spirit, and where the Spirit of the Lord is, there is freedom* (2 Cor. 3:17). Luther stated it quite boldly, because he grasped the true liberty of the freedom of Christ:

> And we refuse to yield the least little bit, either to all the heavenly angels or to Peter or to Paul or to a hundred emperors or to a thousand popes or to the whole world! On no account should we humble ourselves here; for they want to deprive us of our glory, namely, the God who has created us and given us everything, and the Christ who has redeemed us with his blood. In short, we can stand the loss of our possessions, our name, our life, and everything else; but we will not let ourselves be deprived of the Gospel, our faith, and Jesus Christ [*Galatians*, 99].

Christian love is not weak or passive. In our bodies we will be vindicated by God in Christ. How can we not defend this freedom from those who think slavery is more attractive than freedom? This contradiction only shows how fallen man is—slavery to sin is much more appealing than the freedom of faith. This freedom is to know that Christ is greater than all and that He proved His love for us by giving His life for the worlds' sins.

[**v5**] Paul, with holy stubbornness, did not yield in submission to slavery, in the call to have Titus circumcised. To do so would have been to leave the truth of the Gospel—not just for Paul, but for all who heard him. This public act would have undone all the sweet, forgiving words he had preached for close to two decades. One restricting work

would make the Gospel no longer free or salvific. Not even for a moment could he give in.

"Hour" in Greek means "a short period," or, as it means here, "a single point in time." Although our English word "hour" is derived from this same Greek word, the meaning is not quite the same. In ancient times, before digital clocks, time was not divided as narrowly as today. Now, anyone can measure time in seconds or even milliseconds. With specialized equipment engineers and scientists can measure nanoseconds (one billionth of a second) and even picoseconds (one trillionth of a second). We do not think of an hour as a short period of time, but in Paul's day, without incessant media and fast-paced technology, it was. It was their smallest unit of time. While it can also mean "season" in Greek, here Paul indicates that he cannot compromise the Gospel for an instant, that is, for one second, we might say. In the book of Revelation this word is used in the same way: *And the kings of the earth, who committed sexual immorality and lived in luxury with her, will weep and wail over her when they see the smoke of her* [Babylon's] *burning. They will stand far off, in fear of her torment, and say, "Alas! Alas! You great city, you mighty city, Babylon! For in a single hour* [moment] *your judgment has come"* (18:9–10).

Paul's standing up to the pressure of false doctrine was necessary to preserve the truth of the Gospel. An error in doctrine cannot be forgiven like murder or hateful words. Doctrine creates faith, delivering Christ. False doctrine undoes the Gospel, which is the only way to escape eternal damnation. Since it seems that Paul—or rather his Gospel—was being attacked, as if Paul was running in vain, he addressed that opinion head-on. He welcomed the mutual agreement and unity in the doctrine he found at Jerusalem.

Paul again dismisses human distinctions in vv6–9. [v6] Only Christ counts. To have the Gospel means that you can stand up to anyone, even if an opponent has all the honor and respect of the world. God shows no partiality. The Greek could be translated: "God does not receive the face or countenance of man." Those who "seemed to be" or "were thought to be something" are "nothing to Paul." He sees not as fleshly man who cares about appearances and titles, but as God does. *The spiritual person judges all things, but is himself to be judged by no one* (1 Cor. 2:15). "Partiality" means to judge outside of Christ, according to some human standard or law. But we are not God, and it is not given to us to judge people with finality.

The phrase "God shows no partiality" is a Hebraism. It literally says: "God does not receive the face of man." It reflects an Old Testament way of thinking. To lift the face is to grant favor or a request. It is used in the blessing God gave Aaron to bless the Israelites. The last part of the Aaronic benediction is: *the Lord make his face to shine upon you and be gracious to you; the Lord lift up his countenance upon you and give you peace* (Num. 6:25–26). God blesses because He is good, but man, who has a sinful heart, judges by deceptive human standards like beauty, ability, family relations, position, and other superficial things. We are not in the position to grant favor like God, apart from the Gospel. We live and believe only by His generous favor.

We show partiality—receiving the face of man—when we judge by clothes, reputation, wealth, or anything external. God, though, judges the heart, which we are not able to do.

> *My brothers, show no partiality as you hold the faith in our Lord Jesus Christ, the Lord of glory. For if a man wearing a gold ring and fine clothing comes into your assembly, and a poor man in shabby clothing also comes in, and if you pay attention to the one who wears the fine clothing and say, "You sit here in a good place," while you say to the poor man, "You stand over there," or, "Sit down at my feet," have you not then made distinctions among yourselves and become judges with evil thoughts?* (Jam. 2:1–4).

How are we to judge? By a man's confession of Christ, the Word he hears, and the church (and its doctrine) to which he subscribes. We can only judge by outward works, which Paul explains in chapter 5. All who have Christ's righteousness are bothers and sisters—part of the one body of Christ. Do not look down on a part of Christ's own body.

What they were makes no difference to me. Paul has his call from God. No man can override that. He is not being disrespectful. After all, he does meet with them and tell his Gospel. But as important as they may be, they cannot change his calling to the uncircumcised, that is, the Gentiles, those who do not have the written Law or the prophecies about the Messiah.

"Those who seemed" to be something "added nothing to me." The same word translated "added" is used in 1:16: *He was pleased to reveal his Son to me, in order that I might preach him among the Gentiles, I did not immediately consult* [confer, add] *with anyone; nor did I go up to Jerusalem to those who were apostles before me, but I went away into Arabia, and returned again to Damascus.* This word means "to present one's cause for approval; to add to, contribute." Again, the sufficiency of God's revelation is established by Paul's actions. This steadfastness could be called obstinate stubbornness (by the world), but when it is the saving Gospel, it is the Spirit's conviction, clinging to the source of life. Were we all as convinced and passionate about Christ's Gospel as Paul! In his words from 2:5: *to them we did not yield in submission even for a moment, so that the truth of the gospel might be preserved.*

Fellowship is established in vv7–10. [v7] They have here, at the same time, different ministries and the same ministry. They possess the same apostleship. The same Christ was working through the mouths of both parties. They were to preach the same Gospel, which does not distinguish between persons, but showers righteousness on all, bringing God's chosen into His kingdom. The Gospel itself cannot be changed to suit different cultures, but the words and ways of expressing it can vary. The forgiveness of sins declared by the power of Jesus' resurrection, however, cannot be modernized or updated. It remains the only way to God.

[v8] We often want to do other people's jobs, but we are to trust that God works through good order. Paul did not focus on the circumcised— that was not given to him. Though he might have been more qualified, considering his education and background, that was not God's charge. So also we are not to do others' office or function, but the one God has given us. He has put us where He wants us, and we can only be faithful for ourselves, not someone else. "Grace" means most narrowly "the favor of God given in Christ." In the words of one commentator: "Here it is . . . best to take this grace in its widest sense as including Paul's office, his ability, and his marked success" [Lenski, 87].

[v9] The pillars, or weight-bearing columns, of the Church seem to be these leaders, but no one can be saved by a mere man. Only Christ bridged the gap between God and man in His own body. He is the foundation. *For no one can lay a foundation other than that which is laid, which is Jesus Christ* (1 Cor. 3). All leaders in the Church are given a public duty and call, not to add to Christ's Gospel, but to

relay it and apply it correctly. Not even Peter could add to the one Gospel. Without leaders, humanly we might suffer, but the true Church depends only on the promise and work of Christ. He says: *on this rock* [the confession that Christ is Lord] *I will build my church, and the gates of hell shall not prevail against it* (Mt. 16:18). If the invisible Church is not built on Paul or Peter, how little it depends on a pastor or teacher today. It only "seems" to depend on them. If the called men proclaim the correct doctrine, it is enough.

They gave the right hand of fellowship to Barnabas and me, that we should go to the Gentiles and they to the circumcised. "Hand" is assumed, it is not actually in the Greek: "They gave to me the right." The word "fellowship" occurs after mentioning "given to me and Barnabas." In Scripture the right side denotes power, authority, and privilege. We do something similar today in a handshake. This is no mere formality described in this verse, though, but a symbol of spiritual agreement, since they preach the same Gospel of Christ. So they took a public stand against the Judaizers, who would have made Titus submit to that which Christ freed all men from.

[v10] They found common ground in helping the poor, which Paul also talks about in other letters. This act of mercy is not a part of the Gospel, but faith in Christ manifests itself in outward deeds. The Spirit cannot help but be active in us. Our love expresses itself in real, physical ways, but the love of Christ in the Gospel must be the fountain of all true good works. To urge good works, without first freeing from sin and the burden of the Law, is actually to place into slavery. This proper view of works is Paul's ultimate aim in his letter to the Galatians.

This account in Galatians of a conference is similar to what happened in Acts 15. Many commentators think it is the same conference being described. Regardless of the accuracy of that claim, the error is similar, though Acts 15 seems to be a bigger event, since the matter is settled with some finality and in more detail. Paul, for his part, here in Galatians mentions a more informal and private affair. The confession of the truth is the same, though. The entire book of Galatians deals with the same error plaguing the wider church in Acts 15, so it is helpful know what it says there.

> *But some men came down from Judea and were teaching the brothers, "Unless you are circumcised according to the*

custom of Moses, you cannot be saved." And after Paul and Barnabas had no small dissension and debate with them, Paul and Barnabas and some of the others were appointed to go up to Jerusalem to the apostles and the elders about this question. So, being sent on their way by the church, they passed through both Phoenicia and Samaria, describing in detail the conversion of the Gentiles, and brought great joy to all the brothers. When they came to Jerusalem, they were welcomed by the church and the apostles and the elders, and they declared all that God had done with them. But some believers who belonged to the party of the Pharisees rose up and said, "It is necessary to circumcise them and to order them to keep the law of Moses."

The apostles and the elders were gathered together to consider this matter. And after there had been much debate, Peter stood up and said to them, "Brothers, you know that in the early days God made a choice among you, that by my mouth the Gentiles should hear the word of the gospel and believe. And God, who knows the heart, bore witness to them, by giving them the Holy Spirit just as he did to us, and he made no distinction between us and them, having cleansed their hearts by faith. Now, therefore, why are you putting God to the test by placing a yoke on the neck of the disciples that neither our fathers nor we have been able to bear? But we believe that we will be saved through the grace of the Lord Jesus, just as they will." And all the assembly fell silent, and they listened to Barnabas and Paul as they related what signs and wonders God had done through them among the Gentiles. After they finished speaking, James replied, "Brothers, listen to me. Simeon has related how God first visited the Gentiles, to take from them a people for his name. And with this the words of the prophets agree, just as it is written, 'After this I will return, and I will rebuild the tent of David that has fallen; I will rebuild its ruins, and I will restore it, that the remnant of mankind may seek the Lord, and all the Gentiles who are called by my name, says the Lord, who makes these things known from of old.' Therefore my judgment is that we should not trouble those of the Gentiles who turn to God, but should write to them to abstain from the things polluted by idols, and from sexual immorality, and from what has been strangled, and from blood. For from ancient generations Moses has had in every city those who proclaim him, for he is read every Sabbath in the synagogues."

Paul and Barnabas were officially appointed and spoke publicly to the assembly. In Gal. 2, however, it says that Paul went up because of a revelation with Barnabas (taking along Titus as well). The goal of

Paul is not to give a balanced historical account (which is why it is hard to relate it to Acts 15), but to prove his independence from the other apostles. Paul deals with the issue of circumcision later in this letter. The matter is certainly not settled in Galatia. It is a raging controversy. But in Acts 15 the letter coming from all the apostles and leaders seemed to be final word, at least for the churches of Judea.

Acts 15 continues with the content of the letter, the final doctrine agreed to by all:

> Then it seemed good to the apostles and the elders, with the whole church, to choose men from among them and send them to Antioch with Paul and Barnabas. They sent Judas called Barsabbas, and Silas, leading men among the brothers, with the following letter: "The brothers, both the apostles and the elders, to the brothers who are of the Gentiles in Antioch and Syria and Cilicia, greetings. Since we have heard that some persons have gone out from us and troubled you with words, unsettling your minds, although we gave them no instructions, it has seemed good to us, having come to one accord, to choose men and send them to you with our beloved Barnabas and Paul, men who have risked their lives for the name of our Lord Jesus Christ. We have therefore sent Judas and Silas, who themselves will tell you the same things by word of mouth. For it has seemed good to the Holy Spirit and to us to lay on you no greater burden than these requirements: that you abstain from what has been sacrificed to idols, and from blood, and from what has been strangled, and from sexual immorality. If you keep yourselves from these, you will do well. Farewell."
>
> So when they were sent off, they went down to Antioch, and having gathered the congregation together, they delivered the letter. And when they had read it, they rejoiced because of its encouragement. And Judas and Silas, who were themselves prophets, encouraged and strengthened the brothers with many words. And after they had spent some time, they were sent off in peace by the brothers to those who had sent them. But Paul and Barnabas remained in Antioch, teaching and preaching the word of the Lord, with many others also.

The region of Cilicia and the city of Antioch are just south of Galatia—in fact, the regions share a border. The key takeaway from the decision of the Acts 15 council in Jerusalem is the view of the Law: the Mosaic Law does not apply to Christians. It was given to Jews as a shadow of Christ and a tutor. Now that Christ has come, the Gospel removes the burden of those ceremonial laws. *For it has seemed good to the Holy*

Spirit and to us to lay on you no greater burden than these requirements: that you abstain from what has been sacrificed to idols, and from blood, and from what has been strangled, and from sexual immorality. While these dictates seem like new ceremonial laws, they are a prescription for a certain time and people. Except for sexual immorality—which is a part of the moral law, and therefore God's eternal will—these two issues are matters of love. They are not laws dealing with salvation, but guidelines on how to show Christian love. Many Jews were converting to Christianity and their consciences did not need to be pricked by Gentiles eating food sacrificed to pagan idols. Blood carried a strong stigma for Jews, due to the ceremonial division of foods and the requirement of sacrifices. These two guidelines are not binding moral prescriptions for all time, but minimal temporary rulings commanded in love to avoid offense. Like when Paul in 1 Cor. 11 required long hair or a head covering for women, this was a decision for a particular context, so the church would not divide over a lack of love and order, rather than doctrine (the only reason it should). Similarly, Paul in 1 Cor. 11 ties the principle of headship (the ordering of the relationship between men and women), which is still valid, to the custom (of their day) concerning the length of hair and wearing hats. That passage reads:

> *For if a wife will not cover her head, then she should cut her hair short. But since it is disgraceful for a wife to cut off her hair or shave her head, let her cover her head. For a man ought not to cover his head, since he is the image and glory of God, but woman is the glory of man. For man was not made from woman, but woman from man. Neither was man created for woman, but woman for man. That is why a wife ought to have a symbol of authority on her head, because of the angels. Nevertheless, in the Lord woman is not independent of man nor man of woman; for as woman was made from man, so man is now born of woman. And all things are from God. Judge for yourselves: is it proper for a wife to pray to God with her head uncovered? Does not nature itself teach you that if a man wears long hair it is a disgrace for him, but if a woman has long hair, it is her glory? For her hair is given to her for a covering. If anyone is inclined to be contentious, we have no such practice, nor do the churches of God.*

The customs of our day are not those of Corinth. While the principle of headship, that God created male and female for different public and marital roles still stands, that divine order can be reflected in our appearances in different ways. But the Scriptures are clear that man is the head and is to lead: *the women should keep silent in the churches. For they are not permitted to speak, but should be in submission, as the Law also says. If there is anything they desire to learn, let them ask their husbands at home. For it is shameful for a woman to speak in church* (1 Cor. 14:34-35). If women are not submissive, men will not step up and fulfill God's order—that for which men and women were made.

A woman having short hair is not offensive or an act of defiance today. Paul is addressing a contentious, contemporary issue in the Corinthian church, not moralizing for us. That is why he says: *If anyone is inclined to be contentious, we have no such practice, nor do the churches of God.* Paul instructs to not fight over hats, but to hold fast to the Word of God and the Lord's created order, which is revealed in our bodies. The Father did not make a mistake by making male and female unequal and quite distinct.

As in Acts 15, there were sensitive consciences to respect, so certain foods were to be avoided in freedom—not because God really cares (we are free in the Gospel to eat anything at any time), but for the sake of love and weak Christians. God gloriously speaks through Paul of sacrificing externally for the weak who believe—not loud-mouths who accuse true believers of sinning and want to imprison them with ceremonial laws.

> *Therefore, as to the eating of food offered to idols, we know that "an idol has no real existence," and that "there is no God but one." For although there may be so-called gods in heaven or on earth—as indeed there are many "gods" and many "lords"—yet for us there is one God, the Father, from whom are all things and for whom we exist, and one Lord, Jesus Christ, through whom are all things and through whom we exist. However, not all possess this knowledge. But some, through former association with idols, eat food as really offered to an idol, and their conscience, being weak, is defiled. Food will not commend us to God. We are no worse off if we do not eat, and no better off if we do. But take care that this right of yours does not somehow become a stumbling block to the weak. For if anyone sees you who have knowledge eating in an idol's temple, will he not be encouraged, if his conscience is weak, to eat food offered to idols? And so by your knowledge this weak person is destroyed, the brother for whom Christ died. Thus, sinning against your brothers*

and wounding their conscience when it is weak, you sin against Christ. Therefore, if food makes my brother stumble, I will never eat meat, lest I make my brother stumble (1 Cor. 8:4–13).

We should voluntarily restrict our outward actions for the sake of the weak, but when someone demands that we restrict our freedom in Christ to supposedly please God, where He has not actually spoken, we are not to compromise. The latter is Paul's attitude in Galatians. In another context, Paul was fully willing to have Timothy circumcised for the sake of weak Jews who were sensitive about that issue. But in light of the Judaizers who demanded that circumcision be added to the Gospel, Paul says not even an angel from heaven should change our opinion or practice. It is right to stand up to those who demand obedience to false doctrine. To give in at that point is to disobey Christ and give up the true Gospel. The decisive issue is whether one is weak or a perverter of the Gospel. In practice it can be difficult to tell initially. However, by their fruit you will recognize them.

Paul shifts gears. **[v11]** He does not cite agreement with Peter, but disagreement. It really makes no difference to Paul who Peter is—he is only concerned with the teaching of Christ, not appearances. All teachers are sinners. An error in deed can be forgiven and tolerated, when it is done out of weakness, but an error in teaching is much more dangerous. It changes Christ into something other than the Messiah who saves. Then salvation is lost. Having the right practice will not help, since we are saved by what Christ did, not anything we do. Since righteousness is delivered in this Gospel, to change it is to cut hearers off from Christ.

The location of the disagreement in vv11–14 is the city of Antioch. There are two Antiochs mentioned in the New Testament. The first reference is to a large metropolis in Syria. The second, less important, city is in southern Galatia. Paul visited both. Acts 11:23–26 speaks of Paul's involvement with the main Antioch:

When Barnabas came and saw the grace of God, he was glad, and he exhorted them all to remain faithful to the Lord with steadfast purpose, for he was a good man, full of the Holy Spirit and of faith. And a great many people were added to the Lord. So Barnabas went to Tarsus to look for Saul, and when he had found him, he brought him to Antioch. For a whole year they met with the church and taught a great

> *many people. And in Antioch the disciples were first called Christians.*

This large Roman city of Antioch (in Syria) was north of Samaria and Judea.

The second Antioch was not as important. It is called "Antioch in Pisidia" in Acts 13. Evidently, there were many cities called Antioch, founded and named for Seleucid rulers several hundred years before Christ was born. This Pisidia was in the southwestern part of Galatia.

But here, as in Acts 11, Paul is talking about the Syrian Antioch, one of the largest and most important cities in that part of the world. Kephas (Peter) visited there, as it says. Paul refused to yield. He opposed, resisted, and stood his ground. Peter incorrectly applied the doctrine they held in common. Because the truth was at stake, Peter's action needed to be corrected. This holy confidence and doggedness Paul displayed in the first chapter of Galatians (*But even if we or an angel from heaven*) is not new. He resists Peter, the head apostle in the eyes of many.

Paul opposed Peter. He "stood against him to his face" [OJB], that is, directly. When there is a problem, face-to-face is the best way to deal with it. Jesus says the same: *If your brother sins against you, go and tell him his fault, between you and him alone. If he listens to you, you have gained your brother. But if he does not listen, take one or two others along with you, that every charge may be established by the evidence of two or three witnesses. If he refuses to listen to them, tell it to the church. And if he refuses to listen even to the church, let him be to you as a Gentile and a tax collector (Mt. 18:15–17).* The difference here is that Peter sinned publicly against the whole church, especially the Gentiles in Antioch. That is why Paul did not sin by speaking to Peter's face before everyone publicly. A public sin does not need a private rebuke—it can be corrected publicly. Indeed, the truth demands it.

Peter was condemned in his actions. When someone sins, it is an affront to God. It does no good to ignore it or speak non-confrontational words of acceptance. The sin is still there, festering and bringing God's wrath. To be quiet and ignore sin is easy—we do not like to provoke people. But if we have God's Word and know His judgment, it is wrong to not speak up and warn the one sinning against the Lord. The prophet

Ezekiel is told:

> *So you, son of man, I have made a watchman for the house of Israel. Whenever you hear a word from my mouth, you shall give them warning from me. If I say to the wicked, O wicked one, you shall surely die, and you do not speak to warn the wicked to turn from his way, that wicked person shall die in his iniquity, but his blood I will require at your hand. But if you warn the wicked to turn from his way, and he does not turn from his way, that person shall die in his iniquity, but you will have delivered your soul* (Ez. 33:7–9).

We are not to be murderous like Cain—we are our brother's keeper, if we know the truth. Pastors warn by simply speaking the Word of God.

[**v12**] In vv11–12, Peter changed his practice based on who was there to observe it. That is hypocrisy. What is the big deal with eating? It was considered an important honor to eat together, and still is in some respects today. So when Peter excluded some Christians (the Gentiles) for fear of the circumcision party, he was being two-faced and inconsistent. He condemned himself by denying the full application of the Gospel principle in practice.

The false teachers were called "those of circumcision." Their name stands for their major issue or doctrinal vendetta. This is the same type of circumcision party Paul is battling in Galatia with his letter. This account is not as much of a digression as we might think.

Gentiles were not circumcised like the Jewish Christians, who were circumcised eight days after birth. Peter did not want to be associated with Gentiles for fear of persecution. This weakness of Peter was not because of Christ's doctrine. But by fearing people who held false doctrine, he endangered the freedom of the Gospel. Here we see that even the apostles were imperfect and not inspired in all they did, but in their preaching and in the Words of Scripture we have now they were guided by the Holy Spirit. We are continually directed to their teaching, not their actions, personality, or being—since the teaching is from Christ and gives Christ.

This error of Peter is a separate issue from the practice of circumcision itself, though it is related. Titus earlier was pressured to submit to circumcision. The meal in question seems to be a regular table meal, not the special supper Christ instituted for Christians. This issue of eating—normal table fellowship—certainly became a confession of what is important. For Jews, due to their observance and respect for the ceremonial law, Gentile Christians could have easily been thought of as second class citizens. But that contradicts the Gospel, which makes believers fully righteous in Christ. There can be no degrees or levels of righteousness. One's birth, name, works, and flesh are nothing to God—in fact, they must be repented of. There can be nothing better than being righteous—called holy by the Gospel.

Because Peter was an apostle and one of the most public figures in the Church, his actions carried much weight. It would have been devastating to the proclamation of the Gospel for Kephas to continue his public withdrawal from the Gentiles. Paul rightly resists him against his face. Today that would be very offensive, but unless we stand for the truth in public, what is in our heart matters little. The world says to not judge—that it is always wrong to condemn. But that is incorrect—God will judge all. We are not to judge people's hearts, though we should give God's judgment over public sin. Because the Lord has spoken in Scripture against sin, we are merely relaying His judgment—even if we are branded troublemakers and "judgy," which is quite the insult today. Let God be true, and every man a liar (Rom. 3:4).

Notice that Paul does not name the heretics. They are not his concern. One group was from James, though they are not said to be the origin of the problem. Their presence precipitated a change in the actions of Peter. Others were of the circumcision party, who were feared by Peter. The error is clear. Peter separated himself, implying that the Gentiles were unclean—a basic Old Testament concept that Peter, and many Jews, had real trouble letting go of. In another context, Christ dealt with Peter's problem with so-called "unclean" foods:

> *Peter went up on the housetop about the sixth hour to pray. And he became hungry and wanted something to eat, but while they were preparing it, he fell into a trance and saw the heavens opened and something like a great sheet descending, being let down by its four corners upon the earth. In it were all kinds of animals and reptiles and birds of the air. And there came a voice to him: "Rise, Peter; kill and eat." But Peter said, "By no means, Lord; for I have never eaten anything that is common or unclean." And the voice came to him again a second time, "What God has made clean, do not call common." This happened three times, and the thing was taken up at once to heaven* (Acts 10:9–16).

The freedom of Christ was not immediately understood or relished, even by the apostles. You can imagine how laymen would have struggled. The Church of our day is also under satanic attack, which would deny the freedom of Christ's Gospel. Without the Spirit there is no true freedom coming to us in the Gospel.

If we are afraid to speak up because we fear men more than the holy God, we lack the confidence the Spirit gives in faith. Christ said: *And I tell you, everyone who acknowledges me before men, the Son of Man also will acknowledge before the angels of God, but the one who denies me before men will be denied before the angels of God. And everyone who speaks a word against the Son of Man will be forgiven, but the one who blasphemes against the Holy Spirit will not be forgiven* (Lk. 12:8–10). This is not speaking of every single possible opportunity to speak it, but when the truth is known and we become ashamed of the truth due to human consequences, it is a denial of Christ who will judge the living and the dead. In that moment we should be honored and proud to stand with Christ and confront the deniers of the Gospel, exactly like Paul resisted Peter.

[v13] Paul says that the other Jews were "co-hypocrizing"—the most literal translation of that verb. They were committing the same sin of hypocrisy as Peter. Hypocrisy means "to act contrary one's stated beliefs, to put on an inconsistent show for the sake of others." Notice how Paul emphasizes their hypocrisy with a verb and a noun, so that it is underlined. This false impression through a hypocritical practice was so prevalent that even Barnabas was led astray. The word used for Barnabas' error (translated "led astray") is used in a positive and negative sense by Paul elsewhere. Here it is most definitely negative, but he does not accuse Barnabas directly of hypocrisy. He is confused and deceived by popular pressure. Error is always more readily received than truth. Man's sinful nature is attracted to false teaching. The true teaching is only received by God's Spirit in man, but an error committed in ignorance is still an offense against the holy God.

[v14] In Greek, "conduct" refers to outward actions—one's steps. Right or straight footsteps—one's way of walking—is what the root of this Greek word implies. Peter's confession was not in accord with the Gospel, so it was a public denial of what Christ gave them to teach. A minister can undo his teaching by doing the opposite of what he says is

right. We see this in various financial and sexual scandals in our day too. The weak are sometimes not secure enough to withstand these assaults of the Devil. He continues to have a field day among us to this day.

Paul confronted Kephas before all the people. Paul was not trying to embarrass Peter or create a media firestorm. He was merely seeking to preserve the truth of Christ. Peter's sin was public, so he did not need to keep his correction private. Peter had sinned and misled others like Barnabas, a fellow worker in the Gospel. In the same way, Nathan the prophet had to confront David with his adultery and murder, even though David was a man after God's own heart. It is not the magnitude of the sin that separates from Christ, but an unrepentant, unbelieving heart that does not want forgiveness.

In v14, Jew and Gentile are used as adverbs: "Gentilely" and "Jewishly." Peter knew the truth and lived like a Gentile, observing their customs. He had the vision in which Christ told him that nothing is unclean that God has made. For a Jew who lives like a Gentile (not following Jewish ceremonial law), it was duplicitous to make Gentiles do what they were not given. *How can you force the Gentiles to live like Jews?* If Peter did not do this, he was laying a burden on the Gentiles that he was not willing to bear himself. Thus, the hypocrisy of Peter is evident. The issue was not whether one can keep aspects of the ceremonial law in freedom, but Peter's misuse of his apostolic authority and influence. He was implicitly giving weight to false teachers. The doctrinal error was not Peter's, but he was giving credence to it by his public actions—which were a louder confession than his actual teaching during the moment of controversy. He was acting contrary to his own convictions, as a hypocrite.

We also know that Peter, under different circumstances, received Gentiles. When Peter was sent to the Gentile Cornelius, *Peter said to them, "You yourselves know how unlawful it is for a Jew to associate with or to visit anyone of another nation, but God has shown me that I should not call any person common or unclean. So when I was sent for, I came without objection"* (Acts 10:28).

The word at the end of v14 in the original Greek is "Judaize," meaning "to make a Jew." Leaving it last emphasizes it even more. As the Gospel spread to non-Jews (Gentiles), the precise relationship between Gospel freedom and Jewish ceremonial observance had to be worked out. It was a painful process, as the book of Galatians relates. Who would have thought that God would use a Pharisee, Paul—a Jew of Jews—to teach concerning these great matters?

This case of Peter is an example of how tradition and custom often carry more weight with people than doctrinal conviction. Our practices carry so much more momentum than we think, but sometimes we fail to think through our actions and what they signify. If we are confronted by the truth of our hypocrisy (directly or indirectly), we should be thankful. A wise man accepts correction. *Whoever loves discipline loves knowledge, but he who hates reproof is stupid* (Pr. 12:1). Repentance means turning from our sinful ways and thoughts back to God. It is a vital necessity for the Christian, in view of sin which so easily entangles us. We cannot cling to both sin and Christ. Barnabas was just following the crowd and the pull of his own Jewish tradition. But the Gospel is not a matter of doing. The Law condemns man's natural way of thinking and the inclination to just blindly follow tradition, while the Gospel is a freedom revealed directly from heaven.

The Gospel will offend. The key is to offend the right people and not the wrong ones. The circumcision party of heretics would have been offended if Peter had kept eating with Gentiles. Conversely, since Peter did what he did, Paul and the Gentiles were offended. We cannot please everyone. We cannot serve two masters. We should not want to offend the weak, those who trust in Christ for forgiveness and comfort. Yet we cannot compromise in the face of worldly pressure. The strong can seem weak and beg for love. The weak can be combative and ornery, out of ignorance—but they are not trying to suppress the truth or make others do what God does not command.

Christ came to bring a sword, not peace between men. This means that the doctrine of Christ must prevail above human allegiances and political alliances. To love Christ means to suffer persecution for the truth, for it shows that we really hold to the one, true Gospel. And if we must suffer, it should be for the right reasons. Paul called Peter out to preserve the truth of the Gospel and help him personally. It is not easy to speak the truth in love, but if we do not do it, who will? Our light cannot be hidden under a basket. *You are the salt of the earth, but if salt has lost its taste, how shall its saltiness be restored? It is no longer good for anything except to be thrown out and trampled under people's feet* (Mt. 5:13).

This splintering Paul seems to cause is necessary to preserve the Gospel—specifically, the great teaching of Christian freedom. Freedom in God means only love toward the neighbor; it does not hurt or weaken others, but stands in the face of oppression and power plays to limit the freedom Christ earned for us. Freedom is not weak, but bold and sincere. Love is gentle, but it does not bend in the presence of error. This certainly goes against worldly wisdom, which is all or nothing. It flatly rejects everything or completely caves in and welcomes all opinions and vantage points. We are now in an age of "diversity," where differences are practically worshiped. To resist error is to go against the culture. But following Christ does not mean rigidly resisting everything. We are to love with Christ's strong love. Luther says it quite elegantly: "Where faith is involved, there we should be invincible, inflexible, stubborn, and harder than adamant, if this were possible; but where love is involved, we should be softer and more flexible than every kind of reed or leaf and ready to yield anything" [*Galatians*, 103].

Christ does not take sides against people. We simply apply the power of His keys—to forgive sins or withhold forgiveness, which is to bind or retain sins in Christ's name. All people need each key at different times. Those in need of comfort, but misled and searching, can be received and forgiven. This is not about the person or their personality. It is a spiritual judgment based on their confession and whether they are repentant. Consider how differently Christ speaks to "sinners" and to the Pharisees. He received the sinners and tax collectors by eating with them. He condemned and showed no patience to the Pharisees, whose hearts were hard.

We cannot apply the judgment of the Law to ourselves. The Word of God must come from outside ourselves when we are caught in temptation. We often want physical freedom to do what the flesh wants. The Gospel is often twisted to mean that Christ gives us freedom to sin—to do whatever our sinful flesh desires. In this instance we need only to hear Law, God's command and threat against sin. Unfortunately, when we despair and need hope during tribulation, we naturally latch on to the Law and all our failings. We rake our sin over our hearts and minds, ignoring Christ, treating Him as useless—like a drowning person struggling so much that he takes his rescuer under with him.

Intellectually knowing the doctrine of Scripture is a different matter than the art of applying it in order to lead a sinner to Christ. Since the Christian is a mix of old and new, sinner and saint, it is an art that the Spirit must teach.

The issue for Paul was not the personal holiness or sanctification of Peter. He was denying the Gospel in what he was doing. He was not walking *in step with the truth of the gospel* (v14). This public confession and action was causing others to doubt the sincerity of all who were preaching the freedom Christ won and the righteousness that God gives freely to all—Jew and Gentile. In the words of Paul: *Or is God the God of Jews only? Is he not the God of Gentiles also? Yes, of Gentiles also, since God is one—who will justify the circumcised by faith and the uncircumcised through faith* (Rom. 3:29–30).

The main word in v14 is "forced," translated here as "compel." Making people do things by God's command (not orderly discipline) is putting them under the Law and is not compatible with the true love of God. It counteracts the freedom of the Gospel. Paul made such a big scene because the central teaching of Christianity was at stake—not just eating food with others, but the essence of salvation as a free gift. It must be kept free in Christ. It does not depend on any works, including the works of ceremonial cleanness of the Old Testament. Outward distinctions are blown away by Paul—we are all leveled by the Law and lifted to heaven by Christ in the freedom of the Gospel.

Peter implied by his actions that circumcision (the defining mark of a Jew) was required to be united in fellowship, and therefore to be righteous in Christ. He was narrowing the way to salvation that Christ had opened with His own body. Paul was determined to stand against heaven (falsely preaching angels) and hell (Satan's work through the circumcision party). Peter relented, no doubt, so the truth was preserved. 2 Pet. 3:15–17 says:

> *Count the patience of our Lord as salvation, just as our beloved brother Paul also wrote to you according to the wisdom given him, as he does in all his letters when he speaks in them of these matters. There are some things in them that are hard to understand, which the ignorant and unstable twist to their own destruction, as they do the other Scriptures. You therefore, beloved, knowing this beforehand, take care that you are not carried away with the error of lawless people and lose your own stability.*

74

[v15] Peter, Paul, and all believing Jews are Jews by nature, but nature has nothing to add to salvation. Outwardly, it does seem to matter in man's eyes, but God does not show partiality. All are born into sin. Rom. 2:6–11 summarizes the matter:

> *He will render to each one according to his works: to those who by patience in well-doing seek for glory and honor and immortality, he will give eternal life; but for those who are self-seeking and do not obey the truth, but obey unrighteousness, there will be wrath and fury. There will be tribulation and distress for every human being who does evil, the Jew first and also the Greek, but glory and honor and peace for everyone who does good, the Jew first and also the Greek. For God shows no partiality.*

God judges everything, including the things we do and those we fail to do. This includes the thoughts we think and the love we fail to render. Since the first sin of Adam, all are alike condemned.

The value in being Jewish by nature is having God's Word, which forgives and promises the Messiah (what we call the Old Testament Scriptures today). They knew the Gospel, but that cultural fact did not make them righteous before God if they did not believe in Christ. Christ is the Greek word for the Hebrew "Messiah," which means "Anointed [One.]" They did know of Christ, the Lord's anointed, but mere knowledge is not faith. In faith, the Spirit makes us alive by the promise of Christ.

What is a "Gentile sinner?" That makes Gentiles—non-Jews—sound less important than Jews. Here Paul is following the common Jewish understanding. He does not mean "sinner" in a technical sense, as those guilty before God and under condemnation. Gentiles at this time were without the Gospel or the written Law, except for very limited exceptions (since Paul first brought the Gospel to them). They were steeped in sin and idolatry. They worshiped many gods, man-made idols, and were ignorant of God's will. They thought sexual immorality was fine. We might say someone is "pagan" today, even though he is outwardly a good citizen and a decent family man. Here he means that he has no care for or real knowledge of the things of God. Like the term "Gentile sinner," it means that, culturally, God's Word has no impact or relevance for him.

But for the Jews, having God's Word does not necessarily mean they believe it. Not all of God's Word is the same. A true Jew (inwardly) would have accepted Christ. They trusted in Him even before He was born or taught publicly. The promise of the Christ is above cultural and religious practices. Nathanael is the best example of this. He did not know Christ or recognize his face or name, but he did not have to change his beliefs or repent of not knowing Christ. He had the teaching, the promise of the coming Christ, though he did not know He was right in front of Him. Jn. 1:43–49 tells the story:

> *The next day Jesus decided to go to Galilee. He found Philip and said to him, "Follow me." Now Philip was from Bethsaida, the city of Andrew and Peter. Philip found Nathanael and said to him, "We have found him of whom Moses in the Law and also the prophets wrote, Jesus of Nazareth, the son of Joseph." Nathanael said to him, "Can anything good come out of Nazareth?" Philip said to him, "Come and see." Jesus saw Nathanael coming toward him and said of him, "Behold, an Israelite indeed, in whom there is no deceit!" Nathanael said to him, "How do you know me?" Jesus answered him, "Before Philip called you, when you were under the fig tree, I saw you." Nathanael answered him, "Rabbi, you are the Son of God! You are the King of Israel!"*

Nathanael had to be told that Jesus was the Messiah he had trusted in from the Old Testament promises. But this earthly fact did not change his faith in Him.

An account in the Gospel of Matthew deals with Jesus when He was accused of practicing loose table fellowship, which irritated the strict Jewish Pharisees. Mt. 9:10–13 describes it:

> *And as Jesus reclined at table in the house, behold, many tax collectors and sinners came and were reclining with Jesus and his disciples. And when the Pharisees saw this, they said to his disciples, "Why does your teacher eat with tax collectors and sinners?" But when he heard it, he said, "Those who are well have no need of a physician, but those who are sick. Go and learn what this means, 'I desire mercy, and not sacrifice.' For I came not to call the righteous, but sinners."*

Jesus uses "sinner" in a somewhat positive sense, meaning those who know that they are not righteous. They have a great need and desire for forgiveness as sinners, meanwhile, the "holy" or "righteous" (only in their own understanding of themselves) do not need a Savior or forgiveness, and therefore they naturally reject Christ, just like a healthy person does not desperately seek the services of a doctor. A sinner is a person Jesus came to save. Those who are not sinners (in their own mind) reject the Gospel. It is the same today. A "good person" does not need a man to die for them, let alone God's Son. Only the condemned, the forsaken, and the dying need a holy substitute—the risen Christ—to be their sin offering.

The Pharisees even called Jesus a "sinner," meaning He did not keep all their man-made traditions. *Some of the Pharisees said, "This man is not from God, for he does not keep the Sabbath." Others said, "How can a man who is a sinner do such signs?"* (Jn. 9:16). But the answer to the question is quite obvious: a true sinner in God's eyes cannot do such signs. In the blindness of their sin, they thought they were holy and Jesus—God Himself—was a sinner.

The definition of "sinner" changes, depending on how it is used. From man's perspective it usually refers to a group of people defined by their outward behavior and associations. But in the truest, most technical sense it means those under God's judgment—and therefore it includes even the most religious and devout—who do not keep this word: *You shall be holy, for I the Lord your God am holy* (Lev. 19:2; 1 Pet. 1:16).

Paul, though "righteous" by all Jewish standards, said this: *The saying is trustworthy and deserving of full acceptance, that Christ Jesus came into the world to save sinners, of whom I am the foremost* (1 Tim. 1:15). This is a "sinner" in the Christian technical sense: one condemned for not loving God. Everyone is truly a sinner in this sense. No matter how hard we try to cover up our sin, we have not lived up to God's standard and deserve death. This is why Jesus was born into death and suffered in this world for us.

The best understanding of the word "sinner" in the phrase "Gentile sinner" is "godless," that is, without any knowledge of the true God or His will. It has nothing to do with civil life, such as whether one pays taxes or has avoided imprisonment.

In v16, Paul leaves the historical and personal aspect and reaches theological heights. [v16] The definition of justification is crucial to understanding Paul (and all of God's Word). Justification means to declare righteous. This is the Father's activity on account of Christ. It does not speak of intrinsic goodness or outward behavior. It is called an alien, or foreign, righteousness, since it has nothing to do with us—we are not the cause of it. The Gospel opens up a new pathway to God. "Not justified by works of the Law" means that we are not righteous in God's sight by what we do. Instead, by works of the Law no one will be justified. Everyone is a sinner, according to God's just Law.

"Man," as in mankind in general, is whom Paul says *is not justified by works of the law*. This means not just certain people, but everyone. It is a universal judgment. In fact, that is the purpose of the Law: to accuse and bring out our guilt. The Law exposes us.

The counterpoint to works is faith. It is a simple word with many secular and religious definitions, but Paul is not talking about wanting something or thinking an event might possibly come true. Faith is in the Gospel—the same Gospel Paul defends here against the Galatian heresy. Faith is trust in the promise of God's grace in Christ. Faith is "in" something. True belief depends on a particular promise of the Lord. It is not a vague feeling or emotion in ourselves. God's righteousness comes through *faith in Jesus Christ, so we also have believed in Christ Jesus.* Faith latches on to Christ's works, making them its own. Without Christ, there is no true faith.

The classic definition of faith is from Heb. 11:1: *Now faith is the assurance of things hoped for, the conviction of things not seen.* The old KJV has a poor translation of this verse: *Now faith is the substance of things hoped for, the evidence of things not seen.* But knowing what we hope for (and what we know will happen) depends only on God Himself. Paul, in v16, starts with "knowing," so we are to know for certain: *The conviction of things not seen.* Faith is not an intellectual process or rational decision—it is entirely unreasonable (to natural man). We do not see the evidence that we are more loved by God in our daily lives. We do not get less suffering or troubles for believing in Jesus. We do not get younger or better looking as we get closer to the Resurrection. No, we actually become more dependent on Christ. Salvation is outside of ourselves. It is in a promise (which is what the Gospel is) that we are justified and righteousness before God. We rely on the fact that our sins are not held against us—they were taken away by Christ.

Paul uses "faith" (the noun) and the verb "believe" (a verb which has same root in Greek as "faith"). But being "faithful" in English is our action, not a gift. We can believe many things and be right or wrong, but faith in Christ is different. We cannot believe in Him for salvation without the Spirit. "A decision of faith" or "choosing to believe" is an oxymoron—a contradiction in terms. It is God who chooses us and gives faith.

Many today turn faith into a work. It is even difficult to talk about faith in the biblical way, because it is assumed that faith is something we do, manufacture, and increase by our own efforts. To demand it, to think we can make it happen, makes it like circumcision (a work). Then, it adds something to the Gospel, rather than receiving everything through Christ.

True hope is outside of us, or else we would possess it and do not need to look forward to what is promised. Rom. 8:24 speaks of the true, saving hope: *For in this hope we were saved. Now hope that is seen is not hope. For who hopes for what he sees? But if we hope for what we do not see, we wait for it with patience.* Faith in Scripture is a passive receptivity (from the standpoint of the flesh), a holding to Christ and His benefits—the opposite of a self-made feeling. It is active insofar as the Spirit is in the believer working that faith and renewing him.

Paul emphasizes this again at the end of v16: *by works of the law no one will be justified.* One way of rendering this is: "all flesh will not be justified from works of the Law." God through the Law condemns all humanity and shuts off that way to salvation. "Flesh" includes all our abilities, thoughts, and actions. These words could not be more radical. In dismissing everything on earth, Paul is extolling the Gospel. The gift of faith is nothing without Christ. It passively receives the righteousness of God.

Eph. 2:8-10 clearly makes faith not about us or our doing; it is about Jesus, who is our salvation: *For by grace you have been saved through faith. And this is not your own doing; it is the gift of God, not a result of works, so that no one may boast. For we are his workmanship, created in Christ Jesus for good works, which God prepared beforehand, that we should walk in them.* Faith is a gift, created by the Spirit in us, through the Gospel. Redemption was secured by Jesus and the application of that redemption (often called "sanctification" in Scripture) is a work of God the Spirit.

Paul uses the phrase "works of the Law" three times. That includes the ceremonial law: circumcision, Peter's avoidance of the "unclean" Gentiles, and abstaining from "unclean" foods. These ceremonial regulations are not over us today since we are free from these shadows. However, we are bound to civil obedience—being a good citizen, paying taxes, and raising responsible, working kids (Rom. 13). This outward behavior does not count for anything before God. But the divine Law that does apply to us we call the moral law. It is not done away with. It is summarized by Jesus: *You shall love the Lord your God with all your heart and with all your soul and with all your mind.* Being good outwardly is futile as a way to God. The Gentiles, by nature, were open sinners—"publicly," we would say today. It was clear to everyone from their outward behavior what they were. The Jews, on the other hand, were very religious and devout in practice. Still, their works, according to the Law, were just as offensive to God. They were even worse because they used their own works against Christ and made His Gospel something to despise. The superior righteousness of Christ made their fleshly works nothing, which they could not stand. Those who try to do works without the Spirit want to boast in them and use them against God. It is a sin to try to achieve good apart from the holy God, the source of all goodness. This becomes the ultimate rebellion: man's goodness is used against Christ's righteousness. So Paul, in the Spirit, cuts off all works—they have nothing to do with justification. They do, however, play an important part in the life of the Christian who has the Spirit—he does not deny that. But they have nothing to do with salvation or God's favor. The works of man must not even be considered when it comes to justification.

We are good at separating love and works with children, but not with God. We can be proud of our children and boast of what they have done, but it is because they are ours and we love them. We do not base our human affection on their grades or how they act hour to hour. "Good" works of the child always come after the love of the parent. Our love should not vary based on how they are performing. The great danger is not to be evil in deeds, but to use our best actions (human righteousness) against the Gospel and lose Christ, even if we show outward respect and follow the correct religious traditions. Christ is here speaking about faith in the heart and what it relies on. It has nothing to do with works, the outward qualities of a person.

Do not think of faith as a substance or something independent from Christ. Faith takes hold of Christ, so that Christ and His righteous are actually present and received in faith itself. It is not our faith that we treasure in faith, but the risen Christ and all His benefits. So our concern is not some bare, abstract "faith," but the true faith that God gives, which makes Christ our own. In Him, by faith, we have all His gifts, earned by His suffering and death: His forgiveness, His life, His resurrection, and His love. The Christian should not look inside himself (there is only sin there), but to Christ, who gave Himself for our sins. When sins assail us, this Gospel of Christ is the only comfort for troubled consciences—those who know they have failed God and are unrighteous. Even if we are righteous in the eyes of all men, we are condemned sinners in the eyes of the holy Law. But Christ comes in the Gospel and relieves our burdens, turning hell and punishment into heaven and grace.

Paul uses two phrases to speak of faith in Christ: *through faith in Jesus Christ,* and *justified by faith in Christ.* The Greek uses two different prepositions. "By faith" is the same preposition used in the phrase "by/of works of the Law." This parallel between faith and the Law is very important. It is an either/or distinction. We can be justified *by* works or *by* faith. If one work intrudes on faith (so that credit is earned before God), salvation is not *of* faith. So just one work, no matter how distinguished or unimpressive, is damnable if brought into justification. It negates Christ and all He did for us. This includes even the works that God gave and commanded, such as circumcision (which was first given to Abraham). In Christ, we do not avoid good works, but we must first know God and be free in Christ before any work is acceptable in Christ (by faith). All works must be kept free (before Christ) and done in love. They have nothing to do with our status before God, that is, where our hearts rest and find comfort. *For whatever does not proceed from faith is sin* (Rom. 14:23).

"To justify" implies God taking action. He is the one who justifies. The Father makes a legal decision as judge. When we have the right faith in Christ—the incarnate Christ who rose from the dead—we are clothed in Him. We are recognized as righteous, even though we continue to sin in weakness and our hearts produce all sorts of uncleanness. Faith is not a fiction or a leap of faith. It is to rest one's heart directly on the promise of Christ, who died for our sins and was raised for our justification. This judgment happens in time (when faith is given through the Word of

Christ), but looks forward to Judgment Day. Think of the end times description of the sheep and the goats in Mt. 25. The judgment of works comes after the division of sheep or goats—not before. *Before him will be gathered all the nations, and he will separate people one from another as a shepherd separates the sheep from the goats. And he will place the sheep on his right, but the goats on the left.* The sheep are judged by the good works they do not remember. They did not trust *in* them or live *by* them, but *in* and *by* the Shepherd. That is why they are sheep.

We cannot see the difference between sheep and goats now. This is a promise to be hoped in and depended on, not an intellectual curiosity. In God's eyes we are new and not what we appear to be. Our sins have been removed and are now as far away as the east is from the west. Though we seem worse off—our sins are more visible and God appears more hands off—in Christ we are justified. *We also have believed in Christ Jesus, in order to be justified by faith in Christ and not by works of the law, because by works of the law no one will be justified.*

Works for justification are condemned, even though they will play a role at the Last Day. Works that please the Lord are merely the fruit of faith, the result of the Spirit working in us. One does not produce nice vegetables by focusing on the fruit alone, ignoring the health of the plant. Seeking to be justified by works is like hanging pretty fruit on a dead tree with string. Paul directs us away from what we see—the desirability of works to our sinful eyes—and towards Christ. His works were not pretty, but bloody and deathly. Christ's deeds appear wretched to man's natural eyes, so that He appears to be everything evil. But life is found in Jesus' death, which is our life. Faith lives in this promise: Christ kept the Law and did all that God demands therein, so we live *by* faith, not *by* works of the Law.

Verse 17 follows closely v16. [**v17**] "If we are seeking *or* searching to be justified in Christ." The present tense is used—it is an ongoing activity. That can be misunderstood. Justification is all or nothing, and it happens at a point in time. There is no partial forgiveness or righteousness. This righteousness that the believer lives in is ongoing (as is faith). Without its continuance, we would be condemned as sinful. However, we can lose faith and cease be in Christ. The struggle to live in Christ *by* faith and not *by* works of the Law exists until we leave this present evil age. Unlike all other goals we pursue, this righteousness by faith is not about trying harder or using our own resources. We should not seek to be more holy from within. Rather, we hear the Word and become more sinful the more we are convicted by the Law, so we die to our sin and live in the promise of forgiveness by faith. Christ is the author and perfecter of this faith.

The word for "our endeavor" is actually the verb "to seek" in participle form. This verbal is turned into a noun in the ESV. The same verb is used in 1 Cor. 10:24: *Let no one seek his own good, but the good of his neighbor.* We seek by being passive, by giving up our own righteousness and confessing our sin. Christ made us alive and will preserve us by the Gospel promise.

"To be justified" is God's work. It does not happen in us, such as through a feeling in the heart or intellectual reasoning, but in God. In a real sense, when Christ was condemned to die, there your sins died also. You are free from the Law and this righteousness is applied to you through faith in Christ. Your station in the world will not change, nor will your heart, but in Christ you are holy to the Father and have become His adopted child. The Father has decreed it, and so it is true and trustworthy. That is the Gospel message by which we live.

But we are "sinners." Paul includes himself, so "sinners" here does mean not just open, public sinners, like above when he speaks of "Gentile sinners," but those unrighteous before God. All are condemned for their sins, if the Law and its judgment are applied.

Here Paul addresses a human argument. It sounds ridiculous, but it must be addressed. Fallen, fleshly reason argues: "If no works are considered, it does not matter what works we do. We can do anything we want, so sin greatly and live a sinful life to the full." This is how the unbeliever thinks: "If Christ saves only sinners and not good people, people who strive to be holy, is Christ a minister of sin? Is He a deacon of evil, who promotes and encourages sin?"

Both "minister" and "deacon" mean "servant." Of course, this is false; Christ cannot tolerate sin. God is holy and does not approve of evil. It would be blasphemy to accuse Christ (who is God) of promoting sin. That is the danger of the Gospel in man's eyes. It erases sin by forgiving it and removes the Law-based struggle to be good. People will abuse the Gospel (in unbelief), but it is not possible for one to be ruled by Christ and the sinful flesh simultaneously. In reality, the Gospel gives hope to sinners who cannot see how sinful they truly are. Man thinks that the Gospel itself is evil and dangerous, but when the flesh does this, man is just showing his true colors. He is rebelling against God and rejecting His mercy and salvation.

But forgiveness is not approval of sin (that is the human argument) or permission to continue to sin. Christ makes us new, so that we can start to be truly good through the Spirit in the heart and will, out of love for God. We are not just forcing ourselves to do hypocritical acts under the hopeless weight of the Law and the standards of men. It really is a question of where true goodness is located—in the Law or in the Gospel, in man or in Christ.

The more sins we have, the more forgiveness is needed, so some would argue that to sin more is to have more Christ. But that is false, unbelieving logic. Faith is in Christ, and we live in Him. We hate the sin for which our Savior died. It is not an abstract forgiveness we have. It flows from His body and blood, given and shed for sins. Trust in this is love for His suffering on our behalf. To embrace sin in response to the Gospel is to re-crucify Christ and reject Him. *For those who have tasted the goodness of the word of God and the powers of the age to come, and then have fallen away,* (it is impossible) [according to their own will] *to restore them again to repentance, since they are crucifying once again the Son of God to their own harm and holding him up to contempt* (Heb. 6:4–6). Faith is love for Christ and results in thanks for His redemption of our bodies. Love does not spit in the face of Christ who saves us. This passage from Heb. 6 only applies to one who actually had the Spirit and knew Christ by faith—not the pagan who might know the words of the Gospel, but not its power. This is the sin against the Spirit, by one who has the Spirit and His freedom to begin with.

If justification in its entirety is God's work, how can we "seek" it? This is speaking to the redeemed believers ("we", so including Paul himself). We are not puppets, but sinners who believe and are given a new Spirit. The Spirit animates us, so in our minds we want good, even though the flesh prevents that from fully happening. In the Spirit we want to fulfill God's will, but not apart from God. We are not to return to the Law and see works as an obligation. We gain nothing from the Law. We already have righteousness and the Spirit. All is given by faith. Rather, we seek to remain where we are in Christ, though we can certainly remove ourselves from faith.

By the distractions of this world, like wealth and possessions, or by public sin, like sexuality immortality, our hearts can be turned from Christ. If that happens, it is all our doing. It *is* possible to fall away. It is Paul who says: *But I discipline my body and keep it under control, lest after preaching to others I myself should be disqualified* (1 Cor. 9:27). Elsewhere, this is described as restraining the flesh and dying to its lusts. We can never practice this too much, as long as the flesh is hanging around our necks.

"We were found sinners." This is not like accidentally finding a penny. It means that the Law accused us and let us know God's holy judgment which results in death and condemnation. Confessing your sin to the living God is the corollary to being found a sinner. Recognition of sin and confessing it to the Father is a spiritual act. Only a sinner with nothing to offer God trusts in Christ for righteousness. We are condemned in the flesh in order to be judged righteous in Christ, that is, to be justified. Both judgments of the Law and the Gospel fit together, though they are very different standards for achieving righteousness.

Paul answers the first rhetorical question in v17 and then explains it with an earthly illustration in v18: a construction analogy. [**v18**] The Greek original actually reverses the order of the verbs: "if the things which I destroyed, again I build, a transgressor I make myself." The order here is correct. Before Christ we were in darkness, unable to do any good, under the illusion we were something before God that He must respect. After God's Word destroys our human righteousness, we are given faith in the Gospel, as well as the Spirit, so we may live a new life. In faith, we seek to not seek our own righteousness. Righteousness is for us in Christ.

A Christian, insofar as he is a Christian, sins out of weakness. One ruled by the Spirit cannot plan to sin against God, or else he is not led by the Spirit. We do not live the same life ruled by the flesh as before, after we are sanctified by the Spirit. "Sanctified," in Scripture, usually refers to the whole of justification and the new life of faith.

The same verb for "destroy" is also used in Mt. 27:40: *You who would destroy the temple and rebuild it in three days, save yourself! If you are the Son of God, come down from the cross.* When used of buildings, this word means "to demolish or dismantle."

"Prove myself" means "to approve or stamp oneself as a sinner or lawbreaker; to label ourselves the guilty party." It is not the Law's fault we sin—it is ours, even if the Law was the occasion and opportunity to sin. If I condemn my sins by confessing them to God, I do not approve of them. This is turning from transgressions in repentance. It is a negative recommendation of ourselves. It is not saying we are good, but, on the contrary, that we have no good in us. Faith lives in Christ, so we are filled with sin, but desperate to be delivered from the body of death in hope.

The fact that we believe the Gospel does not indict Christ for our sin, but ourselves. Forgiveness is not Christ approving of our sin, but the result of the Father's punishment of Jesus for our sins. He took our guilt and condemnation upon Himself in selfless love. This is the only way to truly hate sin—to embrace Christ's satisfaction for it. In Christ's body, the Father's anger over our trespasses was appeased.

Think in worldly terms. Rebuilding something, after you have destroyed it, marks a change of attitude and ways. No one rebuilds what he believes should never have been there in the first place. We are at fault, so Christ is exonerated (as if God needed it). Unfortunately, this is how sinful men think, so the point is made clear by Paul.

Paul has shifted from his address to Peter to the theological issue of sin and Christ. The transition is seamless. He is talking to the Galatians and us, not Peter, here. But Peter's action would make Christ a minister of sin, if we follow man's flawed logic. Gentiles were assumed to be inferior because they did not have the written Law and its revealed customs. Jews are still sinners before God though, and Jew and Gentiles are both justified in Christ, apart from works. Those who seek to be justified by the Law find themselves enslaved to the Law and sin. So, Paul, as a Jew, speaks for his people: *we too were found to be sinners* (v17).

For if I rebuild what I tore down, I prove myself to be a transgressor. Paul uses the first person here (*I* rebuild, *I* tore down, *I* prove). This admission can be set in the context of Paul's life and conversion, which he laid out in chapter 1. He destroyed the Church (in his own words), the opposite of being a "pillar" and apostle. But Christ called Paul to build the same Church he previously destroyed. Therefore, Paul is guilty, not Christ. The Gospel cannot be blamed for his former persecution of the Church. Paul, the sinner, accepts all the blame. If we rebuild, that is, aim to fulfill the Law in love, we do not approve of our previous tearing down, which was disobedience. It is we who have changed, not God or His Law. Sinners cannot do the Law, though we formerly sought to be justified by it.

Paul's words are simple, but the contrast between faith and works—Law and Gospel—is most difficult to apply to real people. Christians have two natures, or sides. Many Christian churches preach faith, but then immediately after giving Christ take back salvation by adding works of the Law as a condition to salvation, demanding that such works be done to be saved. It is so natural and easy for preachers to teach salvation by works of the Law, and it is also natural to hear them, because we naturally only know the Law. The Gospel is different. It cannot be comprehended by natural reason and must be revealed in the Spirit. If Peter, the great apostle, fell personally at so late a time, certainly no one is exempt from this struggle.

We read much of the Law in Scripture: "Do this and live." But we know we cannot do it. Therefore, the Law is not encouragement or motivation, but condemnation and exposure of our sin that should drive us into Christ's bosom. Doing and inculcating works will always find an audience. People want this, not a Savior who has done everything. The Gospel must be driven into cold hearts like a stake into frozen ground. The Law, and God's wrath revealed in it, helps by breaking down our defense of self-righteousness. Not everyone who calls himself a Christian or preaches Christ has the true Gospel. Paul even had to take a stand against the lead apostle, who some today would even (falsely) call the head of the Church. The head of the Church is really Christ, not a sinful person.

To add one work to the Gospel or create any dividing line between Jew and Gentile undoes everything. Rom. 10:4 puts it another way: *For Christ is the end of the law for righteousness to everyone who believes.* Faith without works is dead (the topic of the book of James). This is true, but it must not be turned around, to make it seem like works make faith alive. No, faith does it all and will produce works if it is the true, right faith in Christ which justifies. False faith produces no works, which is the abuse of the Gospel James warns about. A faith which does not lead to rebuilding what we demolished, but further demolishing (sinning) is not faith at all, even if it is called that. It is satanic, even if Christ's name is invoked. *What good is it, my brothers, if someone says he has faith but does not have works? Can that faith save him? If a brother or sister is poorly clothed and lacking in daily food, and one of you says to them, "Go in peace, be warmed and filled," without giving them the things needed for the body, what good is that? So also faith by itself, if it does not have works, is dead* (Jam. 2:14–17). This is a judgment against Christians using the Gospel to cover up their sin and indulge in the flesh. Since they live without the Spirit, without works, and without true faith, they are to be condemned. But this does not undo Paul's teaching. Each audience must be kept in mind. James is speaking to those who fail to give food to the starving and clothing to the naked (not the poor stranger halfway across the world, but the poor person we actually encounter). Jam. 2:19 goes on to say: *You believe that God is one; you do well. Even the demons believe—and shudder!* This is an intellectual "faith," not a living faith producing good works by the Spirit.

[v19] Here we see the purpose and function of the Law. It is not positive. It does not give life, but the opposite: death. We have here the normal word for death: "to die." What kind of death is this? Not physical, but spiritual. It means to no longer be under the influence and rule of the Law. It is not your boss, friend, or motivator. The Law is good, righteousness, and holy. But we are not. *The very commandment that promised life proved to be death to me. For sin, seizing an opportunity through the commandment, deceived me and through it killed me* (Rom. 7:10–11).

To try to achieve salvation through works is our natural inclination. It is inborn in us, written on our hearts. The conviction of the Law awakens sin in us. This is not the role of tradition and ritual, but the holy, eternal Law, which reveals God's wrath. This is the divine Law in all its forcefulness, which demands perfection under penalty of hell. When we hear the full weight of the Law, it awakens sin in us, because we hate God and are born rebelling against Him. This Law does not produce something new in us, but reveals our miserable condition and makes our sins known to us. We are so turned in towards ourselves, before the Law comes, that we do not have any idea of our poverty before God. So the Law must reveal it by threats and the curse of death.

We all once lived in the passions of our flesh, carrying out the desires of the body and the mind, and were by nature children of wrath, like the rest of mankind (Eph. 2:3). The natural man lives in his passions, blessing them and thinking that they are aligned with God's will, so that he imagines he is good. But the Law—the active, harsh Law—reveals the wrath of God. The way to life (which is what the Law promises, if we could do it) becomes closed, and we die to it. It actually kills us by making us die to our own righteousness and revealing the consuming anger of God. This is at odds with the natural understanding of the Law as a positive power in our lives. The true knowledge of the Law cannot be maintained without great effort.

This death to the Law fits in with Rom. 7:1–3:

> *Or do you not know, brothers—for I am speaking to those who know the law—that the law is binding on a person only as long as he lives? For a married woman is bound by law to her husband while he lives, but if her husband dies she is released from the law of marriage. Accordingly, she will be called an adulteress if she lives with another man while her husband is alive. But if her husband dies, she is free from that law, and if she marries another man she is not an adulteress.*

Paul here uses an example of an earthly law ended by death: marriage. God instituted marriage so that husband and wife are joined as long as they both live. A union can be broken by divorce (by denying the marriage vows and breaking the one flesh bond), but this is a sin before God. This is becoming an increasingly obscure teaching, because we live in a society where divorce is easy and often without just cause. But if God joins husband and wife (as He says He does since the first union of Adam and Eve), then divorce breaks the divine union. This is not the same as legally recognizing that the one flesh union has been actually broken by adultery or denied by permanent desertion. So, divorce cuts a married person in half. As painful as living with another sinner can be, it is always better than physically dividing ourselves—cleaving off our other half. It is not human emotions or romantic love which joins husband and wife, but God Himself for a lifelong union. Divorce, which is properly always adultery, undoes God's work of uniting. We remain united until death—when God breaks the marital union—or until man sinfully does so by adultery. Every marriage must end, but it is to be according to God's gracious will. So, also, death to the curse of the Law leads to freedom in Christ from the threat of the Law. *Likewise, my brothers, you also have died to the law through the body of Christ, so that you may belong to another, to him who has been raised from the dead, in order that we may bear fruit for God* (Rom. 7:4).

Even here, we see that God's Law is unbendable. It does not change to suit our circumstances. But, we have broken it and are guilty. The punishment is death. Christ, though, died to sin for us under the Law, to give us new life. Forgiveness is a gift that removes all the burdens and divine punishments of the Law. Yes, even the sin of divorce, murder, adultery, and every rebellion against God is forgiven. All sin is gone, nailed to the cross of Christ. So you are dead to your sins and the Law which threatens so harshly.

The Law itself works death—the Law is the ministry of death. Its purpose is negative: to kill. What does it say in v19? The goal of the ministry of death is not to die physically, but to die to the Law, so that we live to God by faith. It serves the Gospel as a servant. The Law is like a plow for the ground of our hard hearts. It gets the heart ready for the seed of the Gospel, but does not cause anything to grow on its own. The Law breaks down our pride and self-righteousness and closes the pathway to God of works. The Gospel makes us alive and causes us to be awakened by faith. The Law, on the other hand, awakens our sinful nature, so that we become aware of God's anger and our sin.

How can we who died to sin still live in it? Do you not know that all of us who have been baptized into Christ Jesus were baptized into his death? We were buried therefore with him by baptism into death, in order that, just as Christ was raised from the dead by the glory of the Father, we too might walk in newness of life (Rom. 6:2–4). This death in Baptism is personal. It is not the same as the death Jesus died for all mankind, though it flows from it. This is one we experience daily, though it does not gain us anything, as Christ's did. It cannot be inherited, passed down, or given to us by a friend. Paul uses the first person in this verse. This death is the counterpart to faith. We can believe only for ourselves. Paul, when speaking of these spiritual realities, often switches to first person, setting himself forth as the Christian paradigm. He was not superior to us, but was killed by the Law and lived by grace—just like we do. We are in good company when we die to sin and the Law and rise in Christ by faith. There is no other pathway to life than through death to the power of the Law.

This verse is at odds with much of today's "Christian" self-help advice. Morality, rules, dedication to godliness, and forced obedience is just warmed-over Law, which brings death. It is not the better part of Christianity. By itself, the Law has nothing to do with the revelation of grace and truth in God's own Son. Too often the Gospel is just a prelude to the Law in practice. Sins are forgiven and guilt is taken away by the cross, in order to bind people by all sorts of laws. This is backwards. The Law is not the pinnacle of Christianity, but it is needed in order to kill and destroy our righteousness. The Law is glorious, since it is from God and offers life, but it is a life that no one can partake of. It is like a starving man looking at food through the window of a locked restaurant. It does not bring hope, but frustration. Ultimately the Law should bring death—to the way of works. That path to God becomes dead and we cease trying to pretend that we live by the written code, *so that* [we] *might live to God.*

"Dead to the Law" means that the new man is not controlled by the Law. This does not mean that the Law has no validity or purpose for Christians, not at all. Our old man, along with its passions, can only sin under the Law. So the Law was a deadly force to us before Christ came. But once we are dead to our sins in Christ and live by the promise, we are free according to the new man. We desire to fulfill the Law truly, which is a matter of love. No longer are the commandments separated from the Father who authored them.

This verse turns death on its head. We think of death—including the frustrations of the flesh and not getting what we want—as bad. But in Christ who died we learn to die willingly. It is the only way to live to God. Eternal life is not indulging the flesh. We are to use Christ's death against the attacks of the Law and see death in ourselves as good. So, being killed by the Law is really the opposite of death. It allows for life itself in Christ. That is what Paul says: *For through the law I died to the law, so that I might live to God.* We are not to live according to the Law or strive to be God-like by what is in us. Instead, we are to be Christ-like and die as He died to our sin, so that it holds no power over us. We follow in His footsteps and find death to the flesh most desirable. Even physical death becomes the sweetest sleep in the strength of the Spirit, who will bring us to life at the Resurrection. It is something we long for—to be rid of the filth of our sinful nature.

These are not words that can be understood by human reason—they are entirely spiritual. They are to be lived—they actually interpret us. They are not a rule to dissect, study, and try to follow. It must be God's Law and grace that come to us to kill and make alive. This verse is to be lived—for as long as we are in the world.

Only in freedom from the curse of the Law is there life, but we naturally seek to use it to get to God, unless we die to the Law. We die to it when we believe, and continue to do so because the flesh does not die easily. This ongoing struggle points forward to when we will leave this world, and the flesh, behind.

To be dead to the Law means its threats do not touch us, as far as God is concerned. It is an internal freedom. Nothing external changes when we are brought to life. We die by being shown that we were already dead in sin. But in death (the proper work of the Law) there is life (through Christ's death). These two are separate and distinct, though they are both works of God. We must die and have no sins or guilt on us, in line with God's reckoning. This is a new existence in Christ—totally apart from the Law of God. This is the freedom of the Gospel. It is in the conscience, through the Spirit who gives us life and makes us truly alive. *Truly, truly, I say to you, unless one is born of water and the Spirit, he cannot enter the kingdom of God. That which is born of the flesh is flesh, and that which is born of the Spirit is spirit* (Jn. 3:5–6). The flesh cannot create spirit through the Law. Only the Spirit gives the life of Christ.

Insofar as we are proud and sin erupts in us, we still need the Law, so we die to those sinful passions. The way of living by the Law is to improve ourselves and try harder. But that is not Christian at all—we are to die. We must despair of any salvation that involves our efforts. This fear and dread the Law produces is death to that doorway to God. The Law—not the static information of the Law, but the threatening lightening bolt of His wrath which reveals sin and damns to hell (and is felt in the conscience)—kills us. Only then can the Gospel be glorious and supreme, so that Christ is our God.

We continually die and live. We are not promised in this world a nice, comfortable life. Rather, we go from life to death. We latch on to the Law and think that God is angry and vengeful, but that is ignoring

Christ, so we need to die spiritually through the Law. Until we die to the Law, we cannot live to Christ. It is either one or the other. We cannot see God as gracious and loving in the Law, so we must die to life of, or in, ourselves. We must not be afraid to die physically, and especially spiritually, to the Law's threats. The living promise of the Gospel conquers all doubt, despair, and death, causing us to live with Christ in safety.

Luther writes:

> By paying attention to myself and considering what my condition is or should be, and what I am supposed to be doing, I lose sight of Christ, who alone is my Righteousness and Life. Once He is lost, there is no aid or counsel; but certain despair and perdition must follow. This is an extremely common evil; for such is human misery that in temptation or death, we immediately put Christ aside and pay attention to our own life and our own deeds. Unless we are raised up here by faith, we must perish [*Galatians*, 166].

Luther sets forth the effects of the Law and the inclination to depend on the commands of God—ignoring Christ, who alone gives life.

The preposition "through" is significant. The Law condemns—that is its primary purpose and mission. But not all that condemns is the holy Law. The "through" speaks of instrumentality. The divine commands condemn sins and sinners. In Christ, though, the Law does not condemn. It has no power over the one who has died to it, and in Christ we have died. His death is ours.

[**v20**] Paul uses Christ against the wrath of the Law. So, Jesus is not a new, more intense lawgiver. Neither does He relax the commands for us. He died under the Law to set us free from the Law. Under the Law there is no freedom or life, but Paul says that he was killed. He personally died by Christ's crucifixion, in the righteous verdict of the Gospel. That means that when Christ died, Paul (and you) died to sin. That condemnation came in the Law, but it is taken away by the Gospel. Christ died for us to the Law and all the punishment we deserve. This is the most delectable freedom that Christ won for us, which no one can take away.

What amazing language! Paul is not talking about Jesus' death as a neutral observer. He died *with* Christ on the cross. This only makes sense in terms of the Law and the Gospel. So, we cannot separate Christ and ourselves. We have all of Christ in the Gospel, and so we are alive. We are dead to the flesh, but alive to God. We lead a double life. No one can see our true life in Christ. We must regard the sinful part of us, what is not of the Spirit, as dead and crucified. It is just as much dead as Christ was when He was taken down from the cross. Nothing good can come from the flesh. All righteousness must come from Christ, who is so close, Paul says that He is in us. We are *in* Him if we die *with* Him.

Paul was crucified together with Christ. "Co-crucified" is the most literal translation of this verb. This new life means death to the flesh, but life to God in the Gospel. When we believe, we live in Christ and partake of His death and resurrection. The same word is used in Rom. 6:6: *We know that our old self was crucified with him* ["co-crucified"] *in order that the body of sin might be brought to nothing, so that we would no longer be enslaved to sin.*

It is no longer I who live. The flesh, including everything sinful we were born with, is dead. We are completely new in Christ. Consider these words and live in them. They are living words. Even though you do not feel more alive and they will not cause you to become an Olympic athlete or live an extra 100 years, you live to God. This is an internal, spiritual life, not a temporary one. It is an invisible life, because it is in Christ who we do not see yet. All sins and evil thoughts are crucified—they were killed roughly 2000 years ago. You are no longer you (a sinner), but live in Christ as a holy person. If we believed this fully, we would not be held down by any event in this world. What Christ did is ours: death, then resurrection to life. We are Christ's, and He is ours.

It is not longer I who live but Christ who lives in me. We do not have life in ourselves. The Law demands that we "do," but we cannot make ourselves alive. The situation is much more desperate than we may initially think. Whatever life we have is from Christ, through the gift of the Spirit. Jn. 15 describes us as branches and Christ as the life-giving vine: *Already you are clean because of the word that I have spoken to you. Abide in me, and I in you. As the branch cannot bear fruit by itself, unless it abides in the vine, neither can you, unless you abide in me. I am the vine; you are the branches. Whoever abides in me and I in him, he it is that bears much fruit, for apart from me you can do nothing.* Apart from Christ, even though possessing the Law, there is no good for us.

This is not just a new way of thinking or a "new lease on life," as they say, but the making of an entirely new person. Christ is God for us, and, as a result, is inside of us—joined to us in the baptismal promise. This is the consequence of the Gospel. We are not the source of our righteousness, nor is something inside of us. We are never to take our focus off of Christ who died for us. We only know He is for us in His obedient suffering and the fact that He received the penalty of death—our death.

We live by faith in this world. We rarely feel or see the new man, but we live in hope that God is truthful. His Gospel is our life, because it reveals Christ to us. Faith and the flesh are contrasted. We trust we are alive in Christ, for this is how we become alive—according to the promise of the Gospel. There is no life in doing something, which would be of the Law.

The last part of v20 tells us what we believe in, the very content of Christ's promise: His life for us. Christ, the Messiah, is the Son of God. In Him dwells the fullness of God, since He has always been one with the Father and the Spirit. That fact of His divinity would not help us or be worthy of faith if we did not know why God became man. He died to our sin in love and still loves us. Notice that Paul says "me:" *who loved me.* Faith applies and appropriates the universal promise that God so loved the world to "me," so that Christ becomes "mine." He won us grace by submitting to the Law and to death itself. How humiliating for God to die, we might think, if it weren't our just deserts and what leads us to life. Instead, the death of God, the author of life, becomes our greatest joy in the Spirit. That is why, in all honesty, we can call Good Friday "good." Not in itself, as though death were a friend, but because the Son of God did not stay dead. In dying, Jesus slayed death and gave life through His body.

This new life that Paul describes here is summarized very succinctly by the phrase *the Son of God who loved me and gave Himself for me.* This word for "love" is the verb form of "agape," the Greek term for sacrificial, self-giving love. It implies goodwill and esteem on the part of the one who loves. The object loved is not the cause of this love. Sinful humans often think of love as that which devours and consumes without respect for its object (as when people say they "love" chocolate). But "agape" denotes prizing and delighting in a thing. It has nothing to do with desire or longing: *It is not self-seeking, it keeps no record of wrongs* (1 Cor. 13:5). It speaks of sacrifice, self-giving, and following the direction of the will. This love is chosen and purposed—it is not a feeling which comes and goes (as when people fall in and out of love). It describes the inward attitude of the one who loves as a free and decisive act. This giving, active "agape" is a love that chooses its object, and the Lord chose us to love.

Freedom is knowing God chose you and wants you to live in Him. Though we die to the Law in our flesh, we live to Christ, who loves us, in the Spirit. This verbalized love is what creates faith through the Word. *We are more than conquerors through Him who loved us* (Rom. 8:37). It is a concrete, past, and completed action. We can always know God's will in Christ. This does not mean daily events will demonstrate or lead to that love, but that we trust and hope in a God who is good to us, without seeing it with our eyes. We know that God does love us and will not hurt us. After all, the Son's life was given for you. He gave all of Himself, the holy God, for you. In this only can we know that God is love.

Again, the use of the first person here is meaningful. Paul applies the Gospel to Himself. Christ died in the flesh to rescue us from our sin. His death won us life and forgiveness, which we rely on. In turn, we are led by the Spirit to love Him and live a new life, free from the threats of the Law. *Do not love* [agape] *the world or anything in the world. If anyone loves* [agape] *the world, the love* [agape] *of the Father is not in him* (1 Jn. 2:15).

The Bible speaks of God the Father offering the Son and punishing Him in our place. Here Paul uses "give" in an active sense: "Christ gave Himself." Gal. 1:4 does the same: Christ *gave himself for our sins to deliver from this present evil age.* Here the focus is on the result of that giving—the giving of life and salvation through faith—which has nothing to do with the Law. "Gave himself" is a characteristic Pauline phrase. 1 Tim. 2:6 speaks of Jesus, *who gave himself as a ransom for all, which is the testimony given at the proper time.* Tit. 2:4 also says: *who gave himself for us to redeem us from all lawlessness and to purify for himself a people for his own possession who are zealous for good works.* Eph. 5:25 reads: *Husbands, love your wives, as Christ loved the church and gave himself up for her.*

There is so much here that it can never be exhausted. These words cannot be surpassed. There is no moving beyond dying to the Law and sin and living in Christ by faith. It is the essence of our Christian lives. This is the power of God, given to us, which applies Christ to us.

Verse 21 wraps up the thoughts that began with the controversies involving Titus and Peter at the beginning of Chapter 2. [**v21**] Here Paul makes His strongest argument against the Law: Christ's life and death must mean something. God does not act in vanity or for no reason. He planned from eternity to redeem us from this present, though fading, evil age. But if the Law could save or have any part in our justification, then why did Christ die? His death marks the center of our faith, because in our Baptism we live in that death, freed from sin by the promise.

If the Law does play a part in our righteousness, then Christ died for no purpose. The word for "no purpose" in "Christ died for no purpose" is usually translated "freely." It is not what one might expect. Think of dying for nothing, that is, freely, without reason or motive. That would be the greatest blasphemy and a sin against Christ, who, as an obedient Son, submitted to the Father's will. He struggled to accept the cup of wrath He was given. This same word for "no purpose" (freely) is used in Jn. 15:25: *But the word that is written in their Law must be fulfilled: "They hated me without a cause [freely]."* This verse cites Ps. 69:4, which in the old Greek translation (LXX) reads: "they hated me freely." This shows that this word means "without reason or cause." Consider that the Greek speaking people of this time used this translation (or one close it), unless they read Hebrew. Still, even for a trained Pharisee like Paul, the Septuagint (LXX) would have been the common vernacular Bible during his time. There is precedent for this use of freely, or "giftly," meaning "without purpose."

Paul exclaims: "I do not nullify grace." Others do—many, in fact. Peter was on that road. The Judaizers of Antioch and in Galatia thought that circumcision was a big deal. But if it is added to the Gospel, which is to add Law to the Gospel, Christ is taken away. His death then becomes meaningless and cannot help us. Can there be a worse error? It is worse than the most evil public wickedness, because it takes away Christ, the only source of righteousness.

Even the ten divine words, or commandments, as glorious as they are, are Law. They have no place in our justification. Christ fulfilled them, so we cannot consider or judge ourselves against them, according to faith, which knows no sin or possible punishment. Faith lives in Christ, and Christ is in it. The only worship is to live in Christ, that is, trusting that in this Gospel Christ is for you and, therefore, your sins and the flesh are dead. Now there is nothing but life.

Christ's death could not be for no reason or without purpose. It served the purpose of winning you from death. It had nothing to do with our actions, progress, or works—our life. Jesus fulfilled the Law we are born under. Jesus said of Himself: *Do not think that I have come to abolish the Law or the Prophets; I have not come to abolish them but to fulfill them. For truly, I say to you, until heaven and earth pass away, not an iota, not a dot, will pass from the Law until all is accomplished* (Mt. 5:17–18). Paul uses devastating spiritual logic to cut off all reliance on works and the Law. If it has a place in our new life, then we act like Christ did not fully die for us, and we do not need His entire life and body, which redeemed us.

The "lawless" talk of Paul (think of how it would have sounded to people struggling with circumcision) does not nullify grace. Think of how foreign these words sound to us, because we are surrounded by generic and bland "gospel" language, which does not free us. Though it seems backwards, without the preaching of the full wrath of the Law, the Gospel will be minimized.

The word "nullify" can mean "set side" or "annul." Paul in this letter used it in a legal sense: *To give a human example, brothers: even with a man-made covenant, no one annuls it or adds to it once it has been ratified* (3:15). In referencing human ability, it is used in this way: *I will destroy the wisdom of the wise, and the discernment of the discerning I will thwart* [annul] (1 Cor. 1:19). It can even mean "reject": *The one who rejects* [annuls] *me and does not receive my words has a judge; the word that I have spoken will judge him on the last day* (Jn. 12:48).

Earlier, Paul said that the Gospel does not make the Law meaningless or invalid. Rather, the Law has no power to bring righteousness. The one in the Spirit rebuilds what he previously tore down (as with the converted Jew who previously had the Law of God, but could not keep it). Here it says that grace is not set aside. Though the Law is righteous, no righteousness for us comes from the Law, nor can it produce it in us. Instead, the Law works up the sinful flesh and produces every kind of covetous desire.

We must have the right righteousness—the one which makes us acceptable to the Father. It cannot be from us, since we are condemned sinners. The Law requires love, but you have not loved. It demands putting God first in every thought and action, priority and goal. But this we have not done. However, Christ did what you were unable to do. He freely gave Himself for a purpose—to redeem you. In His death, we have been released from all of God's anger and just punishment. Hell is turned into heaven and death into life, and this grace is now yours through the Gospel. You have God's favorable attitude. Believe that Christ gave Himself to earn it for you. It is yours.

The righteousness given by Christ is imputed to us. "Imputed" means it is attributed or ascribed to us, even though we had nothing to with it. It happened outside of us, in God's view. What was Christ's is now yours: righteousness and life. What was yours, Christ already died to and rose over: death and sin.

We see what Peter's error, originally done out of fear of people, leads to: a denial of Christ. So serious is the stark division between works and grace that salvation hangs in the balance. It is the most serious art of the Christian to know the source of righteousness. To mess it up (by relying on even one part of the Law) is to set aside grace, so that Christ died for nothing. That is why Paul had to correct Peter for withdrawing from the Gentiles.

Either righteousness is all by grace or all by the Law. Yet, it cannot be by the Law, since Christ did die. Grace is established and given on account of His bloody crucifixion. And this Gospel of Christ calls you and includes you in its promise. Grace is yours. You are dead to sin, and your sins are indeed dead. Peace, freedom, and grace are yours. Praise be to God through Christ. Amen.

Chapter 3

Chapter 2 relates Paul's background and begins to detail the role of the Law in relation to the freedom of Gospel. Here in chapter 3, though, Paul leaves aside the introductory material to directly address the Galatians.

[**v1**] "Foolish" is not a compliment. Yet, it does not imply apostasy, a complete falling away from Christ. It is the difference between correcting a child who has done something really wrong, but is still correctable, and one who has rebelled completely and is not even willing to listen. Paul sternly rebukes the Galatians, but in doing so is bringing them back to Christ. Paul must correct them. To do nothing would be pure evil and hatred. How can someone repent if no wrong is presented and God's Law is not used to condemn? The offense must be visible first. Repentance is the goal.

But is Paul going too far? No, he has already established in the first two chapters the seriousness of the issue. To return to any part of the Law is to abandon the one, true Gospel, which is the only path to salvation—one that Christ opened with His own blood.

"Oh" is an interjection in Greek, just like English. Now it is spelled "O-H," but it used to be spelled with just the letter "O," which is exactly what the Greek text has at the beginning of v1. This is a direct address. Paul does the same in Rom. 11:33, in a very different context: *Oh [O], the depth of the riches and wisdom and knowledge of God! How unsearchable are his judgments and how inscrutable his ways!*

You can hear the surprise and disappointment in this verse. "Foolish" means the opposite of wise. The Galatians do not know what harm they are bringing upon themselves. How appropriate for our time. We live in a spiritual age. People are excited and happy to talk about the non-physical. Ghosts, spirits, and even the voices of dead ancestors make for entertaining television content. Zombies, spiritual possession, and objects with supernatural powers are mainstream concepts. Yet, none of this is compatible with Christ's Gospel. Being open to all spiritual talk is dangerous. So much of what passes for "spirituality" is from Eastern religions like Buddhism, which speak of karma (which is basically Law—that our works follow us into other lives through reincarnation). The Galatians fell for the same trick of Satan. The circumcision preachers used the same type of language as Paul—the same phrases and titles for Jesus—but they denied the Gospel.

Christ's aphorism, *be wise as serpents and innocent as doves*, in Mt. 10:16 certainly applies here. There is a time to be innocent (in matters of love) and a time to be as crafty as snakes (when dealing with the truth of God's Word and the foundation of our faith). Wisdom is not the same as intelligence. Knowledge speaks of facts and information. Intellectual brilliance does not mean one can apply that data appropriately. Knowing when to correct, when to be silent, when to inform, when to scold, and when to bear with the ignorant cannot be easily learned. It is nothing like memorizing facts and numbers. Doing what is acceptable or popular cannot lead to wisdom. The lesson of Solomon is relevant here. He could have asked the Lord for riches or a great kingdom, but he asked for wisdom. *Thus King Solomon excelled all the kings of the earth in riches and in wisdom. And the whole earth sought the presence of Solomon to hear his wisdom, which God had put into his mind* (1 Kings 10:23–24). God gives this as a natural gift even apart from salvation or the Gospel. Gamaliel, the rabbi of New Testament times, did not believe in Christ, but showed heavenly wisdom. It is a gift of God wherever it occurs, though wisdom in worldly matters does not save—only faith in Christ does.

The same word for "foolish" is used of the two followers of Jesus walking to Emmaus. Jesus, whom they did not recognize, spoke to these "foolish" men, who did not know what to make of the empty tomb and Jesus' death. He also called them "foolish," like Paul does the Galatians: *And Jesus said to them, "O foolish ones, and slow of heart to believe all that the prophets have spoken! Was it not necessary that the Christ should suffer these things and enter into his glory?" And beginning with Moses and all the Prophets, he interpreted to them in all the Scriptures the things concerning himself* (Lk. 24:25–27). Jesus enlightened them with the Scriptures.

Paul is not talking of worldly standards of wisdom here. This "foolishness" has nothing to do with how much education the Galatians have or how well-read they are. No, he is speaking of the spiritual foolishness of cutting themselves off from Christ. The same word for foolish is used in Rom. 1:14: *I am under obligation both to Greeks and to barbarians, both to the wise and to the foolish.* It is also used in Tit. 3:3, where Paul includes himself, though well educated, as a foolish enemy of God: *For we ourselves were once foolish, disobedient, led astray, slaves to various passions and pleasures, passing our days in malice and envy, hated by others and hating one another.* If we turn away from the Spirit, we are obeying the flesh, which leads to death. The Spirit is given in the Gospel of Jesus to bring the Galatians back to the truth. God must bring us back also, because our flesh can only lead us astray. Wisdom is truly divine in Scripture—it is not a matter of worldly knowledge or experience. The Gospel reveals *Christ the power of God and the wisdom of God* (1 Cor. 1:24).

Our attention is drawn back to 1:6: *I am astonished that you are so quickly deserting him who called you in the grace of Christ and are turning to a different gospel.* Paul beats the drum again in reminding them that they are turning from what they first accepted. It is foolish to turn to something new, if Christ is already yours and you possess the truth in its wholeness. Thus, he calls them back.

O foolish Galatians! Who has bewitched you? "Bewitched" is a strange word. It means, in Greek, "to curse by a spell or an evil eye." We moderns are not generally superstitious in this way, but many people in other parts of the world are, even now. Paul is not saying actual witchcraft has happened. He is saying that their turning from his Gospel was not done knowingly or intentionally. He is actually turning his anger on those who "bewitched" them, allowing mercy for the Galatians, who were overcome by a spell, as it were. But this was no spell. It was false doctrine preached in Christ's name that led them away from true righteousness. Paul has portrayed Christ personally for them by His Word. Instead of saying that he did a poor job and they failed to get it, he shows how ridiculous the situation really is: they were bewitched. It offers a normal human explanation for things we cannot understand.

The truth is that all men are sinners, and their natural flesh constantly rebels against God. *For I know that nothing good dwells in me, that is, in my flesh. For I have the desire to do what is right, but not the ability to carry it out* (Rom. 7:18). If we turn again to anything we have done after conversion and depend on it, as a work to buy God off, we are cursed by God (anathematized). How many take joy in the Gospel for a time, but then are bewitched by false doctrine? Satan is still at work among us, just as he was among the Galatians.

Witchcraft or satanic power is not said to be silly or mere child's play in Scripture. It does exist and can have some measure of power, because the Devil and other fallen angels (the demons) are real. Satan does have a measure of authority and power over this world, but as a created being, he is under God's control and limitations. In Christ, we are to have no fear of this sort of paganism, since our Lord withstood Satan and crushed him by His death on the cross. But neither are we to be involved in it or play with it, as if Satan and unbelief were only games. He is most definitely not safe, but rather looking for people to devour. This is why we stand on the holy ground of faith in Christ—then we are safe and can live without fear of satanic power.

Does the "evil eye" hold any water? Maybe not, but there is an element of truth to the thought that the eye is a window to the soul. Jesus says in Mt. 6:22–23: *The eye is the lamp of the body. So, if your eye is healthy* [single, undivided]*, your whole body will be full of light, but if your eye is bad, your whole body will be full of darkness. If then the light in you is darkness, how great is the darkness!* If the eye is "single"—that is, simple, sincere, and innocent—then so is the body. This speaks of the eye as a reflection and organ of the body that perceives the world. Do we not gaze at and see what we love and are attracted to? But they are usually the wrong things, because our flesh is corrupt. We do not even see correctly. We look and gravitate towards sin and what God hates. The problem is our flesh, not the things we see. If we were not complete sinners, we would not be attracted to them. *To the pure, all things are pure, but to those who are corrupted and do not believe, nothing is pure. In fact, both their minds and consciences are corrupted* (Tit. 1:15). The problem is always inside of us (sin and death), not outside forces for which we are not accountable. We would not be so easily misled or fooled if we saw clearly and loved God.

Some people today trust and rest their heart on horoscopes, tarot cards, and other foolish superstition. Do these have power? Possibly, but how accurate they are is not the right question. Do they try to access spiritual power apart from God's Word? Yes, they claim to, and some people trust in this. But we have all we need in the Gospel and Scripture. If God wanted you to know the future, He would tell you directly. Knowledge is not faith. You do not need to go around and outside God's Word for comfort. Instead, find God in Christ, who died for you.

Trust in Christ and know you have His protection, forgiveness, and righteousness. That is far better than knowing the future, which we know will ultimately end in death. The God who controls all things loves you. God can overcome all your troubles, since He has already overcome death for you and promises you His resurrection. Paul, in 5:20 of this very letter, mentions sorcery as a work of the flesh and something which disqualifies one from the Kingdom of God. There is real danger in these sorts of things. Children should be shielded from all the Devil's works, and adults should search for God where He is found, in the pure Word, and not where He has not promised to be. We see how the Devil tricks people today and leads them to sin against Christ, especially in the great sin of suicide, which has become so prevalent. Unfortunately, if successful, it does not leave time for sober repentance and the application of the Gospel.

Verse 1 moves from "evil eye" to an explicit mention of what their eyes beheld figuratively: Christ. *It was before your eyes that Jesus Christ was publicly portrayed as crucified.* Everyone wants a glorified Christ, a powerful buddy to help them succeed and win. Most would welcome a human model to follow, showing us how to achieve glory and riches. But without suffering, humiliation, and death, glory means nothing and cannot help us. Our glory does not come in this life or by our actions. Jesus was not crucified for nothing, but for sinners. This suffering and death is central to our faith. There, we were redeemed from our great sins and death itself. The punishment for our sins was met and put to death in Jesus' body. Here is the power of the Gospel, which we are given to believe.

Our lives now mirror the suffering of Christ. The glorious resurrection of Jesus is the firstfruits. We do not partake of glory until He comes again at the end of the world. For now, we are to learn to die to our passions, lust, and sinful nature. That is why we must have a Christ who died—any other cannot help us. If Christ did not die in the flesh, then we are still under the Law, condemned eternally. Truly anathema, as Paul says, is anyone who adds or takes away from the Gospel of Christ that he received directly from God.

To the Corinthians, Paul says something very similar, though without questioning their sanity: *For I decided to know nothing among you except Jesus Christ and him crucified* (1 Cor. 2:2). We cannot move on from a dying Christ. That is exactly what we need and what gives true hope, because our sins and condition before God are much worse than we realize. We must continue to die, according to our Baptism, and rise to life when the word of promise comes, because Jesus died and was raised to glory. Without a divine death for the world, glory is not our sure hope. That God should be humbled and die for us is the high point of His love. That action makes His glory accessible and available for us. This is something truly comforting. God sitting in heaven over us, ruling in glory and judgment is not. God's righteousness in Himself does nothing for us—it merely convicts us of our lack of glory. It is the suffering and pain of Jesus we must ever keep before our eyes, so that we know we are cleansed by God's blood.

We are not better than the Galatians. Many of us have known of Jesus since we were little children. But we take our eyes off Christ daily and are "bewitched" by worldly things—whether wealth, position, romance, or fleshly passions. We must continually be called back to Christ. We never outgrow simple reliance on His Gospel, no matter how much we do or the responsibilities we have. The crucified Christ sustains and nourishes that simple saving faith. This means that Jesus suffered temptations, felt pain, and succumbed to death, while still your God. He did not lose or diminish His divinity in this weakness. Only in this Gospel are your sins taken away, your status restored, and righteousness given.

It is dangerous, from a human point of view, to paint the crucified Christ. The flesh and the pride of man will react violently to being told they are so helpless that God had to suffer in their place and die a wretched death. It must be foolishness to the world. Yet, God's Spirit works in this "painting" and gives life though this foolish Gospel of

Christ.

> *Has not God made foolish the wisdom of the world? For*
> *since, in the wisdom of God, the world did not know God*
> *through wisdom, it pleased God through the folly of what we*
> *preach to save those who believe. For Jews demand signs*
> *and Greeks seek wisdom, but we preach Christ crucified, a*
> *stumbling block to Jews and folly to Gentiles, but to those*
> *who are called, both Jews and Greeks, Christ the power of*
> *God and the wisdom of God. For the foolishness of God is*
> *wiser than men, and the weakness of God is stronger than*
> *men* (1 Cor. 1:20–25).

Consider this provocative quote from Luther:

> Sometimes a teacher will scold a pupil bitterly, call him
> names, and beat him with sticks—which the pupil accepts
> with equanimity, though he would not accept it from a peer
> or fellow student. . . . Without severe discipline nothing can
> be done properly in peace or in war [by rulers]. Therefore
> unless a magistrate, a clergyman, a public official or a head of
> a household is angry and scolds when the situation demands,
> he is lazy and useless and will never administer his office
> properly [*Galatians*, 187].

Anger and rebuke is necessary. Being gentle all the time is not very
loving if it constantly tolerates rudeness and sin. So also, Paul says to
a fellow pastor: *preach the word; be ready in season and out of season;*
reprove, rebuke, and exhort, with complete patience and teaching (2
Tim. 4:2). Paul is doing that here to the Galatians and us: reproving,
rebuking, and exhorting. God's true love does not baby us, but gives us
what we need to be joined to Him and produce good fruit, which often
requires tilling, smelly fertilizer, and painful pruning.

Christ was "pre-written," according to the Greek, before the Galatians' eyes. The Lord was laid out before them (before the Judaizers
came with their deathly Law/Gospel mixture). They were not ignorant
any longer. They had Christ from Paul, especially now that this letter
has reached them. We have no excuse, either. God's Word is clear and
powerful. If it is not understood, received, or kept in our hearts, it is
our fault. Guilt is much greater once ignorance is done away with and
faith is given. To turn again to unbelief is simply rebellion against God
and His anointed one—resisting the Holy Spirit.

Paul painted Jesus Christ not with a brush and canvas, but with
words—God's Word. *Faith comes by hearing, and hearing by the Word*

of God (Rom. 10:17). Preaching and teaching is how God works on men. As Jesus said several times: "He who has ears to hear, let him hear." This statement references the Old Testament: *For this people's heart has grown dull, and with their ears they can barely hear, and their eyes they have closed, lest they should see with their eyes and hear with their ears and understand with their heart and turn, and I would heal them.* This passage from Is. 6:10 is quoted in Mt. 13:15.

Paul portrayed not just Christ, but Christ in a certain way: crucified. This does not mean just with flowery language, but as the one who died for sinners, that is, all of us. It speaks to the substitutionary nature of His death—He died in our place. This is necessary, because in this redemption He earned us righteousness, which the Gospel actually gives. We never progress beyond this in Christ. In faith we continue to return to the beginning, to Christ's crucifixion for us in the Gospel, where we died to sin.

We cannot disconnect v1 of chapter 3 from the last verse of chapter 2, which ends: *then Christ died for no purpose.* That is why Christ was displayed before the Galatians—for the very specific purpose of saving them from sin.

Those captive to false belief and doctrine cannot free themselves. We cannot make ourselves believe or come to God, due to the power of sin. [v2] Paul asks a simple question. It can only be answered in one way. "This only I desire to learn from you." The verb translated "to learn" is the verb form of the noun "disciple" (which means "learner" or "follower"). The root of the Greek work is "math," from which we get the word "mathematics."

We are born with the Law written on our hearts. We do works our entire lives. Do we get the Spirit that way? Of course not. It is only from the hearing of faith. Our hearts and minds are opened by the Spirit through the words of the Gospel. We listen and are still. There is nothing we can do—doing is what got us into this mess of sin. Therefore, the Law does not save. For why did Christ die, if the Law has anything to do with getting closer to God?

Faith is brought about by the Word, which we hear. It is not like getting a diploma that one can hang up, while forgetting what was learned. Faith is a living hope in Christ, who promises the redemption of our bodies. Due to the suffering and dying to the flesh we must experience now, we must constantly be fed by the Word and Spirit, or else we will naturally obey our fallen nature. Faith is given and brought about through the promise of forgiveness.

We are given God's verdict in this Word, which changes our status before Him. We cannot believe in what we do not know for sure. Sure and certain forgiveness gives rise to faith. This forgiveness is rooted in Christ's cross and resurrection, the verdict of absolution given to the world. If Christ had not absolved (forgiven) the world of sins, the Word which delivers that forgiveness would be null and void. This is the teaching of objective justification, which tells us that the Gospel can be applied to all people.

The universal character of Christ's atonement changed "the relation in which the world stands to God as far as it no longer remains the object of His wrath" [Lindberg, 260]. In a very real sense, the world has been absolved in Christ. That is why a preacher (and any Christian privately) can proclaim the Gospel and speak for God, through which the Spirit works faith. Forgiving sins conveys the righteousness of Christ, which is a present reality, earned and authorized by Him.

Paul says: "this only I desire to learn." He gives the two mutually exclusive alternatives, though they are so often mixed and conflated. *Did you receive the Spirit from works of the Law?* The Spirit is the one who gives peace, joy, hope, love, and comfort. The works of the Law— that is, attempting to do the commands and trying to obey God—does not bring the Spirit, but the curse, hatred of God, and knowledge of sin. Paul reckons the Galatians as Christians. They heard the Gospel through which the Spirit works. Paul was there, so he knows what they heard—the message of reconciliation in Christ. God's love must first come and make us alive before we are able to truly love or do anything pleasing to God.

The Law is good and was given by God. Moses received the tablets written by the finger of God. But just because something is good, does not mean it is good for everyone. Peanuts are a fine food, but to someone with an allergy to them they can be death. So much more is the Law, which causes death, not in itself, but because of the reaction of a body effected by sin. The Law of works that demands obedience with threats is called the "law of sin and death" in Rom. 8:2. Sin and the Law do not mix. The Law does not grant participation ribbons or honorary medals for trying; it demands holiness in love for God and everyone we come in contact with, especially the ones we do not like. That is where our sin is crystal clear; we have many other gods, since we have failed to listen to the true God, who demands obedience in the Law.

The Spirit produces all good in us. Even our "good works" are properly called "fruit of the Holy Spirit." It is the Spirit of God who leads us into good works and truth. He comes, according to v2, from the hearing of faith. Only in the message of Christ, because of His obedience and fulfillment of the Law, do we gain salvation and entrance into God's kingdom. Before Christ comes to us in His Word, we were enemies of God. But the Gospel declares to us that the war is over, that sin has been taken away and punished in Christ's own body. He was lifted up for our glory. It is a simple pronouncement of freedom, which is why the Gospel is so despised by the world. It seems too easy, but the Spirit works through it to breathe life into old, dead bones. *God's love has been poured into our hearts through the Holy Spirit who has been given to us* (Rom. 5:5).

Again, this is all or nothing. The Law is death when it comes to salvation, but the Spirit brings life to the undeserving, guilty, and cursed through hearing. Unless we are told, we cannot know of God's goodness and mercy. This is the mystery revealed in Christ, who died for the world's sins. This act of mercy opens up God's heart to us when we hear of it. This hearing of faith is entirely passive. The Spirit stirs us up to faith, so we rest in the promises and partake of the peace of God. But works of the Law are never completed and do not give rest. Like the wealth of the billionaire, it is never enough. There is no satisfaction before God in what we do without Him and apart from His Spirit. So, belief is the counterpart to works done under the Law. The Spirit gives freedom from both the burden and curse of the Law.

While it is easy for Law-ridden people to turn faith into a work of the Law (something we must do to be saved), that is a modern day Judaizing. Faith is never demanded as something we must bring to the table in Scripture. It is only created by the Spirit through a promise. Telling someone to "just believe" is pointless. Faith must come from the Spirit, who is personally given to us. It is like telling a blind man to drive a car. It will only cause harm. In contrast, Paul says in 2 Tim. 1:14: *By the Holy Spirit who dwells within us, guard the good deposit entrusted to you.* The Spirit is entirely a gift, sent to renew us in Christ's Word.

Acts 10 deals with Cornelius, who was a Gentile in Cesarea. That the Spirit came apart from the written Law and its observance was surprising to the first Christians, who were Jewish. But the Spirit does not lie. *And the believers from among the circumcised who had come with Peter were amazed, because the gift of the Holy Spirit was poured out even on the Gentiles. For they were hearing them speaking in tongues and extolling God. Then Peter declared, "Can anyone withhold water for baptizing these people, who have received the Holy Spirit just as we have?" And he commanded them to be baptized in the name of Jesus Christ. Then they asked him to remain for some days.* Paul makes the sharpest of distinctions between the Law, that is, the demand for works apart from the Spirit, and the Gospel. We are forgiven in the hearing of the Gospel, which creates faith by the Spirit.

We need to hear often of this distinction. While it is very simple, we often cannot divide it in our own hearts. The truth, inspired by the Spirit here, is a fountain of life. If we could separate these two teachings, nothing would disturb us. But we are weak sheep in need of leading. We must be convicted of our trespasses and made dependent on God's great mercy. The Law must be extolled and used, but carefully, since it cannot bring the Spirit. It must be kept out of justification, the declaration of righteousness that happens in heaven to us. The Spirit does testify within us. He did not come to us by our struggle under a burden, but in the forgiveness of sins offered freely in the Gospel. This means that works do not gain righteousness. However necessary they are for our family and our neighbors in the world, they are cursed before God. In our conscience, we are to rest, be dead to all works, and live in Christ. This happens not in the body, but in the conscience. Only then is there real peace, so that Christ becomes everything, that is, our God.

This message is spoken to our heart: stop doing and listen, for nothing else is needed to procure eternal life. It is already yours, for Jesus has risen from the dead. The payment for sins was accepted, and you are declared righteous. This is how the Spirit comes. The Gospel is despised and hated, except by those of whom Christ speaks: *Blessed are the poor in spirit, for theirs is the kingdom of heaven. Blessed are those who mourn, for they shall be comforted. Blessed are the meek, for they*

111

shall inherit the earth. Blessed are those who hunger and thirst for righteousness, for they shall be satisfied (Mt. 5:3–6). The Law demands strength, but Christ exalts the weak and gives them His life. In the words of Luther:

> Therefore there is in godly people a perpetual struggle between the hearing of faith and the works of the Law, because the conscience is always murmuring and thinking that when righteousness, the Holy Spirit, and eternal salvation are promised solely on the basis of hearing with faith, this is too easy a way [*Galatians*, 215].

This describes the conflict within us that must continue, if the Spirit is to rule.

The point in v2 was even stronger for the Galatians than for us, most likely. Most educated people today know something of Jesus. Perhaps not much, but it is hard not to hear of Jesus, who is God, and that He demonstrated God's love in His death for sin and resurrection to life. But the Galatians, on the other hand, were complete pagans. They had the Law written on their hearts, but not the written code given to the Jews, the people God chose. The Gospel which saves came first to them in Paul's preaching (which has to be heard—it cannot be divined within oneself). Paul merely elucidated the Law that they already knew. He did not bring new ceremonial commands. He offered Christ and strengthened the Law we were born into, in order to condemn sin in Christ. What a simple task—the Spirit does all the work.

If God's Word remains pure, it will work. This is a relief and comfort. Salvation is a free gift of the Spirit, not a legal contract contingent on our performance. Only in the release from the Law and its curse of death can we have freedom. Paul desires to learn in this question what is obvious. The flesh loves to take credit for God's work of grace, but to do so is to not trust or have faith in Christ's life-giving death. The Word of God does all the work, so that we may rest secure in Christ: *And we also thank God constantly for this, that when you received the word of God, which you heard from us, you accepted it not as the word of men but as what it really is, the word of God, which is at work in you believers* (1 Thess. 2:13).

What we begin with—faith in the Gospel—is the only way to stay in Christ. His works must always be the basis for our adoption. This is why the move to works is so cursed in this epistle: it denies the hearing of faith through which the Spirit comes. Because the body of sin is not done away with until physical death, we must live by faith. Only in paradise do we graduate beyond it. There is no need for faith in heaven. We will possess righteousness then, and not need to believe it.

Rom. 10:14–17, which speaks of the reverse order of faith, fits in well here:

> *How then will they call on him in whom they have not believed? And how are they to believe in him of whom they have never heard? And how are they to hear without someone preaching? And how are they to preach unless they are sent? As it is written, "How beautiful are the feet of those who preach the good news!" But they have not all obeyed the gospel. For Isaiah says, "Lord, who has believed what he has heard from us?" So faith comes from hearing, and hearing through the word of Christ.*

We cannot love God or call upon Him for help unless we first know Him and believe He is merciful. We cannot know this unless we are told by God, for why else would we believe it? This Word of Christ, our mediator, comes through men, that is, by verbalized words or some other means of communication. God comes to us in Christ, the Redeemer, not in our trying to ascend to heaven by works condemned by the Law. Paul's point is clear: even the experience of the Galatians shows that the Gospel brings the Spirit, not dead works.

Verse 3 continues the thought of v2. [v3] Paul sets the hook deeper, pinpointing their foolishness. The same word "foolish" is also used in v1: "O foolish Galatians." They began with hearing the Gospel, which brought them salvation and the security of peace with God. Now they are treating that as a mere springboard to the supposed real meat: the works of the Law—that which they slaved under previously without the Spirit. It is like a potty-trained child excited to start wearing diapers again. It is a denial of the beginning, not an improvement.

The Galatians began with the Spirit, but want to complete the race by dealing with the flesh. "Flesh" is a strong term in Scripture. It signifies everything we are born with that is corrupted by sin and under God's wrath. Not just the base passions and lusts, but our false righteousness under the Law. It includes all of our best works and most lofty thoughts. Without the Spirit, everything in us is fleshly—condemned and cursed. Here are a few uses of this term where it means that which is in direct contradiction to God's Spirit and life: *That which is born of the flesh is flesh, and that which is born of the Spirit is spirit* (Jn. 3:6). *The spirit indeed is willing, but the flesh is weak* (Mt. 26:41). The disciples do not watch and pray, but fall asleep without concern in the Garden of Gethsemane. *It is the Spirit who gives life; the flesh is no help at all. The words that I have spoken to you are spirit and life* (Jn. 6:63). The flesh of Jesus is not to be compared to sinful flesh. His body is life-giving and divine, but our flesh is rotten and cannot be made good (even though those who live by the Law try to do that). Instead, in Christ we live a new life by the Spirit, who makes us alive to God by knowledge of the Son. Sin is dead and crucified. It lives out its last breaths in us, but it does not rule or condemn us. Instead, the Spirit, who creates a new man within us, rules us. *For we know that the law is spiritual, but I am of the flesh, sold under sin* (Rom. 7:14).

Paul uses this theological word "flesh" dozens of times in his letters. For example: *Those who are in the flesh cannot please God* (Rom. 8:8). The flesh is not just gross outward deeds, though it manifests itself that way if not checked. It is everything opposed to God, including pride in the Law and one's own righteousness. This applies especially to the outwardly good and those who think that God respects their inherent righteousness. We must close our eyes and not judge by human reason, but by God's Word: *The Lord saw that the wickedness of man was great in the earth, and that every intention of the thoughts of his heart was only evil continually* (Gen. 6:5). This is what God said when He sent the flood to punish man's sin. It still describes man's flesh today.

The "Spirit" in v3 does not have "Holy" attached to it. It can be assumed. The "Spirit" here includes faith in the Word, which is how the Spirit works on us. The Gospel is the power of the Spirit. We are saved in an instant, but as long as the flesh is with us, we cannot turn to the Law to help us in any way. It has no positive power for sinners, though it is God's eternal will. The Gospel must remain our confidence until the flesh is destroyed.

Even circumcision—the ceremonial law shoved on the Galatians— gave an indication of the problem of the flesh: *You shall be circumcised in the flesh of your foreskins, and it shall be a sign of the covenant between me and you* (Gen. 17:11). Why such an invasive sign? It could have been somewhere less sensitive. In and of itself it removed a part of the flesh, giving nothing. But when seen as a promise and seal of grace, not a work of the Law, its true nature is seen. That relates to how Abraham was saved, which Paul deals with in v6 of this chapter. He is moving that direction. He goes from a general perspective of the Law and works to the single greatest issue which threatened the churches of Galatia. In the age of the Spirit, after Christ earned life and ascended, to return to a shadow of Christ is to turn one's back on the Spirit, even though the Spirit and circumcision were originally meant to be together.

The word for "perfected" is perhaps more accurately translated "being completed" or "finished." It is an indicative verb, meaning it is a present, ongoing action. They were going the wrong way, but the way of the Spirit is not closed. They started in the Spirit, but were finishing in the flesh, which is where they were before Christ came in His Word to them.

Paul then examines the nature of their foolishness. [v4] Verse 4 does not just point out their foolishness, but their prior faithfulness in suffering and then asks: "what was the point?" To suffer and then give up the Gospel is to render the pain fruitless—was it for nothing? For what did they suffer? The Word brings earthly suffering as surely as life-giving water brings weeds. Paul draws them back to their beginning and asks: "was it in vain?" We do not suffer for nothing. Athletes suffer in training to gain temporary glory and achieve a human goal, not because it is fun to hurt. So too, every Christian must be disciplined to remain in the Spirit. Suffering is endured and overcome with the joy of salvation.

The same word for "vain" is used in 1 Cor. 15:1–2: *Now I would remind you, brothers, of the gospel I preached to you, which you received, in which you stand, and by which you are being saved, if you hold fast to the word I preached to you—unless you believed in vain.* This word means "without reason or cause." We do not embrace pain and suffering for its own sake (the world calls those kind of people masochists). We gladly suffer in the Spirit because of why we are suffering (as God's elect) and what has been promised (eternal life). *If you were of the world, the world would love you as its own; but because you are not of the world, but I chose you out of the world, therefore the world hates you* (Jn. 15:19).

None of us have finished our race. The struggle is against our flesh, and the boast of its own righteousness is not over yet. We are called to stay firm and live by the Spirit, who came by hearing. What Paul said to some of the same churches in Galatia, in a different context, we should keep near to our heart:

> *When they had preached the gospel to that city and had made many disciples, they returned to Lystra and to Iconium and to Antioch, strengthening the souls of the disciples, encouraging them to continue in the faith, and saying that through many tribulations we must enter the kingdom of God. And when they had appointed elders for them in every church, with prayer and fasting they committed them to the Lord in whom they had believed* (Acts 14:21–23).

We have already mentioned Paul's own personal suffering for simply giving salvation in Christ's name. But to forgive sins, sin must be made sinful. That is why Jesus was rejected. *The world cannot hate you, but it hates me because I testify about it that its works are evil* (Jn. 7:7).

Paul's sensitivity is evident here. He does not condemn the Galatians to hell, but calls them back to when they suffered for Christ's Word. It does not help us to speculate on what kind of suffering this was. The point is that we all must suffer, and the Word will bring it, if we take it seriously. However, we must not interpret this as rejection by God, but a sign of His loving embrace, which drives us from our flesh to the Spirit, who must vivify us daily.

Verses 2–5 go together. [v5] Verse 5 contains another question that can only be answered one way. It is more personal than a direct confrontation—to ask such an obvious question. The one who "supplies" is, of course, God, revealed in Christ. He supplies out of His own. He does not take from another and re-gift. The same verb is used by Paul in 2 Cor. 9:10: *He who supplies seed to the sower and bread for food will supply and multiply your seed for sowing and increase the harvest of your righteousness.* The emphasis is on the Lord's generosity.

"He who gives the Spirit, why does He do it?" Paul has already established that the Spirit does not come by works of the Law, but by "hearing." He ends v5 with the same phrase.

The Spirit works "miracles." The word in Greek is literally "powers," which can take on several shades of meaning in English. "Power" refers to might and strength, as opposed to weakness. It can mean "miracles," as in Heb. 2:4:

Therefore we must pay much closer attention to what we have heard, lest we drift away from it. For since the message declared by angels proved to be reliable, and every transgression or disobedience received a just retribution, how shall we escape if we neglect such a great salvation? It was declared at first by the Lord, and it was attested to us by those who heard, while God also bore witness by signs and wonders and various miracles [powers] and by gifts of the Holy Spirit distributed according to his will.

The context of this passage is close to what we have here in Gal. 3:5: the fruits of the outpouring of the Spirit. We can falsely claim credit for what the Spirit did in us. Our faith is not ours to parade around and boast about. It is the Spirit who works in us, who will also leave us if we embrace the flesh as we did before we were enlightened.

The powers and deeds done by the Galatians (or more properly, by the Spirit in them) were gifts, not works. They were not something they did to win God over. The signs and wonders caused by the Spirit following Pentecost were abundant. History and experience show that these signs are quite rare today. But the main product of the Spirit is faith—confidence and trust in Christ who gave Himself to lift us up to heaven. We now live in God's grace above the Law, which cuts off all human righteousness. Can God do great and impressive things today? Certainly, but perhaps we are too cold to receive them, just as Jesus would not do miracles among the jaded who could not believe (such as among the Pharisees or in His hometown of Nazareth). The Gospel is going out in new places today and is received with joy. It might cause healings, speaking in other tongues, flames of fire, and other works of God. But all good works and powers flow from Christ and His redemption, or else we must see spiritual forces apart from God at work (which would be of Satan). Faith is the preeminent miracle. It opens heaven so that God reveals His love and, in turn, the sinner is made alive by the Spirit. Without this justification, all the signs in the world would be death, since the Spirit has only been promised in the Gospel.

The word for "works" in Greek is a little more colorful than our English word. It shares the root from which our word "energy" is derived. To work within or among is the connotation. Any good impulse or godly motivation is the Spirit's work and occurs because we are justified by the Word before God. The works and their effects were visible, so Paul can appeal to them as a manifestation of the Spirit. *The wind blows where it wishes, and you hear its sound, but you do not know where it comes from or where it goes. So it is with everyone who is born of the Spirit* (Jn. 3:8). We cannot see the wind, but we can see it interact with objects. So it is with people. We can judge a public work of the flesh and know that the person behind it is not ruled by the Spirit, since the Spirit does not lead into sin. If the flesh *does* erupt into sin, causing an unrepentant stubbornness that will not be corrected, that person cannot tolerate the Spirit.

Paul drives a wedge between works of the Law, which are good if they are actually done according to God's Law (out love and fear for Him), and the hearing of faith. This is not morally destructive. It is isolating the source of the Spirit (the Word of Christ which gives righteousness) and His creative work (faith) from other so-called powers (namely, the Law), which do not bring us into God's love. How we start, that is, how the Spirit comes to us, is exactly how we are to finish, if we are indeed going to finish. There is no other way to Christ than this.

Paul is like John the Baptist—a lone voice crying in the wilderness against many popular teachers. God's Word, while it is always persecuted, can never be undone. It is the power of the Spirit and His sword. Paul can stand against angels, as he did in chapter 1, and curse them if they preach another gospel. Works and human righteousness have nothing to do with our justification.

[v6] Verse 6 backs up the one-sided questions with the example of the first man to be circumcised: Abraham. Paul is quoting Gen. 15:6, as he does in Rom. 4 also. *Just as Abraham* are Paul's words, and the rest are the citation from the Old Testament. Abraham believed in God. What did he believe? It was not a generic belief in His existence, but the specific promise that God verbalized to him. This is the context in Gen. 15:3–6:

> *Abram said, "Behold, you have given me no offspring, and a member of my household will be my heir." And behold, the word of the Lord came to him: "This man shall not be your heir; your very own son shall be your heir." And he brought him outside and said, "Look toward heaven, and number the stars, if you are able to number them." Then he said to him, "So shall your offspring be." And he believed the Lord, and he counted it to him as righteousness.*

It is not just the promise of a child given here, but that this child would lead to the Messiah—that the eternal God would be his descendant. This is to be seen as more than a husband of a barren wife wanting a baby; it was about God keeping His promise, which seemed beyond unlikely. Underlying all promises is God's righteousness—without forgiveness for sin there is no approaching or knowing the holy God.

Belief in God must be in a particular promise: that we are accepted on account of Christ. The word for "counted" is critical. The NIV has "credited." Other similar words used are: "accounted," "imputed" (which is a more technical and precise word), and "reckoned." These synonyms are all fine translations. The concept is made simple by our modern means of electronic payment. Funds are debited and credited with the click of a button or the swipe of a card. The action is small, but the invisible result can be large. So it is with faith in the Gospel.

God credits us with Christ's righteousness. Forgiveness viewed from one angle is the removal of sin—not physically, but before the Judge's eye. It is done to our divine account. God does not hold any sin against us. From the other side, righteousness is given or imputed to us. He ascribes to us what is not ours intrinsically or by nature. The result is that we have kept the Law before God (it is credited to us), while every hour we fail to obey the Law and love Him. The Christian hangs on to this promise and is delivered by it. This is what it means to believe in God and be reckoned, that is, considered righteous. The difficulty is that we cannot see ourselves as God sees us. The mercy of God is so great that it cannot be expressed better than in these simple words here in v6.

Abraham is the model believer. It would be anachronistic to call him Christian, but he did believe in the future Christ. He serves as the pattern for all believers and all Christians. Paul spoke about starting in the Spirit and foolishly finishing in the flesh. The Spirit was given to Abraham in the promise, so we do not finish in any other way than how Abraham lived: by faith.

This belief that God's Gospel is true and applies righteousness to us is itself righteousness. If this is not understood, the Bible will be a closed book. God does not see the believer's flesh, or his many sins, but only Christ's righteousness. The verdict is rendered, and we are holy, despite nothing about us being holy to other people or even ourselves. It is applied personally, but not in such a way that the person completely changes outwardly or inwardly. Justification (the root of this word in Greek is "righteous") has to do with God's vantage point—not man's.

The problem is that we assume we think like God. We cannot imagine how God sees nothing bad in us. We look in the mirror and see nothing but evil. But faith trusts God's declared judgment and ignores the obvious "facts" of our sin. We only struggle because we do not fully believe God's Word. Christ Himself is the tangible proof of our righteousness. His righteousness is ours, and we are as alive to God as Christ is risen from the dead. Our sins were on Him (He became sin) to be punished and His life is now ours. Before heaven we believe this, but do not experience it physically. The peace of the Spirit is a valid testimony that God is truthful.

Does it seem fair that God sees a forgiven murderer as he sees you? That is a dramatic claim. Both are considered in faith. The problem is that we do not fully grasp forgiveness. We think in terms of Law and what people deserve (except when it comes to ourselves). We go too easy on ourselves. We do not judge ourselves by God's standard of works. It is God's Law, and He is the judge. He sees our secret thoughts and our deeds done in darkness. These are murderous, because we have been angry and jealous. Do not think that you deserve better. Everyone deserves worse. The Law levels us all. The Gospel is not about fairness. It reveals a divine love that we do not have. It is shown to us in Christ, who suffered in your place, dying for your sins, murder, and hatred. There are no more sins before the Father, when you are reckoned according to faith.

A parallel passage on the righteousness of Abraham is Rom. 4:16–25:

> *That is why it depends on faith, in order that the promise may rest on grace and be guaranteed to all his offspring—not only to the adherent of the law but also to the one who shares the faith of Abraham, who is the father of us all, as it is written, "I have made you the father of many nations"—in the presence of the God in whom he believed, who gives life to the dead and calls into existence the things that do not exist. In hope he believed against hope, that he should become the father of many nations, as he had been told, "So shall your offspring be." He did not weaken in faith when he considered his own body, which was as good as dead (since he was about a hundred years old), or when he considered the barrenness*

of Sarah's womb. No unbelief made him waver concerning the promise of God, but he grew strong in his faith as he gave glory to God, fully convinced that God was able to do what he had promised. That is why his faith was "counted to him as righteousness." But the words "it was counted to him" were not written for his sake alone, but for ours also. It will be counted to us who believe in him who raised from the dead Jesus our Lord, who was delivered up for our trespasses and raised for our justification.

Faith seems so simple and childlike (and it is), but here it is praised. It is the only thing necessary, for it alone receives righteousness as a gift. Believe that God forgives in Christ and you are righteous. Instead of man's worship being an action done for God, the true worship of faith receives everything from Christ as good, since it comes from the good and gracious God—even when it looks bad. God does not need our prayers, hearts, voices, or works. If we do not know God as good and kind, our outward actions must be Law-based and cursed, because they are centered on ourselves and the flesh. The content of faith is not social morality, but God, who will raise our bodies to eternal life. We have no physical evidence to prove it, but God promises life, just like He promised the childless Abraham that he would be the father of many nations. In Christ, Abraham is our father. For we believe just like him, against hope. *In hope he believed* [the promise] *against hope* [any human possibility], *that he should become the father of many nations, as he had been told, "So shall your offspring be"* (Rom. 4:18). There is no other way to the righteous Father than through the righteousness in which Abraham believed.

Faith rests in the Word of God, specifically His promises, which are answered "yes" in Christ. He also gives what we call sacraments, or "mysteries," which contain His Word. We are directed to these tangible places, where the promise of forgiveness is joined to physical elements. Baptism and the Lord's Supper are the two ceremonies to which Christ joins His promise of forgiveness. We bind ourselves to these means, not because they look holy, but because God calls us to them to exercise our faith. The promise of the Gospel is made physical for us to receive and depend upon.

We believe that Christ delivers His salvation to us exactly where He directs us to go, so we may be sure and confident in our justification. He gives the Spirit in water with the Word and forgiveness in Christ's

121

body and blood. This seems rather foolish to the world. Water, tasteless bread, and cheap wine are nothing special, but when the promise of God, which delivers all spiritual gifts is there, there is nothing more holy to faith. In these things we cling to God when we believe, as He has spoken. These gifts give what Christ says they do. We are not to see them as magic potions, but promises to believe which convey Christ's righteousness to us. The important part is not what we do, but what God says He does, even though we see nothing with our eyes. Think of the sacraments as places to exercise faith, not things we do for God.

As long as we are in the world we will continue to sin and cannot have too much forgiveness or believe in it firmly enough. That is why we can never move past the Gospel to anything else (which would merely be Law). All is in vain, unless we continue how we started. *There is therefore now no condemnation for those who are in Christ Jesus* (Rom. 8:1).

Verse 7 states explicitly what Paul means by the example of Abraham in v6. [**v7**] The connection is clear: those of faith (as opposed to those of works) are sons of Abraham. That is, they live by the promise of God— by faith. While Abraham was circumcised—and it was a sacrament for him—it was not without faith. This trust that God is faithful and forgiving in His Word is primary. All our works are secondary—even if commanded by God. Nothing can be done to please God without this faith. *For whatever does not proceed from faith is sin* (Rom. 14:23).

"Sons" is not the same word as the term for "children," despite newer, gender-neutral translations like the NIV. "Sons" speaks of the legal rights and inheritance the Father bestows. Some of that connection might be fuzzy to us due to the loss of the male/female distinction in our culture. Marriage, since it is based on the divinely created differences between men and women, is one place this pattern endures. The man keeps his last name, while the woman traditionally takes on her husband's name. At the time this epistle was written, males received the inheritance. This is a marvelous passage, because it speaks of the righteousness of Christ, which overcomes earthly distinctions. Those who think they are improving the Scriptures by substituting "children" for "sons" are actually watering down the text.

Rich and poor, male and female, are all alike in Christ: completely righteous. Distinctions are necessary now and are wrong to undo on earth. Males and females have their own callings and functions from God—both divine roles are necessary to populate the earth, coexist in marriage, and maintain a well-ordered society and church. In Christ there is no hierarchy, for we possess Him by faith and lack nothing.

It is wrong to turn this freedom in Christ into an earthly liberation gospel, so that outward distinctions are destroyed. Great harm happens when we undo God's created order, as if He made us poorly from the beginning. Redemption does not change our physical bodies or public roles. Knowledge of the Gospel and possession of the Spirit do not give any earthly rights. True freedom is righteousness before God, not before man. It is not what we think is right and fair that counts, but God's righteous verdict, which Christ offers in the Gospel. The impetus to try and make male and female outwardly equal is satanic. It wrecks families and denigrates motherhood and the bearing of new life—the specific blessing and role given only to women. It has led to marriage—a holy creation of Christ—being considered impractical at best and ridiculed at worst. The blessed response to the Gospel is belief, not seizing and enacting righteousness like a child grabbing candy. All such talk of earthly equality and justice is cursed—it is only about man's works. It actually tries to undo what God made good and ordered for our protection. Christ does not work against Himself in the Gospel. The promise of freedom changes us before God in heaven. It is not a license to sin against what Christ designed and made us for.

If we can measure and see our righteousness on earth, it is not God's. That is not the pattern set before us in Abraham. He believed in what he could not see. He tried to do the same as those who want all economic, class, and gender distinctions undone—doing God's salvific work for Him, in this case, by having relations with a concubine, Hagar. Note that he did it in God's name and to fulfill the Gospel promise of a child! But this action was the opposite of trust—it was sinful human righteousness, and it ended very poorly for all involved.

We are called to be faithful to how God made us and to His created order, but also to trust that He will deliver us from its abuses. We are sinful and corrupt, so we need order and clear earthly roles. We do not get to choose our place in this world—that is God's prerogative. As sons of God, we submit, enjoying our status before Him, even if we are lowly and must submit to others in this world. It gives us all the more reason to hope for the redemption of our bodies in the world to come.

That Abraham was justified by faith is not a trivial fact. We are to know it and follow his example. There is only one way to be righteous like Abraham: not dressing like him, going where he camped out, having his name, or being circumcised, but living by God's same eternal promise of salvation. Sons of God (adopted in Christ) do not just happen to have faith, they become sons through faith. The promise which arouses faith in us is the one Gospel.

Another consequence of this statement is that the distinction between Jew and Gentile is not so great. In fact, it is nothing in Christ. Jesus had to deal with the Jewish national pride in their heritage and physical descent from Abraham. While it was of value (they had God's Word and the example of Abraham, who was saved by faith), their tradition and heritage counted nothing before God. To think one has something by birth or action is to live according the Law. Only faith counts as righteousness.

Jn. 8:39–45 describes an exchange between Christ and Jews (who were called "believing"), trusting in their own blood:

> *They answered him, "Abraham is our father." Jesus said to them, "If you were Abraham's children, you would be doing the works Abraham did, but now you seek to kill me, a man who has told you the truth that I heard from God. This is not what Abraham did. You are doing the works your father did." They said to him, "We were not born of sexual immorality. We have one Father—even God." Jesus said to them, "If God were your Father, you would love me, for I came from God and I am here. I came not of my own accord, but he sent me. Why do you not understand what I say? It is because you cannot bear to hear my word. You are of your father the devil, and your will is to do your father's desires. He was a murderer from the beginning, and does not stand in the truth, because there is no truth in him. When he lies, he speaks out of his own character, for he is a liar and the father of lies. But because I tell the truth, you do not believe me.*

The Jews are biologically children of Abraham (as was Jesus and many of the Apostles, including Paul), but because this particular group, as a whole, did not receive Jesus, they were not sons of God, but of the Devil. They wanted to literally murder God—that is, Jesus. Why? Jesus says it clearly: *you do not believe me.* They had the promise recorded for them, but did not live by it.

The world thinks that blood is thicker than water—that a physical relation is closest of all and means the most. But being a son of God cannot be passed down like a baseball card collection or shares of stock. One must first be righteous, which comes through faith in the Gospel. The Spirit creates this belief personally in every believer. Paul's rejection of Christ when he was a proud Jew and merely a genetic child of Abraham, detailed at end of chapter 1, only heightens the force of this section. The sermon of John the Baptist also deals with this boasting before God: *Bear fruits in keeping with repentance. And do not begin to say to yourselves, "We have Abraham as our father." For I tell you, God is able from these stones to raise up children for Abraham* (Lk. 3:8). "Do not even start," the Baptizer preaches. This spiritual pride is against faith, which forsakes all personal righteousness and clings to the Christ, who came into the world in the flesh to put sin to death in His body.

The physical nation of Israel was preached against for their false notion of righteousness. They thought righteousness consisted of doing works like Abraham, and having his blood. But Abraham was a sinner, who had no righteousness of his own to give or imitate. He needed the Messiah's blood. He was promised exactly that and lived by it. [**v8**] So faith is all he had and all that we have too.

Trying to be righteous by works is the same as dressing like someone and thinking this gives you their position. If I wear a police uniform and carry a gun, I get to exercise authority over people, right? No; that would be a very serious crime. To act righteous without the verdict, the promise, is impersonating a rightful son of God, even if all the outward ceremonies are there. This puts going to church in perspective: it is an action anyone can do, but it is not salvation itself. Nothing counts except resting in Christ's righteousness and forsaking everything we do, while certainly not being inactive in love. Faith is internal—we cannot see this trust or measure this hope. It is a living product of the Spirit and is never apart from the external Gospel or Christ who won it.

The same argument is made at the beginning of Rom. 4:1–6:

> *What then shall we say was gained by Abraham, our forefather according to the flesh? For if Abraham was justified by works, he has something to boast about, but not before God. For what does the Scripture say? "Abraham believed God, and it was counted to him as righteousness." Now to the one*

who works, his wages are not counted as a gift but as his due. And to the one who does not work but believes in him who justifies the ungodly, his faith is counted as righteousness, just as David also speaks of the blessing of the one to whom God counts righteousness apart from works.

In v8, the promise made to Abraham is called "the Gospel." That is an important point. Going back to 1:6, Paul says there is one Gospel. It predates the Jewish nation, Abraham, and even the creation of the world.

"The writing" means Scripture, though at that time all they had was what we call the Old Testament. That was the only Scripture for the earliest Christians as well, until the inspired letters, like this one by Paul, were written and gathered together, which was not an instantaneous process. Scripture, having the authority of God Himself, speaks of the Gentiles having the same righteousness of Abraham, thus ignoring nationality and every natural, physical, and personal characteristic. All that matters is the promise.

Acts 2:31 uses the same verb for "foresaw:" David *foresaw and spoke about the resurrection of the Christ, that he was not abandoned to Hades, nor did his flesh see corruption.* This teaches us how to use Scripture. Its scope is not historically limited to a certain time or people. This reading of God's future intention is a strong statement of inspiration, proof that the Spirit did breathe out these words. Although we treat this letter like a human document, written by Paul with human motives and feelings, that does not make it any less than God's full and literal Word. That is the only reason we should take it so seriously. We believe that the Lord is speaking directly to us in these words, and He is—it is His mighty Word. It reaches out and offers salvation to everyone for whom Christ died—for all people. To narrow the focus of God's Word to a particular context or people is to make God limited like a person, not the eternal, all knowing being.

The text says that God "justifies" (present tense) the nations, meaning He is still doing it. The word "Gentiles" means "the nations," an inclusive term used of all non-Jewish peoples. The promised seed, Christ, was promised to Abraham. Jesus, as a man, came through the Jews, so they deserve every respect, humanly speaking. However, the righteousness of faith annihilates human distinctions before God and allows only boasting in Christ, the life-giver, who undoes Adam's first sin.

God alone justifies. It is amazing how people love to judge other sinners by some standard. This is done tragically to celebrities, who are worshiped one moment and then condemned the next. One insensitive tweet or politically incorrect statement can doom one, and there is no apology or repentance that can undo it. This is playing God and being merciless, judging someone and not being willing to forgive. To judge the heart and condemn another person is evil. The world only knows abusive power and all-important public perception. We can and must, at times, judge external actions, but to write a person off for sin is satanic. Christ writes no one off in the Gospel.

Abraham is the fundamental believer and his faith was no narrow fulfilling of his Christmas wish list—child, heir, land and so on—but trust in a redeeming Messiah who would come through him and in whom he was actually righteous. This is how we are to see ourselves as well. All sons of God do the same as Abraham. All other blessings promised to Abraham flowed from this original righteousness, which also makes us beloved sons.

What was the Gospel that Abraham believed? It came in a form that is not preached today, but bore the same content: *In you* [meaning in his descendant Christ] *all nations shall be blessed.* "All nations" also includes the Gentiles, and "blessed" is not about earthly blessings, but the promise of righteousness and salvation in the suffering Servant. Jesus fulfilled that promise, so the Gospel identifies Him directly. The fact that Jesus had not yet been born, did not stop Abraham from believing and being justified by faith, since the promise was the same. It is the same for us, though Christ has already come, died, and risen. We must still believe in Him for righteousness.

The particular word for "preached the Gospel beforehand" is literally "pre-evangelized," which is one word in Greek. It is the only time this word is used in the New Testament. It seems to have no usage in classical Greek and very few occurrences from the time the New Testament was written. It was "pre" (before) the Gospel was fulfilled. Abraham's faith, though, had the same focus as the New Testament Gospel: the promise of salvation in Christ. He had to look forward and trust that He would come, whereas now we have the details and explanation about Jesus, who came. Faith goes behind the historical background of Jesus and rests in the promise that we appropriate His righteousness personally in the Gospel message. This is why the New Testament period is not "pre-evangel" (pre-Gospel)—it is used only of Abraham's faith.

The root of "evangel" (Gospel) is "angel," which simply means "message." It is a positive message, like a victory or the birth of a child—but much greater, since it delivers salvation. It delivers the goods it talks about. In the New Testament, the emphasis is on the power of the message. It brings and delivers its content: salvation in Jesus. It is more than information (a simple message), it is the power of God which brings into His kingdom. It confers the status of being a son of God. It is God's own decree to make sinners His people and bring into His kingdom. Paul says elsewhere: *our gospel came to you not only in word, but also in power and in the Holy Spirit and with full conviction* (1 Thess. 1:5).

Paul does not talk about an abstract Gospel, but *the* Gospel, a concrete truth, the only good news that makes all other good news (like marriage and the birth of a child) mundane and trite. There is no comparison. It works divine faith, so it is to be proclaimed and heard with all seriousness. The Gospel encompasses God's saving action: it forgives sins, takes away guilt, and gives the justification of righteousness. There is no spiritual blessing without this justification in God's sight, even for the patriarch Abraham. Scripture testifies to this in vv6–8.

Note that the word "promise" in Greek has the same root as "Gospel." Faith is based on a message. It is not a vague feeling. It rests on God's spoken word. Without it, we cannot know the goodness of the living God.

The promise given to Abraham actually occurs many times. It is recorded in chapters 12, 18, 22, 26, and 28 of Genesis. There is an important lesson for us in this: since we are weak, we need to hear the promise constantly in order be brought back from doubt and despair. We are not to depend on the Law or any human characteristic, like how faithful we look to man, how impressive or big our church is, or who likes us. God's verdict alone counts, and it comes only by faith in His promise. This means forsaking all righteousness of our own. This promise requires no specific response other than Spirit-given faith, which is a miracle, not a man-made response. *And Peter said to them, "Repent and be baptized every one of you in the name of Jesus Christ for the forgiveness of your sins, and you will receive the gift of the Holy Spirit.*

For the promise is for you and for your children and for all who are far off, everyone whom the Lord our God calls to himself" (Acts 2:38–39).

[v9] This verse summarizes the foolishness of the Galatians and also the axiomatic faith of Abraham. Those of faith, justified by faith and only by faith, are blessed the same as Abraham. One commentator summaries it well: "Paul clarifies that the Gentiles are blessed 'in' Abraham (3:8) by means of his 'Seed,' 'who is Christ' and not just by means of being a people of faith. From Abraham's loins would come the promised Messiah." [Das, 309]. Abraham is not just hoping for a grandchild, but the Savior of the world who will bear his awful sins.

The phrase in Greek for "the man of faith" is difficult to render. "Abraham" is not a Greek word, so it does not tell us how it should be understood grammatically, as with Greek nouns. Another translation of the end of v9 reads: "So then they which be of faith are blessed with faithful Abraham" (KJV). The problem is that this translates two Greek words with the same root (first a noun, then an adjective) in very different senses: "of faith" and "faithful." Since they are used together, it is unnatural to have their meanings at odds with one another. Saying Abraham had some intrinsic quality of "faithfulness" violates the Gospel, which Abraham is said to have believed. That the Gospel of forgiveness is the same for us as it was for Abraham is Paul's whole point. Abraham had the same Gospel the Galatians had then, and we still have today.

The Complete Jewish Bible has the meaning of "faith"/"faithful" both times in both senses in this verse: *So then, those who rely on trusting and being faithful are blessed along with Avraham, who trusted and was faithful.* An active sense (that Abraham did something) does not fit this context. Taking this mediating, cover all the bases position does not clarify the text. Abraham trusted because he was an unfaithful sinner. He was not faithful in his marriage or to God, as Genesis relates. But the passive sense, that he had faith in God's faithfulness and mercy, does fit. The Holman Christian Standard Bible uses this passive sense both times, which fits the conclusion to this section well: *So those who have faith are blessed with Abraham, who had faith.* The New American Standard Bible also has a fine translation: *So then those who are of faith are blessed with Abraham, the believer.* Another translation also ends this verse with "the believer" (OJB). The ESV, which has "man of faith," is not wrong, but it is more of an interpretation, rather than a decisive translation of a difficult phrase.

[**v10**] Paul moves from the example and paradigm of Abraham to a general principle about the Law. This verse is axiomatic in character—it applies to everyone and allows no exceptions. The Law is valid, righteous, and remains God's eternal will, but it does not give righteousness. Instead, it curses all we do—that is its only power for sinful man.

Again we have the phrase "works of the Law." It reads in Greek: "as many are of works of the law are under a curse." The implication is that they rely on works, but the connection to the earlier mentions of "of" (*ek* in Greek) might be lost in translation. For example, in this chapter:

- v2 – "*of* works of the Law did you receive the Spirit or *of* the hearing of faith"

- v5 – "does he supply the Spirit or work powers *of* works of the Law or *of* the hearing of faith"

- v7 - "those *of* faith are sons of Abraham"

- v8 - "the Gentiles *of* faith God justifies"

- v9 - "those *of* faith are blessed with the believing Abraham"

"Of" (*ek*) has a technical meaning here. Often this preposition implies motion: "from or out of." It can denote source, cause, or motivation. Paul so carefully separates works of the Law from the hearing of faith with the word "of" (ek). These are the two ways people seek to be justified, though only one is effective. The Law is self-dependence, while the Gospel, the hearing of faith, is dependence on Christ. This hearkens back to the Old Testament quote which cinched Paul's argument: Abraham believed God, and it was counted to him as righteousness. The "of" refers to the source of our life, that by which we live. Christ's promise, when combined with any legal obligation to God, is entirely Law. Christ did not suffer to burden us, but to free us from sins.

Those of the Law are under a curse. "Under" is a key word in Paul's letters. It denotes a controlling rule, authority, or power *over* us. In Christ, we are not under the Law, that is, its power to enslave and curse with God's anger. Neither do we throw the Law away, though. The curse has been removed—Jesus became a curse for us. The text is clear.

To be under the Law is to be under its curse. It is those who depend on their own actions and see salvation in works who are cursed. All true believers do works, but they do not see them as having anything to do with their status or righteousness in Christ, which is entirely earned and given by Him.

We should not see the Law as a friendly object. It used to be fashionable to post the commandments in public places, but the Law kills and damns with God's righteous wrath. It is nothing to play with. It does not improve us—it is the power of sin. *The sting of death is sin, and the power of sin is the law* (1 Cor. 15:56). That makes preaching a most dangerous task without training, the Spirit, and a divine call.

The Law requires death. That is the curse attached to it. This echoes what God told Adam and Eve in the Garden of Eden: *on the day you eat of it you shall die.* This is no human curse, such as when pagans curse objects that do not work properly. This is God's eternal judgment. Here we see the true character of the Law in one of the strongest verses in the Bible, condemning dependence on works of the Law for justification. All the Law can do is curse man. It cannot justify. In the example of the Galatian Christians we see how foolish it is to turn to the Law after embracing the Gospel. It is turning from life and God Himself to death, Satan, and the curse of hell.

Paul quotes Dt. 27:26. The people of Israel responded in liturgical fashion to the curses pronounced by the Levites. They are blessing, in a sense, the curses of God upon those guilty of iniquity. The whole section reads:

> "Cursed be the man who makes a carved or cast metal image, an abomination to the Lord, a thing made by the hands of a craftsman, and sets it up in secret." And all the people shall answer and say, "Amen." "Cursed be anyone who dishonors his father or his mother." And all the people shall say, "Amen." "Cursed be anyone who moves his neighbor's landmark." And all the people shall say, "Amen." "Cursed be anyone who misleads a blind man on the road." And all the people shall say, "Amen." "Cursed be anyone who perverts the justice due to the sojourner, the fatherless, and the widow." And all the people shall say, "Amen." "Cursed be anyone who lies with his father's wife, because he has uncovered his father's nakedness." And all the people shall say, "Amen." "Cursed be anyone who lies with any kind of animal." And all the people shall say, "Amen." "Cursed be anyone

who lies with his sister, whether the daughter of his father or the daughter of his mother." And all the people shall say, "Amen." "Cursed be anyone who lies with his mother-in-law." And all the people shall say, "Amen." "Cursed be anyone who strikes down his neighbor in secret." And all the people shall say, "Amen." "Cursed be anyone who takes a bribe to shed innocent blood." And all the people shall say, "Amen." "Cursed be anyone who does not confirm the words of this law by doing them." And all the people shall say, "Amen."

The twelve curses and amens speak of the true intention of the Law. "Amen" is a positive word, so how is the Law good? The Law is holy and from God. The problem is not the Law, but sinful men who cannot do the Law, because we do not love God or fear His punishment. That is why this section of curses makes us uncomfortable. The Law attacks, accuses, and brings God's wrath. But the answer is not to ignore it—rather, we should die to it.

The word for "curse" here is a strengthened version of the earlier word for "curse" in v10. It can mean "accursed" or "condemned." So many make the Law into self-help advice—as if we could just motivate ourselves to do better, we actually would be better. But the Law is the opposite: it demands holiness and coerces us into an impossible holiness. But we are not righteous and cannot fulfill the Law. Its true purpose is spiritual: to make us despair of our works. The Law is widely preached, but mostly as soft, cuddly, and helpful. Rarely is it used as the vehicle of God's wrath and the bringer of death. It is a curse upon all men.

Here it refers to the written Law given to the Jews, but we cannot even keep the Law written in our hearts. We feel guilt and shame when we know we have offended God. How good are we at covering our transgresses and rationalizing them—"everyone else does it, right?" But God is not everyone, He is the true judge of all men.

The Law is not grace, it is a strict, divine, legal contract demanding the complete fulfillment of all of its terms. Being decent to other people is not the same as keeping the holy Law. *You who boast in the law dishonor God by breaking the law,* Paul says to the Jews, who have the Law and love it, but are cursed by it (Rom. 2:23). In a marvelous passage, the Law is said to be all or nothing. It must all be kept without any slip up or failure. *For whoever keeps the whole law but fails in one point has become accountable for all of it* (Jam. 2:10). One angry word or one hateful thought brings the full curse of the Law: death.

Those without the blessing of Abraham are cursed. There is no neutral category. The punishment of hell is clearly taught by Scripture. The loss of this doctrine has a lot to with the loss of the fear of God—which is the beginning of wisdom. It does no good to say hell and eternal punishment do not agree with our cultural sensitivities. God's wrath over sin is real—real enough to lead to the death of God's Son for us.

A critical word in the Dt. quote above is the verb "does." Having holy commandments posted everywhere, thinking about them, and dedicating your life to them is useless. It is worse than useless, because the Law brings the divine curse to those who do not keep it. The Law, if understood rightly, makes demands until we die to it. Only then is the Gospel good news to us, when we have no righteousness or goodness in us. This is the spiritual understanding of the Law we are to have. It is a power that curses. The Law is not a practical good, just because we naturally like to use it and try to justify ourselves. It is ungodly to depend on the Law, to be justified "of" or "from" works. Those who think the Law is doable do not worship God, but themselves. They are trying to attain what God has only given in the preaching of Christ.

Verse 10 encompasses all people and religions. Only the Gospel of Christ offers salvation without works or strings attached. Every man-made religion requires some work or obedience we must muster (such as in the five pillars of Islam), devotion we must show, or enlightenment we must find. In some of the Eastern religions there is the teaching of "karma:" what you do comes back to you, in this or another life. All these are forms of Law—judgment according to our works. Only by faith does the true God offer eternal life and the redemption of our bodies. There is nothing to complete or finish. Jesus did it all. Only this doctrine, this Gospel, offers the certainty of salvation. No other religion offers the Gospel—it is only revealed by the true God in His Son. So, do not judge by how old or popular a religion or doctrine is, but by the words of this verse. This alone can cut through all the work-tinged teaching of conflicting religious teachers. But how many judge only by what they see and feel? That is nothing but the way of living "of/from" works. They are accursed, which is the greatest danger for all Christians. Remember that Paul's own congregations, the Galatians, likewise were tempted by this reliance on works, after first receiving the Gospel in faith.

"It is written" is in the perfect tense; it happened in the past, but still stands written for us and all people. It remains an authoritative, eternal Word of God.

The little word "all," which is used two times in this verse, allows no exception. We love to make excuses, but the Law accuses and does not take any tardy slips. "Accursed are *all* who do not remain in *all* which is written by doing them." *For it is not the hearers of the law who are righteous before God, but the doers of the law who will be justified* (Rom. 2:13).

Paul refers to every command of God and all aspects of the Law: moral, ceremonial, and civil. It includes all the divine Law, as surely as it includes all man-made rules. While the Old Testament civil and ceremonial laws do not apply to us, many make them necessary. Today this misapplication of the Law is often shown in honoring the (wrong) Sabbath, which is Saturday, not Sunday. Some churches make tithing a legal demand. For the Galatians the error was circumcision. There are some who think that Paul is only talking about ceremonial law, but the word "all," mentioned twice, does not allow any limitation of the understanding of "Law" here. The moral law curses—it was never meant to bring salvation, even in the Old Testament. The case of Abraham has already been established. He was not saved "from" works, but by faith in God's specific promise of salvation.

To embrace the Law is to abide in it. One cannot be about works and "doing" to gain God's favor and then switch to living in Christ when it is convenient. How many churches make tradition or rules saving burdens, denying the true freedom of the Gospel? It seems as if no one follows this in practice, but God's Word offers you this grace. Christ has done it all—it is yours. We are to live by this promise that we are righteous in Christ.

The Law blinds.

> *Since we have such a hope, we are very bold, not like Moses, who would put a veil over his face so that the Israelites might not gaze at the outcome of what was being brought to an end. But their minds were hardened. For to this day, when they read the old covenant, that same veil remains unlifted, because only through Christ is it taken away. Yes, to this day whenever Moses is read a veil lies over their hearts. But*

when one turns to the Lord, the veil is removed. Now the Lord is the Spirit, and where the Spirit of the Lord is, there is freedom (2 Cor. 3:12–17).

The "book of the Law" refers to the scroll it was written on. From the Greek word "biblios" we get our word "Bible." It refers to papyrus, the plant which was made into paper. The word originates from the city of Byblos, a Phoenician port where papyrus was prepared and exported.

Consider the logic of v10. If one does not do all that is in the book of the Law, he is cursed. This quote by itself could be an invitation to do works, to try harder. However, in the argument of Paul it is the inevitable conclusion. No one can do the Law. We only think we can. It does not stir us to action in the love of God's Spirit, but brings death—the eternal curse of God. No one can do the Law, and it is even worse, the works it requires are all under a curse. This logic could be carried further: what is not of faith is under a curse, because what is not of faith is of works. Scripture says so in Heb. 10:6: *And without faith it is impossible to please him.*

When someone is righteous or good in Scripture it does not mean of works or the Law, unless they were holy and perfect, without the stain of sin. Only Christ fits this description. Instead, it refers to their justification in Christ, the imputed righteousness given to us in faith. The righteous trust in God, not their own works. That is the only way to be righteous. This does not make sense to reason or to the smartest people of our age, but this is the wisdom of God.

> *That is why it depends on faith, in order that the promise may rest on grace and be guaranteed to all his offspring—not only to the adherent of the law but also to the one who shares the faith of Abraham, who is the father of us all, as it is written, "I have made you the father of many nations"—in the presence of the God in whom he believed, who gives life to the dead and calls into existence the things that do not exist* (Rom. 4:16–17).

Luther writes on this verse: "The doers of the Law are believers (not doers of works), who having received the Holy Spirit, fulfill the Law and love God and their neighbor. Thus the 'doer of the Law' is not one who becomes a doer on the basis of his deeds; he is one who having already become a person through faith, then becomes a doer [so that he fulfills the Law spiritually by the Spirit in Him]" [*Galatians*, 259–260]. There is no true doing of the Law without faith.

God accepts no work not done in faith. Without this faith in Christ, there is no good work before God. But in the world, before man, it is the opposite. Faith appears wretched and weak, while pious, hypocritical works of the Law appear righteous and holy. *For the word of the cross is folly to those who are perishing, but to us who are being saved it is the power of God. For it is written, "I will destroy the wisdom of the wise, and the discernment of the discerning I will thwart"* (1 Cor. 1:18–19).

[v11] No one is justified by the Law. The order in Greek is this: "because in/by the Law not one is justified." Paul starts with the Law. The Law corresponds to justification "of/from" works. No one can be justified by the Law, that is, by his works or anything he does. "Justify" refers to the legal verdict God renders. It denotes our status before God—not what we think of ourselves. Only the Lord Himself justifies. The phrase rendered "before God" is used of justification also in Rom. 2:13: *For it is not the hearers of the law who are righteous before God, but the doers of the law who will be justified.*

The end of the first phrase says that this is "evident," meaning "visible" or "plain." This word is used in Mt. 26:73 of Peter's accent, because his speech betrayed his association to Jesus and Galilee. This is when Peter denied Christ.

Next, Paul quotes Hab. 2:4. This verse is also cited in Rom. 1:17, where it talks of the Gospel as the power of God: *For in it* [the Gospel, not the Law] *the righteousness of God is revealed from faith for faith, as it is written, "The righteous shall live by faith."* In Heb. 10:38 it is included in a litany of Old Testament quotes as a conclusion. Heb. 10 begins: *For since the law has but a shadow of the good things to come instead of the true form of these realities.* It speaks of sacrifices especially, but also all the works of the Law: *For it is impossible for the blood of bulls and goats to take away sins.* Then Hebrews speaks of the one perfect sacrifice which ends all sacrifices (and every ceremonial work): *And by that will we have been sanctified through the offering of the body of Jesus Christ once for all.* At the end of Heb. 10, after the quote from Hab. 2:4, it reads: *But we are not of those who shrink back and are destroyed, but of those who have faith and preserve their souls.*

The original Habakkuk quote is a revelation from God to the prophet Habakkuk: *Write the vision; make it plain on tablets, so he may run who reads it. For still the vision awaits its appointed time; it hastens to the end—it will not lie. If it seems slow, wait for it; it will surely come; it will not delay. Behold, his soul is puffed up; it is not upright within him, but the righteous shall live by his faith* (2:2–4). Those who trust in God's goodness must wait. This expecting person lives by his faith in God's certain coming. The Hebrew in Habakkuk has "his faith." One can only believe for himself. But Paul talks of faith in general, as opposed to the works of the Law.

To Habakkuk, God speaks of the boastfulness of the Chaldeans, who will gain control of Babylon and subjugate Israel. Israel's unfaithfulness and the Babylonian ungodliness are distressing for Habakkuk. Chapter 1 includes the complaint of Habakkuk: *O Lord, how long shall I cry for help, and you will not hear? Or cry to you "Violence!" and you will not save? Why do you make me see iniquity, and why do you idly look at wrong? Destruction and violence are before me; strife and contention arise. So the law is paralyzed, and justice never goes forth. For the wicked surround the righteous; so justice goes forth perverted* (1–4). The response in chapter 2, which is cited by Paul and the author of Hebrews, refers to the dependence on the promise of God. Even when it looks like God has dropped the ball and is not going to save His people, *it will surely come* (v3). Faith looks forward to an unseen deliverance, despite all appearances, because God has promised it. Faith clings to this Gospel that God is good and has justified us, even though there is no evidence to back it up. God's Word remains the object of faith and reveals Christ to us, along with all His gifts of salvation. Living by faith is an Old Testament concept, according to the New Testament.

Faith is not a personal power—for that would make it a work. It is a reliance on God who has done it all. The Father sent Christ to die, raised Him, called us in the Gospel, and justifies us. Faith does not exist independently of the Spirit. Paul has already made that connection in v3. Faith is in the Gospel, the promise of God that we are actually righteousness in His sight, and is never apart from it. There is no true righteousness in God's sight and judgment without faith. To live by the Law (which is natural) is to live under God's curse, even if sinners do not realize it. But in Christ we live by faith. Only then is there some true doing of the Law in the Spirit, born of love for the Father.

This faith is a living confidence and hope. It lives above all troubles and sufferings, because we are in God and have His sure word. *No, in all these things we are more than conquerors through him who loved us* (Rom. 8:37). *For everyone who has been born of God overcomes the world. And this is the victory that has overcome the world—our faith* (1 Jn. 5:4). The righteous shall live by ("of/from") faith. It is the source and fountain of life. Life in God is not "of/from" works of the Law. The parallelism in Paul's use of this preposition we have already explored on page 130. The believer does not cease living—we live in Christ and will continue to do so into eternity. The text clearly ties justification (the application of righteousness), which is through faith, to true living—life in Christ.

We must be told what true life is. We think it is having good health, the advantages of youth, food, and comfort, but life is in God. It is not fading, like the flower of the field. It is not temporary, but eternal. It includes righteousness and the future joys of paradise. It is having God's love and never being separated from Him. This is true living. *The righteous will live by faith.* This life we could not desire or know, if it were not given to us and revealed in Scripture. It is to be above the curse into which we were born. This verse is the daylight to our natural darkness.

The Scriptures have much to say about true life. We are naturally dead in sin, so the Spirit must make us alive. This does not mean feeling more holy or spiritual. Righteousness is in God, given in the Gospel to be believed. Describing sin and the corruption of all things, Job says: *Has not man a hard service on earth, and are not his days like the days of a hired hand? Like a slave who longs for the shadow, and like a hired hand who looks for his wages, so I am allotted months of emptiness, and nights of misery are apportioned to me. . . . Remember that my life is a breath; my eye will never again see good* (Job 7). Life is in God. There is no life outside of His righteousness delivered by the promise. Faith looks into eternity and counts on being with the holy God. Ps. 119:50 reminds us that true life is not an easy life on earth—it is having God's favor: *This is my comfort in my affliction, that your promise gives me life.* What a precious verse. We cannot be reminded of the Gospel too much.

Life is more than existing a few decades on this earth. What we naturally think is living, is actually death—living under the Law. Our supposed righteousness (apart from God's righteousness which comes by

faith) is actually death. *For as the Father raises the dead and gives life,*
so also the Son gives life to whom He wills now [through His Word] . . . .
Truly, truly, I say to you, whoever hears my word and believes him who
sent me has eternal life. He does not come into judgment, but has passed
from death to life (Jn. 5:21, 24). There is no life apart from the Son and
the forgiveness of sins in Him. The faith by which we live is in Jesus
and rests on what He has done for us.

There is another way to live. [**v12**] Because the Law's promise of life
is shut off by sin, it only condemns and curses us. This is the reverse of
v11. There is a promise of life in the Law, but for sinners it is a mirage.
It is not possible. We must be convicted of sin, thus the way of the Law
is closed in regards to salvation. Only then can we have true life by
faith.

The citation here is from Lev. 18:5, again focusing on the *doing* of
the Law, not just familiarity with it or caring emotionally about it. It
requires perfect love of God. The Law is spiritual. In Rom. 10:5 Paul
uses this same verse: *For Moses writes about the righteousness that is*
based on the law, that the person who does the commandments shall live
by them. "Based" is not in the Greek text. It is actually "of/from" the
Law, describing the source of righteousness.

Lev. 18 starts:

> *And the Lord spoke to Moses, saying, "Speak to the people*
> *of Israel and say to them, I am the Lord your God. You*
> *shall not do as they do in the land of Egypt, where you lived,*
> *and you shall not do as they do in the land of Canaan, to*
> *which I am bringing you. You shall not walk in their statutes.*
> *You shall follow my rules and keep my statutes and walk in*
> *them. I am the Lord your God. You shall therefore keep my*
> *statutes and my rules; if a person does them, he shall live*
> *by them: I am the Lord."*

Then a list of unlawful sexual relations is mentioned. It covers sins
which some people today celebrate, especially in pornography. It forbids:
uncovering nakedness of any family member. It continues: *You shall not*
lie with a male as with a woman; it is an abomination. And you shall
not lie with any animal and so make yourself unclean with it, neither
shall any woman give herself to an animal to lie with it: it is perversion.
Whether the world agrees is beside the point.

God is holy and gives the holy Law. In our pornographic world nudity and the flaunting of flesh is prevalent and inescapable. In just the last few decades homosexuality has became a dominant false gospel, promising freedom from what God created us to be. But it is an abomination. Performing homosexual acts denies the body Christ gave us and is incompatible with His Spirit. If anyone struggles with those kinds of lusts, there is hope, but no one is to be ruled by them, lest the Spirit be pushed out and faith abandoned. Rom. 1 connects the acceptance of these physical acts with the ignorance of God. Homosexual practices deny the most basic distinction God makes between us: male and female. It does not require Scripture to know this, it is obvious from birth whether we are male and female and our role in marriage:

> *Therefore God gave them up in the lusts of their hearts to impurity, to the dishonoring of their bodies among themselves, because they exchanged the truth about God for a lie and worshiped and served the creature rather than the Creator, who is blessed forever! Amen. For this reason God gave them up to dishonorable passions. For their women exchanged natural relations for those that are contrary to nature; and the men likewise gave up natural relations with women and were consumed with passion for one another, men committing shameless acts with men and receiving in themselves the due penalty for their error. And since they did not see fit to acknowledge God, God gave them up to a debased mind to do what ought not to be done (Rom. 1:24–28).*

All the world's misguided talk of love and commitment cannot undo Christ's good creation.

Paul, in 1 Cor. 6:16–20, relates that what we call "sex" is not truly about an individual's will, body, and choices. It is a divine gift that is supposed to bring a true, physical uniting between husband and wife. It is a uniting act that God works through for the good of marriage. To misuse it causes great harm physically and spiritually.

> *Or do you not know that he who is joined to a prostitute becomes one body with her? For, as it is written, "The two will become one flesh." But he who is joined to the Lord becomes one spirit with him. Flee from sexual immorality. Every other sin a person commits is outside the body, but the sexually immoral person sins against his own body. Or do you not know that your body is a temple of the Holy Spirit within you, whom you have from God? You are not your own, for you were bought with a price. So glorify God in your body (1 Cor. 6:9–11).*

Intentions or emotional connections do not nullify the will of God revealed in nature. What is unnatural is sinful.

Faith does not mean doing what we want or ignoring Christ's will. Sinning against Christ's Law, revealed or natural, is not being led by the Spirit. So many use the Gospel as an excuse to sin, not a promise by which to live. Scripture clearly condemns acting out in gratification of the sinful nature, contrary to the Law of God. *Or do you not know that the unrighteous will not inherit the kingdom of God? Do not be deceived: neither the sexually immoral, nor idolaters, nor adulterers, nor men who practice homosexuality, nor thieves, nor the greedy, nor drunkards, nor revilers, nor swindlers will inherit the kingdom of God. And such were some of you. But you were washed, you were sanctified, you were justified in the name of the Lord Jesus Christ and by the Spirit of our God.* (1 Cor. 6). Not doing these things does not justify—only faith in Christ does. But doing them marks one as without the Spirit, therefore, without faith. In Christ there is forgiveness. According to the Law, there is no reprieve for our past actions. But in Christ we are holy and clean before God, so we live by faith, free from all sins and the flesh which rakes up mud and filth within us. This repentance is a fruit of the Spirit and goes with faith. To repent means we do not want or intend to continue in sin anymore, because we hate it, as the Lord also does.

Next, Paul returns to the curse. [v13] Here we have the mystery of the Gospel detailed. Christ became a curse. God Himself was cursed and sentenced to die. Do not think of Jesus as merely a wise man or prophet. He is God in man (Immanuel) taking the curse of the Law in our place.

"Redeem" is a significant theological word. It means "to ransom or buy back." It was used of slaves to describe the buying of their freedom. This particular form of "redeem" (in reference to people) occurs only here in Galatians. It appears here and in 4:5: *to redeem those who were under the law, so that we might receive adoption as sons.* Elsewhere, we are told to redeem time for ourselves, but this is not God's action, as the form of the word in Galatians indicates: *Walk in wisdom toward those who are outside, redeeming the time* (Col. 4:5). The ESV has a weak translation of this verse: *making the best use of the time.* The sense here is that we are already redeemed, including all our moments and time in this dying world, so they are holy—we just do not believe it fully.

We were originally owned by Satan and under the power of sin. Man cannot escape the curse of sin by his own efforts, which can only be by the Law. *Since therefore the children share in flesh and blood, he* [Christ] *himself likewise partook of the same things, that through death he might destroy the one who has the power of death, that is, the devil, and deliver all those who through fear of death were subject to lifelong slavery* (Heb. 2:14–15).

In Roman society a slave was redeemed from slavery by paying the slave's owner. In certain contexts this was considered a sacred event. A pretend god was sometimes inserted into the redemption transaction, though the slave actually paid the price. Perhaps this was done because we are incapable of freeing ourselves. Freedom must come from an authority above us.

The root of this word "redemption" means "to buy." A useful illustration is the redemption of cans and bottles. An extra fee is assessed in some states for these items, perhaps 5 or 10 cents per can. The redemption fee is exchanged for the empty can. So a can in those places is worth much more than its weight in aluminum. It can be redeemed for the set price. That is a picture of what Christ did for us. He offered not gold or silver, but His precious, holy blood—His very life. Christ redeemed us with something of more value than our sins—Himself.

This particular form of "redeem" was not common in secular Greek. Yet, it is a weighty word in Scripture. The curse of the Law is slavery and death itself, even if it does not feel like it right now. When Christ became a curse under the Law and died, we became legally free from the curse of the Law. Even apart from our believing it, our actual redemption historically took place long ago. The claim of the Law has been satisfied. Paul will talk about what we are freed to possess (sonship and love) later in this letter, at the end of chapter 3 and in chapter 4. Who was redeemed? All the world, and so all people were bought. Christ was the price. Who received the price of redemption? The Father, since He asserted the finality and completion of the redemption when He raised Jesus to life. His anger over sin and His divine justice were both appeased.

A simpler form of redeem, meaning "to buy," is used a few times in the New Testament: *You were bought with a price; do not become bondservants of men* (1 Cor. 7:23); *some will secretly bring in destructive heresies, even denying the Master who bought them, bringing upon themselves swift destruction* (2 Pet. 2:1). Our lives do not belong to ourselves, but to Him who paid the redemption price in full.

"Christ became a curse"—what odd language to our fleshly ears. How can God be cursed? In love, Jesus took our spot under the guillotine of the Law. Why? "For us." Faith takes a hold of this promise and clings to Christ's righteousness as its own. The preposition "for" in "becoming a curse for us" means "on behalf of" or "for the sake of." The idea of substitution is present in it. This preposition is used in Hebrews for the redemption without actually using a form of "redeem:" *But when Christ had offered for all time a single sacrifice for* [on behalf of] *sins, he sat down at the right hand of God* (Heb. 10:12).

"Christ" is the first word of this sentence in the Greek, emphasizing that He—the redemption fee—is the object of our faith. Redemption involves not just Christ, the price that was paid, but our freedom and release from the Law. We are no longer bound to cursed obedience under threat of punishment. Now we have a new relationship to the Law. The curse we were under does not apply to us any longer. Verse 1 of this chapter begins this thought. The tree (it can also mean just "wood" in Greek) proves we are free from the curse. The cross of Christ is our salvation. It signifies the place and way in which Christ's body was paid to redeem you. The parallel to the tree of redemption is the tree of the knowledge of good and evil, which led to our death. The contrast between the tree of sin and the tree of redemption is striking.

The scriptural proof cited here is from Dt. 21:23. The whole passage reads: *And if a man has committed a crime punishable by death and he is put to death, and you hang him on a tree, his body shall not remain all night on the tree, but you shall bury him the same day, for a hanged man is cursed by God. You shall not defile your land that the Lord your God is giving you for an inheritance* (22–23). This Word of God looks forward to Jesus. We should not feel sorry for Him or wish He had avoided this horrible death. Instead, we are to see our sins on Jesus. He became a curse, submitting Himself to the Law for us. The stronger form of curse, "accursed" or "condemned," is used in this quote, as in v10.

Hanging today means killing a man by means of rope around the neck, but back then crucifixion was the common form of capital punishment. Even the way Christ would die was foretold in the Old Testament. We are not to be ashamed of our God's death. Without it, we would not be redeemed and would not have Christ as our Redeemer and God. *And we are witnesses of all that he did both in the country of the Jews and in Jerusalem. They put him to death by hanging him on a tree* (Acts 10:39). Faith believes the Father punished the Son, who offered His life for ours—the righteous for the unrighteous. Is. 53 says very clearly that we esteem, or consider, God Himself as the one doing this action, although it looked like a normal work of civil punishment:

> *Surely he has borne our griefs and carried our sorrows; yet we esteemed him stricken, smitten by God, and afflicted. But he was pierced for our transgressions; he was crushed for our iniquities; upon him was the chastisement that brought us peace, and with his wounds we are healed. All we like sheep have gone astray; we have turned—every one—to his own way; and the Lord has laid on him the iniquity of us all.*

Our freedom from the curse is found only in Christ being cursed. So redemption from the curse becomes the means of God's love. Without being crucified, Christ cannot be our God and savior.

Luther states it quite daringly: "But just as Christ is wrapped up in our flesh and blood, so we must wrap Him and know Him to be wrapped up in our sins, our curse, our death, and everything evil" [*Galatians,* 278]. This is how faith sees the awful death of an innocent man. In this way, when Christ died, so did our sins, the curse, and all our enemies. We are restored to God and free before Him. But God had to become a curse, a sinner, to make this happen. Whatever evil we have done, Christ became that. We were redeemed in His death. What was on Christ, sin, is no longer on us, even as we struggle against our own flesh presently. Only Christ, who is fully God, could do this great work. *For our sake he made him to be sin who knew no sin, so that in him we might become the righteousness of God* (2 Cor. 5:21). Christ became the greatest sinner of all to save mankind from sin.

To return to the Law is slavery. All who do so, ignore Christ who became a curse for us. This reminds us of 2:4: *Yet because of false brothers secretly brought in—who slipped in to spy out our freedom that we have in Christ Jesus, so that they might bring us into slavery.*

[v14] One commentator explains Paul's logic: "we were *under* the curse [of the Law]; Christ took the curse on himself and thus *over* us . . . , so that he rescued us *out from under* the curse" [Lenski, 153]. Christ redeemed all from the curse, therefore the Gentiles, too. Who the Law was given to does not factor into righteousness. It brings a curse to those who rely on it—the opposite of the blessing in faith. Abraham's blessing, the promise he trusted, is fulfilled in us, even if we are Gentiles by birth. All are blessed through Christ—the "all nations" of vv8–9.

"Blessing" is opposed to the curse of the Law. The root for "blessing" in Greek literally reads "good word." While we talk of blessings in a human sense, like money or help, only God can bless for eternal and unequivocal good. *Every good gift and every perfect gift is from above, coming down from the Father of lights with whom there is no variation or shadow due to change* (Jam. 1:17).

The blessing of Abraham comes not from having his blood, but Christ's cleansing blood. It comes in the promise. His actual blood and body are also offered in the Lord's Supper for the forgiveness of sins. Faith receives the promise and the righteousness offered there, as the mouth receives Christ's body and blood. There is no life without faith, though the promise comes in several forms.

The promise to Abraham concerned the Messiah ("Christ" is the Greek equivalent). We are blessed in Him, too. The Spirit makes us alive through the promise, that is, "of" the hearing of faith (v5).

"Faith which receives the promise" has the article in Greek: "the faith," which is not necessary or grammatically correct in English. We can conclude it is there for a reason, since the Spirit does not make mistakes. A literal rendering is: "in order that the promise of the Spirit is received on account of the faith." There is only one faith. It can vary in strength, but if it grasps Christ, it justifies and makes us righteous in God's sight. The foundation of faith is Christ. One is either in Christ and righteous, or outside of Him and under God's wrath. A sinner is either in the one, holy Church by faith in Christ, or outside it, without true saving faith. It is not the personal trust itself which makes one alive to God, but faith's proper object: Christ, the foundation of saving faith. *Everyone who comes to me and hears my words and does them, I will show you what he is like: he is like a man building a house, who dug deep and laid the foundation on the rock. And when a flood arose, the stream broke against that house and could not shake it, because it had been well built* (Lk. 6:47–48).

Here is a great quote on faith from the 16th century Lutheran dogmatician Martin Chemnitz: "If faith is not mistaken in its object, but lays hold of it, be it ever so trembling, with ever so weak a confidence, with only the striving for and desiring of it, such faith is indeed small and weak, but nevertheless true faith" [Pieper, 2:428]. In Him the flesh counts for nothing, we are out from under the curse.

Faith is never apart from the Spirit. The ESV reads: *we might receive the promised Spirit.* The Greek says "the promise of the Spirit." That fits better, because we receive the Spirit in the promise of Christ, which we hear and believe, in the hearing of faith. The curse was extinguished in Christ, therefore there is only blessing. This Gospel is to be distributed to all the world, because it unites with Christ, creates faith, and gives life. The blessing comes in Christ. Outside of Him there is no life, only the curse of being a sinner under the Law. Verses 13 and 14 go together.

The promise of the Spirit is not a New Testament idea. We read in Is. 44:3: *For I will pour water on the thirsty land, and streams on the dry ground; I will pour my Spirit upon your offspring, and my blessing on your descendants.* The Spirit comes not through works of the Law, which are under the curse, but in faith that Christ became a curse for us to redeem us. In Abraham, the very person the Judaizers boasted of following (by requiring circumcision for salvation), the blessing of justification came to the Gentiles, by the same faith he had—"the faith."

The Law is real. It convicts because our sin and sinful nature are real. However, we remain in Christ by faith, outside of the curse. The curse of the Law does not touch us, since we are free in faith. The Spirit has been given to us live in the Law (in love and faith), not under it (as a slave). We live as the true children of Abraham.

Luther describes the boldness of faith: "If Christ is the price of my redemption, if He put Himself under a curse in order to justify me and bless me, I am not put off at all by passages of Scripture, even if you were to produce six hundred passages in support of the righteousness of works and against the righteousness of faith" [*Galatians*, 295]. Luther means that the passages are inspired and true—meaning the Law is real—but they do not apply to us. In faith we are outside the curse and reside in Christ where there are no threats. The Law has no ability to accuse Christ or those righteous in Him. This is the key to understanding Scripture. Without this knowledge it is a closed book.

Paul now shifts gears. [**v15**] Notice that Paul calls the Galatians "brothers" for the first time since 1:11. He does so frequently from this point on. The promise of life still applies to them. He is not accusing them or calling them foolish here. He has made his point and disciplined them. Now he teaches patiently—he is not their adversary.

"I speak according to man." A covenant is a legal agreement between two parties. It must be ratified by both participants. The perfect tense is used here for "ratified." The covenant stands and remains in effect. If ratified, it cannot be changed. Any legal contract works by that principle. One cannot unilaterally void the contract because it is unfair at a later date. It is common to hear of a bitterly divorced spouse who inherits over the current spouse at death, because the named beneficiary was not changed. In the same way, intentions or feelings do not trump the divine Law. The Law is a legal contract, sealed with blood: *Therefore not even the first covenant was inaugurated without blood. For when every commandment of the law had been declared by Moses to all the people, he took the blood of calves and goats, with water and scarlet wool and hyssop, and sprinkled both the book itself and all the people, saying, "This is the blood of the covenant that God commanded for you"* (Heb. 9:18–20). The New Covenant is more properly a testament, a one-sided promise, not an agreement between equals. Like a last will and testament, it stands firm. Even a spouse or child cannot undo what has been ratified. If it could be changed after one's death, it would mean little.

"Covenant" is a much misused word in Christian theology. There is even the term "covenant theology," referring to various covenant schemes Reformed theologians posit in Scripture. The problem is that covenant is a legal word—it basically means "contract." It is two-sided. Both parties must keep and obey the terms of the covenant. It demands the specified works, or else it is not in effect. Therefore, it is of the Law. So the Jewish Law was a covenant, but it came after the promise. At all times, including those of the Old Testament, God's people were only saved and became God's people through the promise—the same, exact faith the Spirit works today.

147

[v16] Verses 15–17 should be read together. The Gospel came first, so it has priority. The Law does not undo the prior promise. They existed side-by-side for a time, but only the Gospel gives eternal redemption from the curse. The Law supports the promise, in a negative way, by exposing sin and wickedness so that we realize our need for the Savior who is delivered in the promise.

On the other hand, "testament" is a Gospel word. It only gives, because its terms were already fulfilled by Christ. A last will and testament enacts a gift, even without the beneficiary knowing about it beforehand. It requires nothing but ratification. It is entirely one-sided. The simple word "will" fits well here without the legal baggage of the word "covenant." The Gospel is for sinners, but its terms were between the Father and the Son. Thus, it is nothing like a worldly, two-sided covenant.

But even a man-made "covenant" cannot be nullified, set aside, or declared invalid. The Law is not set aside or ignored—Christ fulfilled it. Christ uses this word "annul" of Himself: *The one who rejects* [annuls] *me and does not receive my words has a judge; the word that I have spoken will judge him on the last day* (Jn. 12:48). Paul himself uses the same word in 2:21: *I do not nullify* [annul] *the grace of God, for if righteousness were through the law, then Christ died for no purpose.*

Paul argues from the lesser to the greater. If a human contract cannot be changed, surely God's will cannot either. This is something evident to all, which is why he uses it to prove his point. The second word translated "or adds to it" can also be used as a legal term for adding a codicil. A will can be modified or added to today by a codicil, but it does not undo or change the will, except where explicitly stated. It must be newer and ratified in the same way as the will (perhaps with a notary public and two witnesses), but after the testator is dead, nothing can be added.

The testament he is talking about is not the Law (since it cannot save), but the promise of the Spirit, the blessing that Abraham first believed. The Law was made most concrete in the Decalogue, what we call the "Ten Commandments," but this was not given until 430 years later, through Moses.

While the Gospel is called the "New Testament," "new" does not refer to its age. Rather, it makes us new by giving the Spirit, even though it is older than the written Law. It is primary, since it offers righteousness. *Therefore* [Christ] *is the mediator of a new covenant, so that those who are called may receive the promised eternal inheritance, since a death has occurred that redeems them from the transgressions committed under the first covenant. For where a will is involved, the death of the one who made it must be established* (Heb. 9:15–16). The Gospel promise existed before Christ died, but His death was necessary to fulfill and ratify it.

The promise refers to a "seed" (singular). It may seem nit-picky, but no word of the Spirit's Scripture is without purpose for us. The "seed" testifies to Christ, rather than referring to all people. All nations are not the promise, but all nations will be blessed in Abraham's seed, that is, his one promised offspring: Christ.

"Promises" (plural) is used here. The promise was spoken many times, with some variation in wording, but there is only one God, who promises the one eternal salvation. That promise can come in many forms and wordings. The one faith in Christ is the only saving response the Spirit generates in us through the promise. The seed is Christ. He was promised long ago to Abraham, which is why he could believe in Him for righteousness.

The word for seed in Greek is "sperm," from the verb "to sow [seeds]." God refers to one seed: the Christ. Although Isaac was Abraham's immediate offspring, his near sacrifice on Mt. Moriah shows that another sacrifice was needed. Isaac was a sinner born of sinners, but Christ was conceived holy by the Spirit, able to fulfill the Law. This very promise was chronologically given slightly before circumcision and 430 years before the tablets of stone. There is a great difference between the Law and the Gospel even for the Jews—over 4 centuries of storied history. Paul uses the father of the Jews, Abraham, as his battering ram to defeat any talk of adding the Law to the Gospel, as if it were a codicil offering some improvement.

[v17] This first testament (the promise) was not ratified by a man, but even a man-made covenant is impossible to change. The author and fulfiller of this testament is God Himself. The Greek word for "ratified" here is slightly different than the "ratified" in v15. The prefix "pro-," meaning "before," is added to it. The Gospel promise was in effect before the Law came. The Law does not change the Gospel in the least.

Christ reigns over the Law, as do those in Him. We are not under the Law.

The word for "does not annul" in Greek is "a-ratify," or "un-ratify," we might say. The later Law does not make the promise idle or fruitless, emptying the cross of Christ of its power. Paul uses this word of himself: *When I was a child, I spoke like a child, I thought like a child, I reasoned like a child. When I became a man, I gave up* [abolished] *childish ways* (1 Cor. 13:11).

Here "the promise," with the article, is used. In our consciences too, the promise is to rule over the Law. Our flesh needs the Law because it is unruly and does not let us fully follow the Spirit. But "the promise" is the only life-giving source for us. The curse cannot save.

A will or testament designates an inheritance, while a contract does not. The Gospel is a testament, not a covenant. **[v18]** Paul points out the contradiction of relying on the Law. It is not a promise, so it does not offer freedom. It demands works—that all of our works are holy.

In Acts 20:32, "inheritance" is used of our spiritual blessings: *And now I commend you to God and to the word of his grace, which is able to build you up and to give you the inheritance among all those who are sanctified.* Paul speaks of our promised rights, which we have, but do not fully enjoy now. People fight over worldly goods, but all the ungodly do is die and leave them to others. In Christ we have a much greater inheritance: being cleansed by His Word.

Again, the same "ek" preposition pops up: "of/from" the Law; "of/from" the promise. There can be only one cause of salvation. It is of God (in the Gospel) or of man (under the Law).

The word for "give" has the connotation of grace. Its root denotes "freely," that which is given as a gift. It is used for forgiveness in Col. 2:13: *And you, who were dead in your trespasses and the uncircumcision of your flesh, God made alive together with him, having forgiven* [freely pardoned] *us all our trespasses.* Every spiritual gift of grace He now gives us through a promise. What distinguishes a promise? It is to be believed, so it requires faith. But faith is not a legal obligation, it is the Spirit renewing our will, according to God's love. To tell someone to love God, as a command, is fruitless. But God's love is freely proclaimed, so that holy faith is worked by the Spirit where and when He wills.

It seems at this point that Paul has destroyed the Law, so that it is nothing and should be completely ignored. But that is not true. It is just that, in comparison with the promise, the Law has no role in justification. It should not be trusted in or relied upon. So what is the point of the Law? Paul obliges us. [**v19**]

The external supremacy of Law had a set time period. This includes the whole Jewish legal code, rules for worshiping God, and all civil penalties for disobedience. Beyond that time period, the Law was meant to promote and extol the Gospel. This sounds almost ridiculous after Paul has attacked the Law so much.

There are several different definitions of the word "Law," so we must keep them straight. In Paul's writings especially we see a variety of meanings. Consider the contrast between the two "laws" in Rom. 8:2: *For the law of the Spirit of life has set you free in Christ Jesus from the law of sin and death.* Law, as in doctrine, can mean the entire content of God's Word. In the Psalms we often have this definition of "law": torah, instruction, teaching, and guidance. *Blessed is the man who walks not in the counsel of the wicked, nor stands in the way of sinners, nor sits in the seat of scoffers; but his delight is in the law of the Lord, and on his law he meditates day and night* (Ps. 1:1–2). When used in the phrase "the law and the prophets," it means the first five books of the Bible, the Pentateuch, written by Moses. This is the common Jewish way to refer to the Old Testament: Law (Torah), Prophets, and Writings. *But now the righteousness of God has been manifested apart from the law, although the Law and the Prophets bear witness to it* (Rom. 3:21). The Gospel is shown in the example of Abraham, recorded in the "law"—the first book of the Bible: Genesis. "Law" can also just refer to the text of the Old Testament: *But the word that is written in their Law must be fulfilled: "They hated me without a cause"* (Jn. 15:25).

The Law, in our context, usually refers to the moral law, which is eternal. *Owe no one anything, except to love each other, for the one who loves another has fulfilled the law. For the commandments* [this word is not in the Greek text], *"You shall not commit adultery, You shall not murder, You shall not steal, You shall not covet," and any other commandment, are summed up in this word: "You shall love your neighbor as yourself"* (Rom. 13:8–9).

We hear "law" and think of commands—what we must do or not

do. That is part of it, but in the accounts of the giving of the tablets at Mt. Sinai they are not called commandments at all, but rather the "ten words." Neither are they numbered for us, which is why there are several major divisions. The main Jewish numbering today has the first "word" as Ex. 20:2: *I am the Lord your God, who brought you out of the land of Egypt, out of the house of slavery.* This is not a command at all and does not apply to Gentiles, since they were not delivered from physical slavery in Egypt. We can actually trace the introduction of calling the ten words "commandments" to the 1560 Geneva Bible, which was then incorporated into the KJV. Older English translations before the KJV used "ten words" instead of "ten commandments."

The Law was not just revealed on tablets of stone. It is also written on our hearts, so that we have it by nature. Rom. 2:14–16 has this important passage: *For when Gentiles, who do not have the law, by nature do what the law requires, they are a law to themselves, even though they do not have the law. They show that the work of the law is written on their hearts, while their conscience also bears witness, and their conflicting thoughts accuse or even excuse them on that day when, according to my gospel, God judges the secrets of men by Christ Jesus.* The Law is familiar to man because we were created to know it. Everyone knows guilt, the recognition that we have broken the divine Law.

"Law" is a multifaceted word, so we must pay close attention to the context to recognize which use of the word is before us. The word "law" is often used in different senses close together: *The Law and the Prophets were until John; since then the good news of the kingdom of God is preached, and everyone forces his way into it. But it is easier for heaven and earth to pass away than for one dot of the Law to become void* (Lk. 16:16–17).

Paul often uses the word "law" to speak specifically of the Law's curse: *For the law brings wrath, but where there is no law there is no transgression* (Rom. 4:15). The Law is a power, similar to the Gospel, except it brings death instead of life. It is the power of sin, not the power to make a person good: *Likewise, my brothers, you also have died to the law through the body of Christ* (Rom. 7:4). It even brings sin to life and awakens it in the conscience. So, also, the Gospel is something that reigns in the conscience, by which we live. We are free from God's condemnation and wrath over sin, revealed by the Law. We are not to live under God's displeasure and the curse of death, but under grace by faith in Christ. The Law as a restraining power has no role for the new man.

Now we know that the law is good, if one uses it lawfully, understanding this, that the law is not laid down for the just but for the lawless and disobedient, for the ungodly and sinners, for the unholy and profane, for those who strike their fathers and mothers, for murderers, the sexually immoral, men who practice homosexuality, enslavers, liars, perjurers, and whatever else is contrary to sound doctrine (1 Tim. 1:8–9). This is the external force of the Law, similar to parents disciplining little children. It is not a spiritual use of the Law, but the threat of civil punishment and public shame. Christians ruled by the Spirit do not need this use of the Law, which is called a curb. It does, however, impede violent outbursts of sin somewhat, but this power does nothing to address the seat of sin—man's heart.

Then what becomes of our boasting? It is excluded. By what kind of law? By a law of works? No, but by the law of faith (Rom. 3:27). "Law" is not bad in itself. We must look to how it is used. Later in Galatians Paul turns what is painted so negatively into a positive "law": the fruit of the Gospel: *Bear one another's burdens, and so fulfill the law of Christ* (Gal. 6:2). So the Law is not done away with as a moral standard. It is, at its essence, God's eternal will. External customs, traditions, and rituals were done away with when Christ made His sacrifice for sin. The Law is really about love. We have greater clarity, since we do not need the ceremonial law.

The issue so far, in Galatians, is not the Law in itself, but its purpose. What does the text say? Is the Law only a negative power, which is eradicated and overwhelmed by the Gospel, as some theologians say today? No, it is good, righteous, and holy. But in regards to salvation, the Law can only bring a curse upon condemned sinners. The Law actually supports the Gospel, though in a completely negative way, by exposing sins. It increases trespasses. This is the first phrase recorded after the question, "why then the law?" Its purpose, when used rightly, is to increase the need for the Gospel by multiplying sins. But since the Law is God's will, it does not cease to be eternally good. What the Law is, in itself, is different from its effect when applied to sinful, Law-loving, self-justifying men under God's wrath.

The Greek word translated "increase" can mean "to add, join to, or give in addition." It is used in this sense in Lk. 6:27: *And which of you by being anxious can add a single hour to his span of life?* This is helpful, because sin was already there. The Law does not create sinners, it simply reveals what we already are. It does not actually bring or increase evil in pure creatures. It brings trespasses—the guilt and knowledge of what we are and do before God. It reveals that we have trespassed (gone beyond) God's boundaries and will. It only appears to increase sin because we were previously unaware of what our Creator requires of us. This speaks to our guilt before God. We become conscious of it through the ministry of the Law. It is most necessary to be cursed and without hope of life, so that Christ's death will be good news for us. The Law closes up all other vain ways to God. This is the reason Paul says "because of transgressions."

"Until" means that the Law as a dominant power was given for a specific time and period. It has a limited extent, not just chronologically, but in our lives—that is, until the hearing of the Gospel. Paul, later in this letter talks of the Law as a guardian or tutor for children. The Law as a ruling force and controlling influence is outgrown in faith. This is the topic Paul attacks in the first half of Galatians, not the Law itself as God's holy will. This aspect of the Law, which defines what is good, does not change. It is the attitude and heart of man which must be changed before the Law can be seen as a positive entity. The problem was never God's Law itself, it was man's rebellion against the author of that Law. Without the Spirit of Christ, the Law cannot be used lawfully. *For God has done what the law, weakened by the flesh, could not do. By sending his own Son in the likeness of sinful flesh and for sin, he condemned sin in the flesh* (Rom. 8:3).

Was the Law meant to be primary and tyrannize for all time? No, just "until the promise to Abraham of a seed [the Redeemer] was born." This promise was fulfilled in Jesus of Nazareth, who suffered on the wood of the cross as a curse and sacrifice for all people. Now that you have this message, the Law as a controlling power is not meant for you. Our flesh, the sinful part of us, needs the Law. But our minds are to be ruled by the Spirit, not the dictates of the Law. The Law, as ruler, can only make us hate God, due to its revelation of sin in us. In the

Gospel we are forgiven and have God's love in the promise. If we live in the promise, we are not under the Law. We certainly do not set the Law aside, either, but in the Spirit we begin to spiritually fulfill it. The fulfillment of the promise, the Gospel given to Abraham, Adam, and you, is Christ. Without sin, there is no need for the Law. If our flesh was righteous, we would naturally do good by the Spirit, so there would be no separation from the Lord. Taming the Law or making it doable does not eradicate our sin. We either are holy, according to the Law, or condemned in God's sight. But Christ's sacrifice under the Law was necessary and it brought us life and a real righteousness that satisfies the demands the Law makes.

The Law does not bring us closer to God—that is Paul's point. The Law is not a positive force for sinners. It is for God, but we need it as a stick to provoke us. The demands of the Law do not soften our heart or cause us to love. Who likes being told what to do? Attaching threats to a command worsens it—we rebel against and hate the one who makes demands upon us. Rules and laws are somewhat effective outwardly, but they cannot change the heart. Children are usually more honest than adults. A father can demand with threats that a child clean his room. He might do it, but it will not be done in love or with a willing spirit, but grudgingly. Yet, without this sort of law, which brings a father's wrath, children would rarely do anything productive. Likewise for us. The Law *does* serve a purpose and must be preached to rebellious flesh, but it cannot produce any good or bring the righteousness of the Gospel. *For the law brings wrath, but where there is no law there is no transgression* (Rom. 4:15).

Grace is the main thrust of Scripture, but unless sinful man is confined by the Law, he will reject grace. The Law must add trespasses—it must kill us before the just God. *Is not my word like fire, declares the Lord, and like a hammer that breaks the rock in pieces?* (Jer. 23:29). *But now we are released from the law, having died to that which held us captive, so that we serve in the new way of the Spirit and not in the old way of the written code* (Rom. 7:6). There is no condemnation, no curse, no sins, no death, and no separation from God in Christ Jesus. That is why the Law was given, for the sake of grace, for the uplifting of the Gospel of Christ.

The moral law is eternal. But what is not eternal, though, does not apply to us. There is no longer a certain day or physical way to worship God, it is only done in Spirit and truth. While we must have customs and traditions to coexist with other sinners, they are no longer a burden and law from God (as the ceremonial law was for the Jews). Man-made order can be followed in the law of love. *True worshipers will worship the Father in spirit and truth, for the Father is seeking such people to worship him. God is spirit, and those who worship him must worship in spirit and truth* (Jn. 4:23–24). We please the Lord only with faith, which is only from the Spirit of truth.

Angels are a topic we do not know how to discuss today. This is a nonspiritual, materialistic culture that only thinks in terms of physical objects and motivations. Angels all around us, protecting us, does not compute. What we cannot see or measure is not real to us.

Angels are simply messengers, which is what the word "angel" most simply means. Here we are talking of created, spiritual beings without a body. They are servants of God, created by Him to minister and serve us. They are mentioned several times in the Gospels, telling of what God will do and what He has done in Christ. They give messages that point to God in Christ, functioning as heavenly preachers. They only have male names in Scripture, such as "Gabriel" and "Michael." Their role is to protect, so strength and power are assets. They are not pictured as feminine or cute babies in the Bible, but as masculine soldiers who can kill whole armies without breaking a sweat: *And that night the angel of the Lord went out and struck down 185,000 in the camp of the Assyrians. And when people arose early in the morning, behold, these were all dead bodies* (2 Kings 19:35). The Lord still sends these messengers to do His will and serve us at His bidding, just as He sent the angel of the Lord to keep His promise to King Hezekiah, made through the prophet Isaiah.

Angels are not to be worshiped, they are mere creations of God. 2 Cor. 11:14 says: *for even Satan disguises himself as an angel of light.* We should not be fooled by appearances, but test the spirits. Not every white light and near death experience is of Christ. An angel from the Lord will not contradict Christ's Scripture.

The role of angels in delivering the Law is clear in the New Testament: *Therefore we must pay much closer attention to what we have heard, lest we drift away from it. For since the message* [the Law] *declared by angels proved to be reliable, and every transgression or disobedience received a just retribution, how shall we escape if we neglect such a great salvation?* (Heb. 2:1–3). Stephen, in Acts 7, accuses the unbelieving Jewish religious leaders: *Which of the prophets did your fathers not persecute? And they killed those who announced beforehand the coming of the Righteous One, whom you have now betrayed and murdered, you who received the law as delivered by angels and did not keep it* (Acts 7:52-53). From three separate texts we know beyond a doubt that the Law was given through angels. What does that mean? The Old Testament texts do not exactly say. We know it was not a peaceful, pleasant scene: *Now when all the people saw the thunder and the flashes of lightning and the sound of the trumpet and the mountain smoking, the people were afraid and trembled, and they stood far off and said to Moses, "You speak to us, and we will listen; but do not let God speak to us, lest we die"* (Ex. 20:18–19). The Law is good, divine, and holy—the angels themselves delivered it. But the Gospel is from Christ the Lord Himself, and it offers a righteousness the Law cannot produce.

One reference to angels giving the Law is from Moses, right before His death: *The Lord came from Sinai* [where the Decalogue was given] *and dawned from Seir upon us; he shone forth from Mount Paran; he came from the ten thousands of holy ones, with flaming fire at his right hand* (Dt. 33:2). Just like Christ will come with His angels at the Judgment, so the Lord's glory is revealed in the giving of the Law. But, for sinners, the Law can only increase trespasses. There is no glory for us in the Law, even though it was given in glory.

Regardless of the actual role the angels played in giving the Law, they are clearly intermediaries. This means that the Law, though holy, is secondary and subservient to the Gospel. In Christ, God reconciled the world to Himself. In Him we have access to God's loving will and righteousness, which He gives through the promise. He ratified it by His own death. The angels are divine, as is the Law, but God Himself came to us in Christ to die our cursed death and bring us into His kingdom. There is no comparison between the angels and Christ, between the Law and the promise of life. *He is the radiance of the glory of God and the exact imprint of his nature, and he upholds the universe by the word of his power. After making purification for sins, he sat down at the right hand of the Majesty on high, having become as much superior to angels*

157

as the name he has inherited is more excellent than theirs (Heb. 1:3–4). The book of Hebrews makes much of the contrast between angels and Christ, which is used to show the relative glory of the Law compared to the Gospel.

Besides the angels, Moses was also an intermediary or mediator. Moses represented Israel before God, since no one else went up to receive the Law. The text says "through the hand of a mediator." Moses' hand took the tablets and carried them down Mt. Sinai. Then he proclaimed to the people what God had revealed. The true mediator between God and man is Christ, who is fully both. Moses himself said: *The Lord your God will raise up for you a prophet like me from among you, from your brothers—it is to him you shall listen* (Dt. 18:15). This is speaking of Christ.

[**v20**] A mediator brings two parties together. He is the go-between. This is not the same as a legal judgment, in which one party is right and one is wrong. It implies some compromise, which the reconciler or mediator facilitates. God the Son was our sacrifice, bringing us to the Father. He facilitated this reconciliation on our behalf.

The Greek text could be translated: "but a mediator is not one, but God is one." The Father did not make a covenant with Himself, though through His Son He gives us righteousness. This recalls what is called the "Shema" (the word for "hear" in Hebrew): *Hear, O Israel: The Lord our God, the Lord is one. You shall love the Lord your God with all your heart and with all your soul and with all your might* (Dt. 6:4–5).

Christ, as man and God, stood between sinners and the holy God. He mediated by suffering and taking the Law upon Himself willingly and fulfilling it, even while suffering its curse. He became the curse of the Law, as Paul says in v13. *But as it is, Christ has obtained a ministry that is as much more excellent than the old as the covenant he mediates is better, since it is enacted on better promises* (Heb. 8:6). God *desires all people to be saved and to come to the knowledge of the truth. For there is one God, and there is one mediator between God and men, the man Christ Jesus, who gave himself as a ransom for all* (1 Tim. 2:4–6). Christ as both God and man is the one mediator and savior of mankind.

We should not think of God in the abstract, in His bare glory outside of Christ's atonement. That is to walk into a consuming fire because of our sins. We have Christ as mediator for us. He is our access to God, the hinge between God and us. He is gentle and welcomes sinners, having suffered all things for us. This is one reason we pray in Jesus' name. Without the Son we would not know the Father. There would be only the Law and its curse without His body of flesh and blood. Without the redemption price there is no redemption.

The Law itself does not mediate anything. It does not change our status before the Father. This is why the promise is primary and came first. In logical order, we can say that the Law is first, because we must first have awareness of trespasses before Christ's death becomes sweet to us. The Gospel is called "new" because we are born in slavery to the old covenant of the Law. The Gospel must be revealed to us, as it was in dramatic fashion to Paul. *Therefore [Jesus] is the mediator of a new covenant, so that those who are called may receive the promised eternal inheritance, since a death has occurred that redeems them from the transgressions committed under the first covenant* (Heb. 9:15). However, the Law is younger, so that the Gospel does not come after it to supersede it. The promise was always the only way to life. The Gospel was not tacked on by God after Law was given. The Gospel preceded the Law.

[v21] This verses relates the Law to the Gospel. They are not opposed, if the Law is used properly or "lawfully," but man naturally tries to justify himself by the Law. The Law and the promise are not against one another, if understood rightly. The Law was not given to save, or else God would have contradicted Himself. This is why people are so often confused by the Bible. They hear the demands of Law and think: "I must be able to do them," or they misuse the Gospel and think: "now that I am Christian I can do the Law by my own efforts." That is the problem with the Galatians. They are returning to the Law. The Spirit is necessary to fulfill the Law, who only comes by the Gospel. The Law and Gospel are not opposing forces—they have complementary aims if used rightly. Their immediate purposes, however, are completely different: one brings life, the other death.

"May it not be" is a phrase that means "perish the thought, it cannot be." It is a very strong denunciation. In Rom. 3:6, it is translated: *By no means!*

Promises, in the plural, is used here, even though there is only one Gospel. It can come in many forms and wordings, but all deliver the justification of God. Some Greek texts we have state "promises of God," but the "of God" part is questionable textually. One early manuscript does not have it at all. However, this textual difference does not affect anything of importance. The promise, of course, is from God, not man. Only He can give the eternal inheritance, even if the text does not explicitly say so.

If a law, any law, could make alive, righteousness would be from the Law. It would have power to help sinners. Salvation would be "of/from" the Law. But that is not possible. The Greek word modifying the infinitive verb "to make alive" suggests power or capacity. The holy Law, given by God through angels, cannot give righteousness. It is foolish to turn to the Law for help. Though, in itself, it is far from useless for the Christian. We are only speaking here of righteousness, our status before God. Our new man delights in the Law of God because the curse has been removed.

We are dead in sins. The Law cannot make us alive, since it merely demands what we cannot give: holiness. The issue is righteousness—our status before God. We are to forget what things look like and consider this Word of God. We need to be made alive, but the Law kills. It makes us aware of our desperate condition. We are born under condemnation and the curse of death due to our disobedience, since we are born apart from God, without the Spirit. *For through the law I died to the law, so that I might live to God* (Gal. 2:19). But without the Law we would never have this useful knowledge of sin.

"To make alive"—it is one word in Greek—is God's action. It is used of the Resurrection in 1 Cor. 15:36: *What you sow does not come to life unless it dies.* We are spiritually dead before the Spirit makes us alive. He comes through the promise, not through the written code of the Law. If the Law brought righteousness, then we could make ourselves alive, but dead people do not do anything. If they can, they are not dead. *And you were dead in the trespasses and sins* (Eph. 2:1). So the Law is great, like many things in this world—cars, clothes, computers, food, and marriage (which is also divine)—but none of them save or give righteousness. We do not, for that reason, throw them out and trample them in the street. It is the same with the Law. It has nothing to with righteousness, rather, it destroys our false sense of self-righteousness. Our saving hope is in the promise, which makes us alive by the Spirit's work.

There is no Law that can give life. This includes all the works of man done under the Law and the obedience performed to win God over. This also means that all traditions and customs—even if biblical, ancient, and respected—are dead, condemned works, if done without faith. Nothing we do without the Spirit can make alive what is dead.

Verse 22 shows how the Law "increases" or "adds to" trespasses. **[v22]** The Law is for everyone. It is written on everyone's heart. Its true purpose is to imprison and close up all under sin. It reveals our guilt and God's just anger. Only when we despair of our own righteousness, does the Spirit have room to work faith in us. The only thing we can do is stop working against God. We call this repentance. Natural man can only work works which are sin to God. The Law is used wrongly when people strive toward righteousness through outward rules or dictates of conscience. Then God's Law is used against God and the righteousness revealed in His Son. Because of sin, the Law has power, but the Law is not therefore evil. Once we are alive, even if our faith is weak, we are given true freedom from the curse—not to be strong apart from the Spirit, but to know Christ in the promise and be a helpless sinner who lives according to the Law in the Spirit.

The Greek word for "imprison" means "to encircle, close together, or restrict." The same word is used in Rom. 11:32: *For God has consigned* [restricted] *all to disobedience, that he may have mercy on all.* It is also used in Lk. 5:6: *And when they had done this, they enclosed* [restricted] *a large number of fish, and their nets were breaking.*

"All things" are mentioned. This refers to not just people, though it certainly includes people. All things are cursed in this world. "Everything is Broken" is a song by Bob Dylan that illustrates this. Here are two verses:

> Broken cutters, broken saws/ Broken buckles, broken laws/ Broken bodies, broken bones/ Broken voices on broken phones/ Take a deep breath, feel like you're chokin'/ Everything is broken/ Broken hands on broken ploughs/ Broken treaties, broken vows/ Broken pipes, broken tools/ People bending broken rules/ Hound dog howling, bullfrog croaking/ Everything is broken.

The creation itself is in bondage and slavery to decay: *For the creation was subjected to futility, not willingly, but because of him who subjected it, in hope that the creation itself will be set free from its bondage to corruption and obtain the freedom of the glory of the children of God* (Rom. 8:20–21).

The Law imprisons, so why does Paul say that Scripture does? He is speaking here of the Law, which is revealed most fully in Scripture. This is one work of Scripture: to imprison and kill. That makes it dangerous. The Bible is no toy to fool around with—instead, it is a sword that should be used most reverently. The Bible is like a table saw that can sever a finger with ease, if it is not used properly. We must understand the relationship between Law and Gospel in order to not read the Scriptures as a hodgepodge mixture of contradictions. In the Bible God speaks to us, but we should not expect to find in it everything we want. God's Word kills and makes alive. Without the Spirit, the Bible's message of salvation cannot be comprehended.

Why all the imprisonment? Why are we harassed by our trespasses and the sins of our youth? We should be; that is God's work, the result and intent of His Law. We are to become exceedingly sinful. It is God's work to condemn and make guilty by the Law. We are not to try to outrun the condemnation of the Law. Once there is no good in us and we have given up hope of righteousness by works, Christ can be everything to us. Faith in the promise is everything. The Law came because of the promise. The Gospel did not come because the Law failed in its original intention. Paul is so clear here, but we are confused when confronted with our own evil deeds and half-believing hearts. You are called to rely only on the promise that Christ is yours and you are His. Live in this, because it has made you alive.

Only by faith are we alive, and in God's heart by His grace. Whether we fully realize it or not, all are imprisoned so that we would partake of the glory of being God's children. The Law shows us the true nature of things from God's own perspective. But we must be personally condemned to recognize the full truth of the promise. Knowing and loving God is a matter of faith, not works. The promise is life itself. The only true worship is to hear and believe the Gospel, so that we hold to the Father's love in Christ, while forsaking our own works—even our religious works and sacrifices. All is for the sake of Christ, who is our righteousness, because He became a curse for us in the flesh.

Faith is Jesus Christ. There is no other faith that the Spirit gives. Jesus is the content of faith. Faith is not something we add to Christ's words and person, as if He did not do enough for us. Christ justifies, not our belief. Faith receives the promise, and is itself created through the promise by the Spirit. Faith is the Spirit's work, not our own.

[v23] This verse restates v22 from the perspective of the effects of the Law and the Gospel: before the faith came to us and made us alive, we had to be imprisoned, miserable, frustrated, and a slave, so faith could come to us. Not all believe, but the Law imprisons so that not all would be deluded by their own self-righteousness. We were dead without God's Spirit, so it is only right that we feel dead and powerless before the demands of the Law. The Law continues to coerce and imprison as long as it has power—that is, until we die to it.

Faith is revealed in Christ, so we cannot separate faith from Him. Faith is in His name and receives His righteousness. It can be thought of as the personal application of righteousness—justification. When Christ came, faith was revealed in the Gospel to all. Not that it did not exist before, but it was freed from its Jewish context and ceremonial trappings.

We were under the Law—its authority, curse, and condemnation—which leads to hell and eternal punishment. No one naturally thinks they are bad and without goodness, so the Law must break us and cause us to despair of ourselves. This is a spiritual work, though it feels like death—because it is death to our flesh. That is the only way to eventually be made alive by the Spirit.

This verse is not just speaking of the relative ages of the Law and the promise or the first instance of a command or faith. Rather, Paul is explaining why the Law was given and seemed to be dominant from Moses until Christ. The problem was not the Gospel, but that the Law was falsely relied upon.

This passage can also be used to depict the role and order of Law and Gospel in each person's conscience. The Law always precedes the Gospel by convicting of sins. Without guilt, there is no need for forgiveness. But this order is not about verbal presentation or how the words of a sermon are chronologically arranged. It speaks to the work of the Spirit, who is working on the heart through the Word. The Spirit does the real work, not the human speaker. They remain God's words.

The word for "captive" is not as negative in Greek as it sounds in English. To be a captive means being taken prisoner, but the word here means "to guard, keep safe, or hold in custody (as with a child)." Here is a positive use of this word: *And because you belong to Christ Jesus, God's peace will stand guard* [take captive or take charge] *over all your thoughts and feelings* (Phil. 4:7). His peace can do this far better than our human minds. In faith, we trust God's loving will over our flighty, sinful wishes. If God is watching out for us, and we have His favor, we do not have to preserve or justify ourselves.

Some aspects of the Law are natural to us, but faith must be revealed. Faith is the reception of the promise and does not come apart from the promise of life. This promise delivers the Spirit, who renews us. If He came outside of the Word, we could produce the Spirit like a genie from a bottle, from our own works—and therefore of the Law. If it depends on anything we do, it is not of the Spirit. Faith receives the promise as true and believes that Christ will keep His word.

The word for "imprisoned (together)" in this verse is the same one used in the previous verse. This could be related to the history of Israel, especially in regards to the ceremonial law. The Jews were never without the promise and the favor of the Lord, but the Law, including all ceremonial practices, seemed dominant. That was not actually the case, but it did seem that way until Christ came. The ceremonial laws, which restrained the flesh, but did not justify, are no longer needed. They did their holy job of guarding until Christ came. This puts physical Israel in a respectful place, but not a place to boast. They have no claim of superiority over any other people, despite having the Law. Through them came the promised seed, Christ. But they were like children before Christ. They have no reason to boast in the holy Law or their ancient traditions, because now all have access to true righteousness in the Gospel. To return to the Law or think that it can help before God is foolishness (which is what Paul calls it earlier in 3:1, 3) or childishness (what he is implying here). The Galatians are new adults longing to return to an immature, childish state by running to the Law that Christ freed us from.

The word "until" is not there in Greek. Instead, there is a preposition which indicates purpose and direction. Before faith came we were held by the Law, imprisoned "for" the coming faith to be revealed. This word translated "for" can also imply entrance into a state. Faith now rules. While the Law, on the surface, was dominant for a time, it was merely a placeholder, a temporary guardian. The Law and its dominion were never intended to be permanent. They have always been subservient to the glorious grace of God revealed in the Gospel of Christ.

[v24] Here is a positive use of the Law—not for justification, but for guarding. The word translated "guardian" means "instructor of children." It signifies not just a teacher or a trainer, but one who closely supervises a child in regards to living and morality. This was a technical term for an attendant (a slave) who supervised a boy, ensuring that he did what was required to become a man. He protected and watched over him, so no harm would come. He was supposed to stay close by the boy's side, to keep watch over him and restrict his freedom—by discipline if necessary. This explains the outward necessity of the Law.

The Law is a custodian and tutor, for a brief time. But a 35 year old does not need a tutor, or else there is no hope of him ever becoming a man. A custodian or nanny is normally needed only for a set time. For the same reason, a parent should discipline a child when he is young. Spanking a 40 year old to wake him up from his foolishness is not proper or productive. We do it when children are little, so they will be able to self-correct as adults. Discipline has a certain goal and aim in mind—it is not a perpetual state. It has been said that the job of a parent is to put oneself out of a job: children are to grow out of being childish. The Law (as a power and ruler over us) is not a master for long. Children must be kept by rules and threats, but the Law subserviently serves the purpose of freedom, if it is used properly and wisely. Christ, through Paul, makes it clear that the Law is not the problem—rather, it is the misuse of it that requires such careful separation of it from the promise, especially in our own hearts.

The Law imprisons—it locks up and restricts. It does not prevent sin or make holy, but it does restrict outward displays of sin, to some degree, as do civil laws today. The threat of punishment does make decent citizens do the right thing, even though they might not sincerely want to. The fear of humiliation, social pressure, and jail (the loss physical freedom) will achieve results. No love of God can result from those restrictions, only sin and resentment. It is like keeping a dog on a leash. It restrains, but does not address the cause of the behaviors: a sinful heart and rebellious will, which hates God.

We are enclosed so that we may escape sin in Christ. It is like forcing cattle onto a truck: if you restrict all other options (the way of works), the way of the cross is all that is open. The Law truly closes all paths to righteousness, all salvation by works.

Prison prevents crimes, at least in the case of those imprisoned. It rarely makes people better, though it can be an opportunity for the Gospel. Imprisonment itself causes frustration and hatred. So does the Law. God's Law causes us to hate Him. It brings our sin to the forefront. We initially blame everyone else, including the holy God, for our desperate situation. There is only wrath in the message of the Law, no matter how much we try to avoid it; hell and the outer darkness is all it offers. This is the spiritual effect of the Law. Many in this world are too lightly imprisoned by the Law. They feel the pressure to look like decent people, and they certainly do not want go to jail. But goodness is not avoiding punishment from the government—it is not God. Civil laws do not address the heart, which must love and fear God. Most unbelievers do not know that they are slaves to sin and cursed under the Law. They do not experience the spiritual effect of the Law. They do not see it as a guardian or tutor, but a false savior that sets aside the death of Christ, our God.

Because our flesh remains with us until we leave this world, the Law always has this purpose: to terrify and imprison our sinful flesh. This is a divine work, so that we might have real hope elsewhere. This happens inside the Christian as the preaching of the Law works on us. We are daily being killed and raised to life. This is the way of faith. We are killed in the flesh to be made alive by the Spirit.

The Law was our leader and our tutor. For a period, the Law reigned over the Jews by its burdensome regulations. Read Leviticus and note all the detailed regulations. There were burnt offerings, grain offerings, peace offerings, sin offerings, and guilt offerings. There were specific unclean animals that they could not eat. Everything had be done correctly, down to the smallest detail. The laws never stop, just as sinners do not stop sinning, but they had a purpose: to protect and imprison under sin, not to make better. The Law increases awareness of sin. But when Christ came, the need for the Law as a tutor stopped. To cling to the tutor after becoming an adult is backwards. That is simply returning to the Law—a rejection of Christ.

The "in order" of the ESV shows that the Law was given to lead *to* faith, not practically or directly, but indirectly through its cursing and condemning. The result is that faith is exalted and more needed, because the Law has exposed the depths of our sin. The Law, properly used, exalts Christ. This verse says that the Law was given for faith—not faith for the Law. This order must be kept straight. The Law remains a servant to the Gospel. When the Law is misused, it is promoted as a positive power, so that the Gospel is abused and perverted.

The first word of this verse in Greek is a coordinating conjunction, translated here as "so then." It expresses the result of the previous verse. The logical connection made in this verse is powerful. "The faith" refers to the revelation of Christ. Our justification happens through faith, not by works of the Law. There are not differing schemes of salvation. Paul never says that the Law saved, even when it was a tutor and Israel was under its dominion. No one is saved unless he is saved like Abraham—justified by faith. Faith is opposed to works done under the Law, but true faith produces works in accordance with the Law in those justified.

There is no way to stand before God without the promise that delivers Christ. True righteousness revolves around justification—not improvement, betterment, or effort. Justification is pure, life-giving righteousness, which is necessary for anyone to be received by God. The Law says "do this or die," but the Gospel gives righteousness through Christ by connecting us to Him. So faith—trust in the promise of God—is better than forced obedience. True obedience is always in faith, never outside of Christ.

We can see how Paul moves from destroying the Law as a tool to justify—in place of Christ—to explaining the positive role of the Law and its subservience to the Gospel promise. What does the text declare? There is a negative function of the Law, but in light of our sin it is actually positive for us. The Law, in itself, does not contradict the Gospel. Jews, who formerly kept all the regulations, dietary rules, sacrifices, and cleansing rituals did not have to deny the Law after Christ came. The problem was not the outward acts or God's demands, but the heart that could not do anything in love. Faith has come in its fullness, though it was always the source of life.

[**v25**] It is a historical fact that Christ came. He was born of a virgin, taught, suffered, and died. On the third day He rose and then later ascended to heaven. Then the Spirit was given. We are not under the Law, but freed by the Gospel. This is rooted in biological reality—the flesh of Jesus crucified in our world—not ideology, the world of mental concepts.

We are no longer under the Law as a custodian or disciplinarian. No more does the Law rule and direct us, because freedom in Christ reaches us individually in the promise. When it is articulated to us and received in faith, we throw off the tutor and become God's child, free in Christ. Faith has come, and it is still here. This is a statement to believe and find comfort in. No matter how imprisoned we seem by our situation, the freedom we really need is in Christ, and it is ours now in the promise.

Here is part of a sermon on this text by Martin Luther. It is a marvelous application of how we are free from the prison of the Law:

> The 'shutting up,' the confinement, of the Law should teach us to desire faith and to recognize the evil tendencies of our nature; for faith is a spiritual freedom, liberating only the heart. To illustrate: Suppose you were confined in a prison, where you were very reluctant to remain. Your captor might release you in either of two ways: First, he might give you physical freedom by destroying the prison and letting you go where you desire. Secondly, he might make you mentally free by bestowing many blessings upon you in this prison— illuminating and enlarging it, making it pleasant in the extreme, adorning it richly and to an extent rendering it more desirable than any royal palace, more to be desired even than a kingdom; and by so reconciling you to your surroundings, so altering your mind, that you would not, for all earthly possessions, be removed from that prison, but would pray for its preservation that you might continue therein, it being to you no longer a prison, having become a paradise. Would not the latter be preferable? The former liberation would leave you but a beggar, as before. But in the latter case, your mind being free, you would possess all you might desire [*Church Postil*, 3.2:275].

This illustrates how true Christian freedom is peace with God, right where we are. It does not exist in possessions, earthly comforts, or new government laws, but in having God's love. Nothing external has to change at all. Justification marks our change to the Father in heaven. All fruits of faith flow from this freedom from sin and the curse.

Where there is faith, there is true freedom. It is in the conscience, not in moving to a new house or country. There is no need for the Law as a condemning power over us. We were under its thumb, until Christ came under it for us. God no longer demands, He instead opens the gates of heaven wide for us. Our God comes in the person of Christ when we hear the promise. The Gospel delivers the Spirit, which makes us alive. We can never hear this too much or know it too well. Because of Satan and the temptations we face, the Word of Christ is always to be honored. There is no goodness for us apart from Christ.

If we are not children under the guardianship of the Law, what are we in faith? Sons of God. [**v26**] Human faith is not an idea or emotion. Through the promise God creates a new reality, calling us new. We are something, even though we are nothing. Those who are called become His people. A son is free in the Father's love.

The first word of this verse in Greek is "all." Faith erases all the human distinctions that we care about so much: looks, race, wealth, and social status. In faith, we have God's approval and righteousness. This freedom in the Gospel is described here as being a son. This is "through" faith. This reliance on Christ establishes a new relationship with God. No longer are we at odds with Him due to sin. We are now part of His family as His beloved children.

But the word "son" denotes something different than "child" or "daughter." "Son" speaks to one's place and position in the household. The son is the heir and is the one who will rule and inherit everything. Before God we are sons in faith. This includes all males and females, by faith. This is not of works or any other characteristic (such as sex or race) we may have, but through faith in the promise. The Spirit creates faith through the Gospel, the only way we have to be a son of God.

Faith is not a feeling or emotion. It is the holy reception of Christ. One does not become justified by feeling close to God. One can only be free, a true "son of God," by faith. This means to live in and by Christ's righteousness. To be in Him is to have died to the Law and no longer be compelled by it. In the place of the Law, we are ruled, according to our new man, by the love of the Father.

This freedom is full because we are fully sons. One cannot be half a son. Neither does God disown. But the realization of this new status before God is partial, from our perspective. It is through faith, but we do not believe it fully. As we believe the promise of Christ, we are sons. There is nothing between us and our Lord—the barrier of sin has been removed, but in unbelief, which resides in the flesh, we do not fully believe. This why we do not feel like sons, and at times we think we are distant from God. We do not completely believe the promise. We believe weakly—fully justified in heaven, but not fully rejoicing in this heavenly work. No one believes fully or does not struggle with the sinful flesh, but we are sons *in* faith, not *in* ourselves.

The flesh does not go away when we start believing—instead it fights hard against faith and asserts its religion of works against faith. *I believe; help my unbelief* is the cry of all believers, because no one fully believes (Mk. 9:24). We cannot even convince ourselves—if we do, it is by the Law and cursed. It must be God's Spirit that convicts us and makes us sons. Faith is knowing that God's Word is true, even when all the world and our own experience tell us the opposite. It is being a son before God. What could be more impressive and practical?

The opposite of a son is a slave, that is, a worker who must perform bitter labor, without a choice in the matter, and get nothing for it. While we appear to be hard-pressed and are given difficult duties in family and vocation, we are to believe that we are free sons. A slave has no choice. A son, however, is given opportunities to please the Father. Outwardly, these two roles can appear exactly the same—the difference is the motivation. We are filled with God's love and live in Christ by faith, but a slave must obey under punishment of death. How many are slaves and seem happy to be in the world's slavery? Verse 23 says that the Law holds captive, as in a prison. But the freedom we have is not to lord it over people or to do what we want, but to serve in love, with the love we have as blessed sons. There is nothing more precious than faith.

The "in" preposition is critical: *in* Christ we are sons. Outside of Christ we are slaves, under the Law and God's wrath. We live in Christ by faith, justified in God's eyes. We are not to look at what happens in our lives to determine our status and value. God says we are sons—all are sons *in* Christ. There is no distinction—nothing can be done to improve our position before Him. Works of the Law try to win God over and impress Him, but this is to treat God as an unloving tyrant. The Law can never make anyone a son—it is the wrong way. It is only a guardian. But faith has come, and in faith we are completely free—we are in Christ, holy and clean. Whatever appears evil, like suffering, is not in our Lord. It is called discipline—it must be for our good and growth. If we look outside of Christ, there is only death, sin, and the damnation of the Law.

Thankfully, faith is safe in Christ Jesus, outside of ourselves. He has already fulfilled the Law and taken away the curse. A new life, a life as a son, is given in the promise. It is yours. It is through faith in Christ Jesus. One can be a son without realizing it. Now you have been given this knowledge, so live as a son in faith. Satan's temptations always revolve around the paradox that we are cursed outside Christ but are sons in faith, so nothing more can be done to elevate us. The natural inclination to depend on the Law, to value ourselves, is a great evil to resist.

How delightfully Paul erases the distinction between Jew and Gentile! It is nothing in Christ. There is nothing that can boost our status— not works, genetics, or heritage. All is loss and not worth considering compared to the knowledge of Christ. The ceremonial aspects of the Law the Judaizers promoted were meant by the Father to enslave, so that Christ could free. In the Spirit we are fully sons, no longer in need of a tutor. We are free in the Spirit to love in kind. Paul is not putting down the Law or deriding it. No, he praises it, but not in comparison to the Gospel. It cannot make you a son, but the Gospel reveals faith. The Law is powerless to justify, but, by faith, we are fully sons, not criminals on probation. We have all the rights of sons. We do not have to be in fear of God. If we are sons, God is our Father, who has bestowed sonship on us. *And if children, then heirs—heirs of God and fellow heirs with Christ, provided we suffer with him in order that we may also be glorified with him* (Rom. 8:17).

No longer children, we do not need the coercion of the Law. *For all who are led by the Spirit of God are sons of God. For you did not receive the spirit of slavery to fall back into fear, but you have received the Spirit of adoption as sons, by whom we cry, "Abba! Father!"* (Rom. 8:14-15). This freedom is from the guilt and reign of sin. It comes from being reconciled to God. Jesus says much the same in Jn. 8:34–36: *Truly,*

truly, I say to you, everyone who practices sin is a slave to sin. The slave does not remain in the house forever; the son remains forever. So if the Son sets you free, you will be free indeed. Our permanent place is secure. We are not hired hands, but rightful sons in Christ. But if we think salvation is ours outside of Christ, we fall from grace and become slaves. Whatever is not of Christ, is of the Law. We are always sons *in* Christ, *through* faith. Those little prepositions mean everything.

The shift in person is almost lost. Note carefully how Paul switches from "we" to "you" in vv25–26. He applies this blessed sonship in Christ to the Galatians. He starts the chapter with calling the Galatians foolish, then frees them from slavery personally, in order to make them sons of God.

How do we become sons in Christ, through faith? **[v27]** The promise is the key, but God gives His promise in several ways. The issue of Baptism has divided Christians for the last 500 years or so, but the Scriptures are clear. Baptism is not a work you do, or else you would be under Law—the worst curse. Notice how positively Scripture speaks of Baptism. It speaks of water and Christ's word the same way as it does about the Gospel, and even Christ Himself: *John proclaimed a baptism of repentance for the forgiveness of sins* (Lk. 3:3). *We were buried therefore with him by baptism into death, in order that, just as Christ was raised from the dead by the glory of the Father, we too might walk in newness of life* (Rom. 6:4). *Baptism, which corresponds to this, now saves you, not as a removal of dirt from the body but as an appeal to God for a good conscience, through the resurrection of Jesus Christ* (1 Pet. 3:21). A power is clearly attributed to Baptism, but that power is none other than the Gospel. Certain misinformed people get worked up over Baptism, as if it were a magic act. But it is simply a promise, with water attached. It is a foothold for faith to cling to Christ. There is no Christ for us without a promise given directly to us.

Jesus said Baptism is how the Church makes disciples. Christ, through it, takes away sins, joins to Himself, gives new life, and makes His disciple. *All authority in heaven and on earth has been given to me. Go therefore and make disciples of all nations, baptizing them in the name of the Father and of the Son and of the Holy Spirit, teaching them to observe all that I have commanded you* (Mt. 28:18–20).

Despite prejudice against God working with and through basic earthly elements, Paul says that Baptism justifies. It is the application of the Gospel. Through faith, it clothes with Christ's righteousness and gives us the status of being a son of God. But there is only one Gospel, as Paul said in the first chapter. Being baptized is the same as wearing Christ, being covered with His righteousness. Sheltered from God's anger over sin, we look like Christ as we live *in* our baptism. Water and the Word work this miracle. Baptism should be very precious to us. This promise is for faith.

We do not have to be re-baptized each time we doubt. If so, we would have to do it more than a hundred times a day. The promise is applied tangibly to us in water, so that the promise remains ours for a lifetime. This is a place faith can turn to: "I have been baptized by Christ Himself."

A baptismal certificate can hang on the wall. However, we cannot see our righteousness or the Spirit in us, though we can know that God has given those in the gift of Baptism. When we trust in this promise, we live in Christ. The true gift of Baptism is not a reality we can see—it is the application of the Gospel. We can see the water and know who has been baptized, but we must trust the promise that we are truly *in* Christ. We can rely on it only if it is God's work, not ours. In Baptism Christ comes to us.

We are clothed with Christ. We put on His holiness as easily as donning a sweater. It comes by faith and requires no works or effort. However, it can only be given. We can trust in our Baptism, even after sinning and falling away from Christ, because the promise remains firm. Our Father's grace is certain in Baptism. Paul directs us to the tangible promise: Baptism is something we can latch on to and rely upon. No one can seize Christ's divinity by force, but we can hear and know the promise and have all of Jesus in our own Baptism.

Many in Christendom turn the comfort of Baptism into a work. Because they do not do it with pure intentions or cannot follow through on their commitment to God, they assume they have to redo it over and over. They make it into a human work, so Baptism can never be righteousness, but merely condemning Law we fail to live up to. But Baptism is the application of Christ—see v26. There are no conditions. It is as monergistic as Christ's death on the cross. If Baptism cannot save an infant, it can save no one, and the resurrection of Christ is lacking. He does everything in Baptism—that is why faith can rest in it. To trust in your Baptism is nothing other than trusting in Christ, who has been given to you—the Christ who died and rose to make you a son of God.

The word for "clothed" is in the simple past tense. In Baptism we wear Christ and are covered completely by His righteousness. It is already an accomplished fact. Faith latches on to this promise, given in Baptism. We cannot extol Baptism too highly, especially for children. They are always being directed to their works and burdened with laws, but Baptism is God's work. Parents should remind them of the gift the Spirit of God gave. Baptism is the Gospel. It means we have died to sin by dying Christ's death. It raises us and grants life before the Father, because Christ rose from the dead. Baptism should never be separated from Christ's work of atonement. It simply gives the fruit of that work on the cross. So, without faith, Baptism is a promise ignored. It can be returned to, but we are not free from the Law just by virtue of having water applied to us, outside of faith. Baptism is not an external work that can be done and then forgotten. It is a promise to live in. It clothes with Christ, who offered His life for your sins.

Since Baptism is a physical promise that offers Christ, it prompts and gives faith. That is why children can be baptized. The Spirit works in the promise to create faith. There is no Gospel or faith without the promise.

In another epistle, Paul calls Baptism a spiritual circumcision: *In him also you were circumcised with a circumcision made without hands, by putting off the body of the flesh, by the circumcision of Christ, having been buried with him in baptism, in which you were also raised with him through faith in the powerful working of God, who raised him from the dead* (Col. 2:11–12). It is a circumcision made without hands—not by man, so it must be done by God.

The conclusion of being a son has been explained. Now the implications are explained. If we are sons, then we are not what the world categorizes us as. [v28] This verse is critical. It is perhaps the most misinterpreted verse in the Bible. Many read the first part of this verse and ignore the last. Without reading "in Christ Jesus" at the end, the meaning is radically different than what Paul actually wrote.

This verse speaks of the result of Baptism (v27) and faith (v28), which go together. The result is that we are all one in Christ. The status and role we have in the world is both nothing and everything in faith. Clothed with Christ, we are all one—the same and equal before God. There is nothing better than being clothed in righteousness—being a son of the most holy Father.

There are three pairs of opposites in the text, at least from a worldly perspective. "Greek" (meaning "Gentile") is opposed to "Jew" (the physical descendants of Abraham). In Christ they are one. One is not at a lower rank. Both are sons, and covered with the same righteousness of Christ in Baptism.

A particle not translated is used with "Jew," "slave," and "female." It means "there exists" and it is used with a "no" to negate it. It is then even stronger than it reads in English: "There is not Jew; there exists no slave; there is no female in Christ's righteousness." These do not count before God in regards to righteousness. Being of Abraham is nothing at all. Why? In faith, we are reckoned as righteous before God. Even Abraham himself counted for nothing—he was saved by faith. This is not before man, the critical mistake of many who misinterpret this verse. They ignore justification and think only in terms of physical freedom and civil righteousness—making impossible demands in their quest for worldly equality.

If we are outside of faith, then we are outside of Christ and not one. There are differences in this world—the body does not change when we are converted. To claim Jewish descent and privilege when you are not genetically Jewish is wrong. A female does not become physically male in faith. That is not the point of this verse. It deals with righteousness *before* God, the equality of sonship, which all believers have. It does not erase distinctions in this world. The Gospel does not deal with what we see.

This verse is used to support liberal feminism, along with homosexual and transgender lifestyles. But we live in Christ by faith, not in how we deal with one another in our bodies. How God created us—male or female—still applies in this world. In Christ, there is neither male, nor female, since He died for all, and all are fully sons of God in faith. Our bodies were redeemed by Christ, but we do not leave our bodies or this world in faith. We are not free to use them any way we see fit. Sin has corrupted us, and culture indoctrinates, but improper lusts for the same sex cannot be given into. Lust for the opposite sex is also sin—both are adultery in the heart. Marriage is the only place God has given us to share our bodies—and God unites only a male and female into a one flesh union. Does that mean that the Christian will not struggle with same or opposite-sex lust? No, the flesh will continue to rage within us. But we are not to let the flesh rule and drive the Spirit out. Depend on the promise, and you are clothed with Christ. All your sins are covered. You are dead to your sins in Baptism. Still, the body must be restrained—it cannot be given license to sin, which is all the flesh can do.

Our vocation, the station or place we occupy in this world, does not change because we are spiritual in Christ. Faith is internal—it does not demand outward changes. A pilot is not magically a plumber, and a teacher is not suddenly a military sharpshooter in faith. We are not free in Christ to usurp another's job—we are supposed to do our own. The strongest example is right here in this verse: there is neither slave nor free—neither exists in faith. In Christ, a slave and a free man are one in righteousness. However, Paul does not erase those distinctions in the world, outside of Christ. Paul tells slaves to submit to their masters, as being physically under a master does not impede freedom in the Spirit: *Bondservants, obey in everything those who are your earthly masters, not by way of eye-service, as people-pleasers, but with sincerity of heart, fearing the Lord. Whatever you do, work heartily, as for the Lord and not for men* (Col. 3:22-23). Even if master and slave are both believers and righteous in Christ, the outward, worldly order is not undone: *Those who have believing masters must not be disrespectful on the ground that they are brothers; rather they must serve all the better since those who benefit by their good service are believers and beloved. Teach and urge these things* (1 Tim. 6:2).

Slavery was part of Roman culture, economically and legally, but Christ did not come to change government laws. Since even the divine Law cannot bring anyone to God, changing human laws has nothing to do with true righteousness, either. Instead, Christ came to redeem and bring us God's peace. We can be in God's kingdom without changing a single external thing (that is not against God's will). Submitting as a slave, wife, child, or employee is not a sin, if it is proper, lawful, and done in faith. In fact, submission to Christ's appointed authorities is pleasing to Him in faith. It is to be done for the sake of Him who institutes all authority. The equality and sameness is all in faith—how we are righteous in Christ.

Were you a bondservant [a more palatable word for slave] *when called? Do not be concerned about it. (But if you can gain your freedom, avail yourself of the opportunity.) For he who was called in the Lord as a bondservant is a freedman of the Lord. Likewise he who was free when called is a bondservant of Christ* (1 Cor. 7:21–22). We are in Christ by faith, but in the body we are in this world. They are two separate things. The flesh needs restraint and should not get what it wants. Paul has not one ounce of worldly rebellion or undoing of the social order in his teaching. A human justice can only go against Christ's righteousness, which is received passively by faith. External equality in the body concerns human laws and relationships, not righteousness in Christ by faith. How many were changed from within by the emancipation proclamation? Even today the struggle for true equality continues—but it can never happen outside of Christ; there is too much hate in man's heart, and God's creation is not ours to remake in our image. True freedom is not a matter of laws, human or divine. Only Christ can free hearts from worshiping worldly issues and bestow true freedom in the Gospel.

Human slavery as a legal and social institution is a political issue, not a religious one. It is not the freedom Christ gives. He said to render unto Caesar what is Caesar's. Paul demands that Christian masters treat their slaves well. True slavery is sinning against the Lord, not in being physically restrained and forced to work. If we have God's love, what can man do to restrict us? We are free in Christ, and faith is not opposed to doing physical labor. Paul also said by the Spirit: *If anyone is not willing to work, let him not eat* (2 Thess. 3:10). Our body needs restrictions and specific duties to keep it occupied. But all the while we are to remain free *in* Christ.

Too many make the Gospel a battering ram to bring on civil reform or to legalistically enforce man-made ideas of human rights. But no works of man, even in the political sphere, justify or forgive sin. *But thanks be to God, that you who were once slaves of sin have become obedient from the heart to the standard of teaching to which you were committed* (Rom. 6:17). True freedom is hidden in Christ. If we have

177

earthly freedom from a job, children, or marriage, it should be used to serve Christ, the same God who created this world and put us where we are. Christ speaks to us His will in these earthly roles we do not get to determine for ourselves. They are where the Lord would have us serve and show Him our thanks, and we can do so in complete freedom, even if we look like slaves to the world.

While the world is corrupt, governments will rail against Christ. Freedom in the worldly sense hurts people—the only thing worse than a bad government is chaos and no rule of law. It is the same with marriage and its specific gender roles. Nowhere does the Bible give license to mistreat women—quite the opposite; they deserve greater respect. They are to submit to their husbands out of love—not by force. *Likewise, husbands, live with your wives in an understanding way, showing honor to the woman as the weaker vessel, since they are heirs with you of the grace of life, so that your prayers may not be hindered* (1 Pet. 3:7).

Christ works within a person through the preached Gospel. Changing laws can never change the heart. We are one in Christ Jesus. This is a spiritual freedom we gain by wearing Christ's righteousness, given in Baptism. The unity of freedom is in Christ's sinless body, not in human laws or movements.

There is an element of truth in the human crusade for changes in morality, civil laws, and relationships between people. We long for a sinless, perfect world. This will always be an unfair place, but less order means more sin, because we are naturally slaves of sins. Only God can bring true justice: *For to us a child is born, to us a son is given; and the government shall be upon his shoulder* (Is. 9:6). We long for paradise. Now, God rules believers personally by the Spirit in the Gospel. But in heaven, punishment and rules will not be needed to force men to be decent to one another. Jesus gives us a reliable, better hope: *For in the resurrection they neither marry nor are given in marriage, but are like angels in heaven* (Matthew 22:30). Our roles will be equal in heaven, so we are to trust our Father, who made us, and not rebel against what He did in creating us. Embrace physical difficulties in faith, knowing you are one in Christ by faith.

In our disappointment with this world, we try to change things and usually make them worse. Order, even if imperfect, is good in itself. The purpose of government is to punish evil-doers, not to make the world a better place. Order is necessary for sinners, so they do not hurt and kill each other. That does not change their hearts, but allows us to coexist in outward peace. Then God's Word can actually free internally by the promise of life in Christ.

The verb here in v28 is in the present tense: "you *are* all one in Christ." All things are had in faith presently. To summarize this verse: In Christ— that is, by faith—we are one. This means that no differences matter to God. Outward characteristics and callings are not erased. Faith is in Christ. For complete change, we must wait for the Resurrection and the new heaven and new earth.

[**v29**] Verse 29 makes the connection back to Abraham, recalling vv5–7: *Does he who supplies the Spirit to you and works miracles among you do so by works of the law, or by hearing with faith—just as Abraham* "*believed God, and it was counted to him as righteousness?" Know then that it is those of faith who are the sons of Abraham.* Since we are in Christ by faith, not by works or a change of our bodily nature, we are "of Abraham."

The distinction between Jew and Gentile has already been erased— they do not exist in faith. Being of Christ by the promise is the same as being of Abraham's seed, who is Christ. Paul says we should find comfort not in the work of circumcision, but in the seed, the one offspring Abraham was promised. We live by the same promise—our status as sons of God far exceeds being a physical descendant of Abraham or following the traditions he followed. We are heirs according to the promise. Faith and the promise are connected. Faith grasps Christ by the promise. We become Abraham's offspring. *Know then that it is those of faith who are the sons of Abraham* (3:7).

"Seed" here is singular. "Offspring," in English, is like the word "deer." It can mean one or more than one, but the Greek word is definitely singular, not plural. That distinction is important. If it is just one, it refers to Christ (3:17). Christ is the seed, so we are the offspring of Abraham in Christ and wear Him by faith. Our connection to the Lord is so close that we are called the seed ("offspring" in the singular), though not according to the flesh. In faith, we believe we have a new status, birth, and name. What we were born and what we do is not relevant in Christ—all are one in Jesus. We are not inferior to celebrities and presidents: we are much more in faith. This does not mean in the world or in our flesh. This promise nurtures our inner man and renews our mind. *Put off your old self, which belongs to your former manner of life and is corrupt through deceitful desires, and to be renewed in the spirit of your minds, and to put on the new self, created after the likeness of God in true righteousness and holiness* (Eph. 4:22–24).

Consider Baptism: *he saved us, not because of works done by us in righteousness, but according to his own mercy, by the washing of regeneration and renewal of the Holy Spirit* (Tit. 3:5). Baptism happens once, just as there is one Christ and one promise, but faith continually clings to the promise applied to us. We return to the promise against sin, doubt, and suffering. The struggle is not to do or become, but, instead, simply to *be* a son of Abraham, a son of God by faith.

How we are heirs? God gives the inheritance in the promise. A human heir receives money, possessions, and property, but God gives spiritual blessings. Abraham was promised land and a child, but mainly the Christ. All blessings are through Him, the seed. Christ died to leave us life. He swallowed up death for us, eating the curse, so we may wear Him in faith. Eternal life is ours, as is forgiveness. All these blessings come through faith. We are to hold the promise that we are heirs in Christ dear. Although we are not equal to the mighty and powerful of this world, in Christ, we are above all the offices and honors of this world.

This last verse references 3:18. Paul has made his case. We have holy logic here, above all human ways of reasoning.

Chapter 4

This chapter break does not mark a substantial division in content. The first verse flows from the previous chapter. [v1] This explains what was just said in 3:29.

What is an heir? One who is promised something. But an heir does not possess everything yet, even though it is his. This explains faith. We know the Gospel and rejoice in our status before God, but we do not see our righteousness, and neither does our neighbor. We feel like slaves at the mercy of an uncaring world, but we live in the promise that our God is gracious. Through difficulties, we rely on the Gospel, which reassures us of our status and place in Christ. What we experience is far different. For trusting God's Word we are called naive, sheep-like, and foolish. This directs us all the more to the promise.

The word here is not the usual one for "child;" rather, it means "infant"—a young, helpless child. Jesus uses the same Greek word for infant: *Out of the mouth of infants and nursing babies you have prepared praise* (Mt. 21:16).

A child does not enjoy the benefits of ownership, whereas an adult might. But in this context, Paul speaks of our inheritance from God. The promise bestows everything on us. But under the Law, this freedom was limited. Outwardly, an infant heir is not much different than a slave. He has people carry him around against his will, and he must take orders from his parents and caretakers. But the ownership and position are his by birth. Our position is likewise by faith.

"Owner," here, is "kurios" in Greek, usually translated "lord" or "master." Not long ago, gentlemen were called lords, meaning they were the master of a household or estate. For example, Lord Byron was a poet of the 19th century. He took a seat in the British House of Lords, which required a certain title and name. In contrast to men, the Lord Christ is lord of everything—heaven and earth.

Placing a three-year-old in charge of wealth and adults would not be wise, but he is truly the owner, if he is the heir, according to his father's will. He is the true son and heir, but, as a minor, he needs a guardian or tutor. Even today, a child cannot sign contracts or conduct business apart from a legal guardian. Again, we see the temporary and secondary role of the Law illustrated.

Paul returns to the role of the Law in relation to that of the Gospel in vv1–3. The minor heir is under two classes of people: 1) a governor, which can also mean "steward, manager, or foreman;" and 2) a house-manager or treasurer. The word "house-manager" is used in 1 Cor. 4:1–2 of ministers of the Word of God: *This is how one should regard us, as servants of Christ and stewards of the mysteries of God. Moreover, it is required of stewards* [house-managers] *that they be found faithful.* It is not enough know the mysteries (doctrines) of the Word—they have to be apportioned out, explained, and used in the right way for the benefit of the flock.

But, just as with the outward rule of the Law, the time the child heir spends under guardians is limited. In a legal trust, the beneficiary owns everything, but cannot access it directly until the appointed age, possibly until 30 or even 35 years old. Giving a large inheritance to an 18-year-old is not wise, so its enjoyment is restricted. The trustee is the steward, who manages for the true owner. It is not his, and he can be held legally accountable if he mismanages it. Using it for his own benefit would legally be stealing, since the trustee is only a manager. The Law of God had a very valid purpose, but only for the spiritual minor. Those who are childish are not able to live independent of a guardian. To seek a guardian as a legal, functioning adult would be ridiculous. Likewise, the traditions and ceremonial laws are all done away with, now that Christ has come. Faith reigns, and in Him we are sons, not children subject to strict management.

[v2] The key word in this verse is "until." The Law bound the Jews, who were inheritors of God's blessings and salvation. The promise of Christ, given to their forefather Abraham, was theirs, but the Law was needed until the time of Christ, when the promise would became fully known. The Law was fulfilled and set aside as an outward, compelling

force and tutor of man.

We see here a positive use of the Law, even though it remains a coercer and governor over us before faith comes. The time set is when everything takes effect. The ownership was there, it just could not be exercised. "The date set" translates a word only used here in the New Testament. It is defined as "a day appointed beforehand." It is not arbitrary, but fixed. So also, the fulfillment of the promise of a seed to Abraham was set by the Father before the world began. Since Christ has been born and has redeemed us from under the Law, the Law should no longer be our guardian. We live free in faith, not under the thumb of the Law to be ruled by threats and the punishment of God. Christ has come, and the date of legal maturity has passed. Both true sonship and our spiritual inheritance is here. We are now sons.

[**v3**] *We were* as children—legally. The word translated "children" is used for "infant" in v1. Paul includes himself, along with all the physical descendants of Abraham, under this title. This does not mean that the promise did not apply to the Jews following Abraham. Faith did not skip from Abraham to us; rather, the Jews could not enjoy the full use of their freedom.

"Elementary principles" is an abstract phrase for us, but the key here, as elsewhere in Galatians, is the preposition, which is "under." We were under the Law—even those who did not have the written Law. It ruled over us. It is the basic position of people in this world. Man's heart is born of flesh, without the Spirit.

The Greek word for "elementary principles" speaks of the basics, the ABCs of this world. "Elementary," as in "elementary school," speaks of the rudimentary foundation, but in this case, the implication is that it is childish and should be put away once the full age of maturity is reached—when Christ came to free us from slavery to the Law. *Truly, truly, I say to you, everyone who practices sin is a slave to sin* (Jn. 8:34).

The Greek word for "elementary principles" is used in several other places in Scripture. *See to it that no one takes you captive by philosophy and empty deceit, according to human tradition, according to the elemental spirits* [elementary principles] *of the world, and not according to Christ* (Col. 2:8). Human tradition and the wisdom of men hold people captive, away from Christ. They are Satan's tool. Our natural reason and feelings are imprisoned by the Law, without knowledge of the mystery of Christ. Apart from the Gospel, we can know nothing of faith as the way to righteousness. Colossians also uses the same Greek word, though it is similarly translated as "elementary spirits:"

> *If with Christ you died to the elemental spirits [elementary principles] of the world, why, as if you were still alive in the world, do you submit to regulations—Do not handle, Do not taste, Do not touch (referring to things that all perish as they are used)—according to human precepts and teachings? These have indeed an appearance of wisdom in promoting self-made religion and asceticism and severity to the body, but they are of no value in stopping the indulgence of the flesh* (Col. 2:20–23).

These outward regulations are a product of guardianship. They do not lead to God. They must be cast off in Christ, so that we are ruled only by the Spirit, who comes by the promise of Christ.

These three passages, Gal. 4:3, and the two from Col., speak of the elementary principles of the *world*. Our infantile state, living under the Law without Christ, is contrasted to eternal life in the Gospel. We are called to live a new life in Christ, not in the world or according to worldly, elementary principles. These enslave and represent the power of the Law—its curse and negative effect. The Law can only kill.

Christ brings a new knowledge and way of living. Now, He has freed us from the curse and the elemental principles of the world, which prevent us from loving God in the Spirit. Here is a helpful quote: "These worldly principles were not the Law itself but the earthly things with which the Law had to do" [Lenski, 196]. This explains all the tedious commands concerning physical objects in the Old Testament: the Jews needed a tutor to enslave them for a time, but full adulthood in Christ is not about dealing with foods, sacrifices, days, or certain words. The ceremonial law dealt with human things that are passing away, not the soul and heart. None of the physical things of the world—apart from Christ—can reconcile to God, but without the Spirit, that is all we can trust in. Only Christ actually saves. Paul lays out quite clearly that the Law is not opposed to the Gospel. But the Law must be kept in its proper place. It was never meant to permanently rule in this world.

Luther describes Moses as the guardian: "because the time had not yet fully come, Moses, our guardian, manager, and custodian, came and held us captive, to prevent us from taking the upper hand and gaining control and possession of our inheritance" [*Galatians*, 360]. There is no salvation in worldly objects, apart from faith, though there is much sin available to our flesh, which would separate us from God.

In one way the explanation in v3 applies only to Jews before Christ, but each person is born into sin, and therefore enslaved by elementary principles. We think changing our behavior will change our course and fate. Everything we think and do is according to elementary principles, which enslave. We cannot free our selves or give ourselves an inheritance. Christ comes to us personally to free us in the Gospel, though not to redeem us—that has already been finished on the cross. Until faith comes to us, though, we do not know of it and cannot trust in it—we are still enslaved. We are truly freed from works, that is, everything required of our body to achieve sonship. Everything is now holy to His sons. We do not need ceremonies, rituals, or mosaic customs to purify us—they are for infants, not those who know the full revelation of Christ. True faith has nothing to do with human traditions or anything man does or says. Only the Word of Christ counts for righteousness. The Law closes off all human righteousness.

The first verses of this chapter set up the glorious entrance of Christ in history. [**v4**] "The fullness of time" is a beautiful phrase. The world was made for this moment. All things led up to it, and all things look back to it. In Christ's birth and earning of our salvation, we find God most definitely at work. Salvation is not an idea—it is an accomplished reality in Christ's crucified body.

"Fullness" implies completeness, that there is nothing lacking. This word is also used in the same sense in Eph. 1:9–10: The Father made *known to us the mystery of his will, according to his purpose, which he set forth in Christ as a plan for the fullness of time, to unite all things in him, things in heaven and things on earth.* Christ is the fulfillment of the world, though we could never guess this mystery from the elementary principles of the world alone. There is too much in this Word of God to express. The best human explanation, apart from the divine words, is a mere grasping at straws, but the promise is delivered even in feeble attempts. This knowledge of Christ delivers the Spirit and frees from all that enslaves. It transports to heaven by forgiving us before God and robes us as a son of God, with all the righteousness of Christ.

The fullness of time—time is something we are stuck in. We cannot wrap our heads around eternity—it is above our minds and experience. Yet, God did the reverse. He became like us in all ways, except sin. Jesus, God Himself, came to us in our form and flesh, to undo the curse. The eternal Son of God was born. No one can exhaust these words. Here is where we are to find God for us—not in laws or lofty thoughts, but in a helpless baby. This baby did not have a human father. It says "of woman," generically, meaning not of man. Jesus was born of a virgin, Mary, but was conceived by the Spirit without a biological father. The word for "sent" is more official than the typical word for "sending." We can even say "commissioned," which means "to send out with a purpose or mission." This word is used of Paul's apostleship to bring the Gospel to the Gentiles: *And he said to me, "Go, for I will send you far away to the Gentiles"* (Acts 20:21). We are to remember that God did this with us in mind. All kingdoms and great nations were mere pawns in the lead up to this revelation of faith which benefits all nations.

This brings tremendous comfort, no matter what difficulties we are facing. This fullness of time trumps any temporary sorrow. What we think is the central and the most important moment in our lives is trivial compared to this good news. God came for you in Christ. All that we have suffered, Jesus also faced under the Law, but without sinning. Luther personifies faith for us: "Law, I shall not listen to you, because you have an evil voice. Besides, the time has fully come. Therefore I am free. I shall no longer endure your dominion. The most difficult thing of all is to distinguish the law from grace; that is simple yet a divine and heavenly gift" [*Galatians*, 365].

In chapter 3, we saw how crucial it was that Jesus took the Law from our backs, including the curse. He fulfilled the Law, releasing us from its slavery—not just Jewish law, but the divine Law that enslaves. [**v5**] This verse states why Christ, our God, was born. He redeemed us. This takes us back to 3:13: *Christ redeemed us from the curse of the law by becoming a curse for us—for it is written, "Cursed is everyone who is hanged on a tree."* And who is under the Law? All people, though not all realize it. The true glory of the Law is to convict people of sin, making them aware of their wretched condition. Christ was ransomed for all humanity; He was the price of our freedom, born to redeem by His precious death, which won us life. We receive this by faith in the promise of Christ for us.

This was the promise made to Abraham. The Old Testament Scriptures testify to this. *Israel, put your hope in the Lord, for with the Lord is unfailing love and with him is full redemption. He himself will redeem Israel from all their sins* (Ps. 130). If the Law does not serve this purpose, however negatively, the Bible and God Himself are contradictory.

The word for "adoption" in Greek is related to the word for "son." The connection to being a son of God in faith is evident in this adoptive "sonship." We are given the status of sonship in Christ. We are accepted because of the sacrifice of Christ's body. Therefore, the inheritance is ours. While by faith we are acceptable to God, we still wait for the throwing off of the flesh: *And not only the creation, but we ourselves, who have the firstfruits of the Spirit, groan inwardly as we wait eagerly for adoption as sons, the redemption of our bodies* (Rom. 8:23). The article is used with "adoption:" "the adoption, the bestowing of sonship." We receive this by faith. The Gospel is succinctly put in vv4–5.

The "might" included in the ESV translation seems to weaken Paul's words. Christ did redeem those under the Law, all of them, but many have not received the result of it yet: the adoption. Some have rejected it, but God desires all to receive it. No sin went unpunished in Christ. He received the whole curse of the Law. The subjunctive mood of the "to receive" verb simply states that it is by faith. It comes to us in time through the Gospel. We receive sonship, or adoption, before the Father in time, through the promise, which is still going out today. The Father wants all be rescued from the punishment of sins and inherit the promised sonship. Christ said: *for I did not come to judge the world but to save the world* (Jn. 12:47).

Paul's words, granting freedom from the governorship of the Law, condemn much of what passes for Christianity. While Jesus is said to have died for sins, the real power of Christianity is often made to be what we do for Jesus. Many say we have to accept Jesus, invite Him into our hearts, have an emotional experience, or be faithful to win His approval, as if we could improve our standing apart from the Gospel. Even the precious gifts of Baptism and the Lord's Supper are often turned into works we do for God, as if the Law still reigns. Jesus is often said to be the new lawgiver in the mode of Moses, not the Redeemer from the curse. Paul uses the phrase "offense of the cross" later, in

5:11, to summarize the offense this freedom causes. To be free from the burden of the Law and live by the Spirit in the promise are the highest things one can teach and hear. Christ is not had apart from the proclaimed freedom that we are already sons by faith. This excludes all works, no matter how religious they seem, since all rests on Christ. This complete freedom in the Gospel is despised by the Devil, the world, and our flesh. It always requires a great fight to view the Law according to the words of this epistle—as childish, temporary, and impotent.

Verse 6 turns to the effect of this adoption as sons. **[v6]** Without the Spirit, the Law condemns and coerces, but with the Spirit we begin to love the Law and even start to fulfill it in faith. This speaks of the Spirit in us, given personally to guide us. The Spirit is "sent," or "commissioned," the same word used of Jesus in v4.

Because you are sons—the Spirit is a consequence of justification, of being granted sonship by the Father's grace. Too many seek the Spirit apart from the Gospel and the promise that Christ has accomplished our redemption. The Spirit does not speak on His own, but enables us to hear and believe Christ. *When the Spirit of truth comes, he will guide you into all the truth, for he will not speak on his own authority, but whatever he hears he will speak, and he will declare to you the things that are to come* (Jn. 16:13). Without the Spirit, there is no goodness or life in us. There is no worship or faith without this Spirit (Jn. 4:20–26). As said in 3:2: *Did the Spirit come by works of the Law or by the hearing of faith?* The Spirit is to be sought in the Word of Christ, by believing our new status—that we are righteous in Christ.

The Spirit is called the Spirit of the Son, because He witnesses to Christ, not Himself. We find the Spirit, not by focusing on the Spirit in the abstract, but by believing that Christ's redemption has been applied to us. That is why He is the Spirit of the Son. The Spirit works in the message, which brings relief from the curse of the Law. The Son is "his Son," God the Father's Son.

"Abba" is not a Greek word, but Aramaic, the common language of Jews in Judea at the time. "Abba" occurs three times in the New Testament. Jesus uses it in the throes of His suffering in the Garden of Gethsemane, knowing what He has been given to do for us: *And going a little farther, he fell on the ground and prayed that, if it were possible, the hour might pass from him. And he said, "Abba, Father, all things are possible for you. Remove this cup from me. Yet not what I will, but what you will"* (Mk. 14:35–37). "Abba" is a personal address, like the one we find in the Lord's Prayer: "Our Father who art in heaven." In Rom. 8:14, the connection between justification and the Spirit is made: *For all who are led by the Spirit of God are sons of God.* One cannot be a son without the Spirit, yet we cannot lose sight of the fact that Christ is the Redeemer, not the Spirit. Only a son, one in Christ, can call God Father or "Abba." It is because of our new status in Christ that we can actually love God and see Him as a generous and completely loving Father. This is to know God by faith in Christ, outside the burdens of the Law.

"Crying" (present tense) is a continual activity of believers. We rely on Christ and His righteousness. We never have anything of ourselves to rely on. Even the Spirit is simply an undeserved gift. "To cry" does not mean here "to weep," but "to call out loudly and forcefully"—to make ourselves known. When a child seeks to be comforted he cries out. The result of faith—the new life in Christ—is not fear and punishment, but life and forgiveness. The Spirit leads us to call out in trust to the Father, because of the Son. *In my distress I called upon the Lord; to my God I called. From his temple he heard my voice, and my cry came to his ears* (2 Sam. 22:7).

The Aramaic and Greek appear right next to each other in repetition: "Abba [Father], Father." It shows the new way God is seen and the change that occurs in the believer. There is a real spiritual power in the Gospel, because the Spirit is there, wherever Christ's redemption is given. The typical Jewish address for "father" in Aramaic and the common Gentile address in Greek for "father" are used by side-by-side, illustrating again that in Christ there is neither Jew nor Gentile (3:28). The repetition emphasizes that our new relationship to God is paramount.

This exclamation is something a slave could never say, but, free in the Son to be sons by faith, we have God apart from the threats of the Law. We know Him as the Father who sent the Son to bring us out of slavery. This is a joyous release from the power of sin. There is no spirituality, no faith, and no life without the Spirit. Without the Spirit, it is impossible to believe or pray. While emotion and feelings of the heart are never the basis of faith (or else the pressure would be on us to produce them as works), the Spirit does work on us and affect our will and heart. We are renewed. In the midst of great trials and temptations, the Spirit cries out in us to the Father: *The Spirit himself bears witness with our spirit that we are children of God* (Rom. 8:16). We are to hold on to the promise and not look with our eyes at the sin we see, but to behold only what we are in faith. The Devil presses and harasses all believers, but we can rely on the Spirit's help, especially in times of need and distress: *And when they bring you before the synagogues and the rulers and the authorities, do not be anxious about how you should defend yourself or what you should say, for the Holy Spirit will teach you in that very hour what you ought to say* (Lk. 12:11–12). Or, as it says in Rom. 8:26–27: *the Spirit helps us in our weakness. For we do not know what to pray for as we ought, but the Spirit himself intercedes for us with groanings too deep for words. And he who searches hearts knows what is the mind of the Spirit, because the Spirit intercedes for the saints according to the will of God.*

[v7] This joy of the Spirit is the result of knowing the Father and being reconciled to Him in the body of Christ. Paul has made a drastic move from slavery under the Law to sonship in the Spirit. The son is an heir, whereas formerly we inherited only eternal punishment. God has shown great love to us in Christ and blessed us with His own Spirit, so that our bodies have become the very temples of the Holy Spirit.

A slave is one who must work without a reward, but a son is an owner and future heir. They work for entirely different reasons. The Gospel gives and declares to us a new status in Christ. It is a new way of relating to God—to know Him as our true Father and not just a master who gives laws and demands obedience. The Law/Gospel difference is spelled out by Paul to the Galatians in practical terms. An owner and heir has much more incentive to work than one who is simply working out of necessity. This change of status through faith, which has nothing to do with works, allows true works to be pleasing fruit to the Lord. Children who are convinced they are sons have every incentive to please the Father in what they do.

Through God is another prepositional phrase that Paul uses to witness to Christ's superiority over the Law. As God, He won and gives this adoption to sonship. We are excluded from causing it—it is entirely God's work. It is not of man's works, but *through God.*

Verse 8 shifts gears slightly. It begins a personal application of the distinction Paul has laid out between the Law and the Gospel. [v8]

What does the natural man know of God? That He exists and is eternal, but that is not what Paul means. Knowing *of* someone by reputation or gossip and actually *knowing* someone are completely different. An acquaintance is someone you know *of*. But a friend is someone you have insight into and with whom trust has been built. Companions share personal information and emotions—they have more than just a business relationship. To know God is to have His Son. Only in Christ, who took on flesh and suffered, do we know the Father. Paul is arguing that the Galatians (and all fleshly people) do not really know God, because they only know Him through the Law as a demanding slavemaster. We can even pretend to love the wrathful God, but slavery is slavery, no matter how much it is dressed up.

If not the true God, then what were we enslaved to? Things that are not actually God: "not being gods." This includes things directly called "gods." If we are enslaved by the sinful nature, we worship and devote our energies to deities which cannot help. How many gods are there—that are by definition false? There are as many so-called divine beings, religions, and spiritual pathways as man can imagine. But gods that are not God, we call false gods. These pretend "gods" take the place of the true God in our heart. If we are in slavery to the elementary principles of the world, then we must serve or worship what is not the true God. Religions of enlightenment and the worship of images, food, objects, and idols cannot give knowledge of God. God is known only in Christ, through the Gospel.

Idols were common at the time this letter was written. Temples, sacrifices, and rituals filled the pagans' days, and their longing for the divine. Today, we do not call the things we serve by nature "gods," but sometimes they are labeled idols (such as in the TV show "American Idol"). All unbelievers have them and offer them meager praise. Fans show reverence and have elaborate rituals to honor their sports teams. Games are life-or-death to them, something they serve as a slave. People even bow down to and honor athletes and celebrities by waving their arms in reverence as the pagans did before the idols. Even if it is done in jest, worship is a constant activity of man's heart. We must have something to love, fear, and trust. Even the most pathetic idols and activities take the place of the Father of Christ for unbelievers.

Everyone has a god—the question is whether or not it is the true one. By nature we are enslaved to sin, and therefore actual slaves. *Therefore, just as sin came into the world through one man, and death through sin, and so death spread to all men because all sinned* (Rom. 5:12). All such slaves serve what is not God the Father. Whether it is their hobbies, job, family, or themselves, something must take the place of the true God. Even if they are good gifts of God, which those things can be, if they are elevated above the true God, then they become false gods—tickets to destruction. Slavery is not the way to the true God, to truly knowing Him. To know God means that the Father knows us, that is, that we are justified and counted as righteous. The point is not what we think intellectually, but who in our body and heart we serve. Only the Gospel of Christ covers our sins and forgives the false service we offered as slaves.

"Enslaved" is a good translation. In Greek, it is a verb with "slave" as the root. An unbeliever is enslaved; he is not free to love God, nor can he free himself. *No one can serve two masters* [lords], *for either he will hate the one and love the other, or he will be devoted to the one and despise the other* (Mt. 6:24). Slavery is real, external bondage. Feelings or thoughts cannot free a slave. Freedom must come from above—it is never the fruit of bondage.

The take-away is that a slave must serve. Man was made to worship the true God by faith, but not really knowing God, we invent false gods. "By nature" means by the natural order of things, apart from any revelation. The same word is used in Rom. 2:14: *For when Gentiles, who do not have the law, by nature do what the law requires, they are a law to themselves, even though they do not have the law.* We serve as slaves under the Law, even when there is no written Law to tell us what to do.

Even outward worship naming the true God, apart from the Spirit and the promise of Christ, turns the true God into a false one in our heart. Faith grasps the knowledge of God and His loving will for us, not our own personal knowledge of Him. Whatever service we offer that God does not want is false worship. A slave cannot serve willingly, that is, worship the Father in the Spirit. There is no free service or true worship until we are freed by the Spirit and adopted as sons. God desires this spiritual worship, not slaves falsely impersonating sons.

How often have we done things for God that He has not explicitly said that He wanted? "Formerly," Paul says, so that is not the case anymore. We are by nature unspiritual: without the Spirit. But now you are not a slave to sin. No longer are you only able to sin, but you are a son, an heir, and free in the Spirit to know God.

Now, we are not slaves because we know God in Christ. [v9] Paul makes explicit what justification means. It means acceptance by God. If *we* accept God, what do we gain? Does the holy God care about our judgment? Not at all. Who are we to judge Him? It is *His* verdict that matters. The language of "accepting Christ" is contagious among people who believe that they are free and have never been slaves. It can be used properly, in that the Spirit causes us to appropriate, or accept, the gift of Christ's righteousness, but it is often used of our works, that God reckons what we do as righteousness, apart from Christ's forgiveness and without the Spirit. If thought of as a work for God, this human "faith" reeks of spiritual pride—as if God wants our weak acceptance of Him! Rather, He offered His only Son on our behalf. He did it all. Faith is not a work—it is God's work in us.

When we know God, we are in Christ, clothed with His righteousness. This is how we have the Spirit and the inheritance of sonship. True worship is faith—knowing God and resting in His promises. *But if anyone loves God, he is known by God* (1 Cor. 8:3). Knowledge of God is not about facts and details, but trusting that He loves us and chooses us to be His in Christ.

Now, Paul applies the illustration and asks the Galatians (and us) a rather pointed question. Paul highlights the exact folly of their foolishness: *How can you turn back again?* "Turn" is used for "repent," at times. When we turn to God, we turn away from our sin. But to repent of following Christ is to turn away from life. To turn "again" to slavery, to works of the Law, even if it has the imprimatur of the impressive Galatian teachers, is true bondage. In the larger context of the letter, this section turns from the abstract issue of freedom and slavery to the specific instances of slavery to which the Galatians were tempted to turn.

These *weak and worthless elementary principles of the world* are unable to save from slavery or give the Spirit. "Beggarly" is the common word for "poor," meaning "without wealth or substance." Ceremonial laws were the main issue, part of the larger problem of using the Law as a way to God. They had a place for a time, but to return to them after hearing the Gospel is foolish.

Remember that, as Gentiles, the Galatians did not have or follow the ceremonial laws before faith. Why would a freed slave, knowing both slavery and freedom, volunteer to be a slave again? The Law was useful as a restraint for the flesh, as a tutor and guardian, but it has nothing to offer one rich in Christ. Our power is in His sacrifice, not in the Law. Though we uphold the Law and condemn sin against it, it cannot free us from slavery. It reinforces our slavery. It cannot help sinners who are, by nature, slaves.

What strong language is used to describe the Law! This is, perhaps, why some get the idea that the Law is evil and should be ignored by Christians, but that is not the case. The Law is to be respected and remains God's will. The problem is that being under it means we are under a curse and rejecting the gift of Christ. It is holy, but leaves us still in slavery, not knowing God. Why turn to it again? The impulse to get to God by works, by the supposed power of the Law, remains with the flesh. This is the Devil's trump card. We must die to the flesh and our false power to achieve righteousness, so that Christ's life is our only hope.

The "weak and poor elements" are the same "elementary principles" mentioned in v3 and defined on page 183. The ceremonial laws deal with things of this earth, not the true knowledge of God by faith. Paul has used several metaphors and illustrations to make this point. Why become a child, a slave, again, as if you did not know God? The Gospel is exciting for many the first time it is heard, since it does bring the Spirit and real hope. But the flesh wants to be enslaved, so the pull of doing the Law and ceremonial observances as sacrifices for God is strong. We must be extremely vigilant to preserve Christ's Gospel freedom. Christ does not lead us into slavery again. We remain in God's grace by the promise. The Law is the power of sin—it must be weak and beggarly in regards to salvation.

Verse 9 ends with "again you desire to be enslaved to these things," that is, to childish and powerless things. Christ did not die and then ascend to heaven so that we may be concerned only with touching and eating. To return to slavery means that Christ did nothing significant.

Paul accurately portrayed Christ and the power of His resurrection from the dead—to free slaves. Jesus states His mission by quoting Is. 61:1: *The Spirit of the Lord is upon me, because he has anointed me to proclaim good news to the poor. He has sent me to proclaim liberty to the captives and recovering of sight to the blind, to set at liberty those who are oppressed* (Lk. 4:18).

Luther states the same: "Whoever defects from this doctrine [of Christ's righteousness applied to us in the promise] will necessarily fall into an ignorance of God and an ignorance of the righteousness, wisdom, and proper worship of God. He will be an idolater, remaining under the Law, sin, death, and the rule of the devil" [*Galatians*, 397]. If we serve the name of Christ in our own way, by works, through the elementary principles of the world, we make Him into a false god, an idol for ourselves.

Not all that man calls "worship" is accepted by God. Only in faith is anything we do not a work of the Law. "In faith" means it is done out of love for Christ and in our status as sons. Otherwise, we are slaves, trying to please the master through the Law to which we are enslaved. This slavery seems very reasonable to natural man, who is without the Spirit. "Christians are just people who try to be good," we so often hear, but Christ's sheep are actually known by God and righteous in His sight. It is one thing to wax poetic about God's creation, eternity, and goodness—it is quite another to know with certainty His eternal will for you and to be filled with His own Spirit. Our activity, knowing, and choosing mean nothing if Christ has not chosen us and given us His righteousness to wear. Therefore, life must be of the promise. It must be an inheritance received through faith. It has nothing to do with the beggarly elements of this world that people get so worked up about. The Law itself is weak and beggarly for salvation. How bold is that!

[**v10**] These outward things have to do with the body, not the heart. They do no touch the righteousness by faith. They are part of the elementary principles of the world, and therefore they are of the Law.

This verse is not talking about human rules to provide order among people. It does not mean we cannot use a calendar or plan a schedule. When done in freedom these things are fine. But laws were being preached to the Galatians as the way to God's righteousness. We go to church on a certain day, but do we have to? Will we lose our inheritance if we do not? No—we are free in Christ from the elementary principles. Everything not against the Spirit and the Lord's will is free. We should have faith every day, not just on the Sabbath (Saturday) or Sunday, the Lord's day. Our observance in the body is not the same as internal faith. The two must be kept distinct. Although we need external order, our outward observances have nothing do to with the freedom of the Gospel.

In the Greek, the first word of this verse is "days." The verb used here, in this context, means not just "keeping," but "observing closely and legalistically for salvation." Many make it seem as if God cares what day we join together to hear His Word. This can be a hard verse to hear, due to our own traditions. Easter is no different than Labor Day to God. He made both 24-hour time periods, and Christ's righteousness is had by faith both days. It is an act of mercy that we do not know the exact day Christ was born. Today, we have a different calendar than the Jews. The exact date of Easter is one of the reasons why the Greek Orthodox and Latin Roman churches split around 1000 A.D. What a silly thing to split over. The Gospel is not about days or months or times or years. These are elementary things, powerless to save or help before God. Slaves are bound to certain days as laws. The Gospel, on the other hand, gives freedom every day for all eternity.

The Jews, before Christ, had all sorts of significant holy days. They were necessary under the Law, and their outward observance was required. The Old Testament mentions Passover, Feast of Booths, the Day of Atonement, etc., but Christians should not seek to be enslaved by relying on the Law. Externally, the body needs order, but we are not to believe that these works have anything to do with righteousness, which is found only in Christ. Here is an exceptional passage detailing our Christian freedom: *Therefore let no one pass judgment on you in questions of food and drink, or with regard to a festival or a new moon or a Sabbath. These are a shadow of the things to come, but the substance belongs to Christ* (Col. 2:16–17). Too many Christians act like Israel in the Old Testament, thinking we had it so good in slavery in Egypt (under the Law), with all those wonderful foods (or ceremonies)—why do we have to be free in the Gospel?

Are we slaves since we observe church holidays? We are to do them in love for others and to keep order. We must have some structure, or else we could never gather together and hear God's Word. We cannot expect to be moved by the Spirit to all show up at church at the same time, without some orderly planning. But we do not make it necessary for salvation. Only Christ is necessary. He comes to forgive us in the Gospel, not our works. But for others, especially the weak, we should sacrifice in love. If the Word of God is preached rightly, everything else can be endured.

We may keep days outwardly with our bodies while being free in the mind and conscience. We can do things without considering them in regards to our peace with God. The Law has a valid application in keeping unruly and fleshly people in check and it should be used to curb outward disobedience and disorder.

> *Now we know that the law is good, if one uses it lawfully, understanding this, that the law is not laid down for the just but for the lawless and disobedient, for the ungodly and sinners, for the unholy and profane, for those who strike their fathers and mothers, for murderers, the sexually immoral, men who practice homosexuality, enslavers, liars, perjurers, and whatever else is contrary to sound doctrine* (1 Tim. 1:8–10).

The Law has no ruling function for the new man.

Parents and governments should discipline and use threats, but, when administering God's Word, the Gospel should rule. We conform ourselves to the expectations of others, not because God requires it, but because we are free to do so in the freedom of the Spirit. All things are free, including material things, once we are free to the Father. So we do not do anything because it affects our righteousness in Christ or because others command it. When someone requires a work God does not, tying it to salvation, we must *not* do it, to preserve our Christian freedom. This is the place circumcision occupied for the Galatians. But Christian love, worked by the Spirit, is good and pleasing to our Father. To personally refrain from food or observe a day in freedom is good if done willingly in faith. But when commanded in God's name or forced upon others, it becomes death and cuts off Christ's grace. This liberty or freedom of the Gospel is so important that Paul goes to great pains to explain it.

This doctrine of Christian freedom applies to all external things—the beggarly elements which cannot make righteous. Some churches have

Jewish rules about food, forbidding certain foods on certain days. This is a very evil thing, because it puts words in God's mouth. It takes away the Gospel and imposes the Law, which only has the power to curse and bring death. It destroys the preaching of the Gospel, because sinners naturally trust in what they do. Some people think they are good Christians because they did not eat red meat on a certain day. But God is clear in this verse. These external things have nothing to with true righteousness granted in the Gospel. Christ redeemed us—we do not redeem ourselves.

[v11] The truth can be undone with one false teaching. If a work of the Law is added to the Gospel, it stops being the true Gospel. Paul poured himself into preaching and evangelizing the one Gospel. But, in no time, false teachers threatened to undo it all. Paul could not rest on his previous work—the Galatians needed more instruction. So, also, this letter is directed at all. Though we have cars, computers, and phones, we are not better in our sinful nature than the Galatians were. We, too, must be vigilant and need to be led by a called servant of Christ, if possible. If we are to have the Spirit and enjoy freedom in Christ, the Word of God must correct us.

The historical church on earth has often buried the fullness of the Gospel. It is always in danger of being lost and encrusted with cursed demands for works. Observe the feeling and emotion in this verse: Paul is distraught. All he fought against now looks so enticing and threatens to enslave the Galatians again. Consider that this is Paul, the apostle to the Gentiles, they are turning from—not a regular pastor. Ultimately, it is the Gospel and the knowledge of God they are rejecting—that is, Christ Himself. This is the great struggle still today. Paul highlights in his letter, not the ever pervasive goal of being a better person, but how God continues to work among us in the Gospel.

Paul fears for their souls. The first part of this verse says: "I fear for you"—that is, their whole person, body and soul. He is not just lamenting that he has wasted his time on them. He desires their salvation, just as the Father does for all people. Without Christ's righteousness, we are under wrath and dead in sins. Paul is being personal here. He uses the first person ("I") to show his concern for them in Christ. He is not just working to ensure his legacy. He knows that if the doctrine of Christ is lost, everything is lost. He does not want to have labored in vain among the Galatians—that is not why the Spirit called them by the Word of Christ. Every preaching of the Gospel is meant to be fulfilled in the Resurrection from the dead.

The last part of this verse could be translated: "lest somehow I have labored in vain among you." The Gospel cannot be ineffectual—it is the power of God—but Satan works mightily to disrupt it and return people to things they can see and touch: the weak and beggarly elements. Paul intimates that His work in Christ cannot have been in vain, but it is his fear. He did labor, though certainly not under the Law.

In v12, Paul returns to his previous labor among them. [v12] This marks a change in tone. The Galatians are not lost, despite the doctrinal wavering on their part. Paul became like them. As a Jew, he adapted himself to their Gentile ways. Now he "begs," or "entreats," them to be like him, free from the elementary principles of the world. He again calls them "brothers," alternating from displeasure and astonishment to fatherly counsel and brotherly love. He carefully portions out rebuke and comfort, not in a formulaic way, but back and forth, exactly as they need it. He is a true pastor. He does not whisper sweet nothings in their ears; he speaks the plain Word of God, even when it could be taken as an insult from a worldly point of view.

In this verse, Paul beseeches them. This word is also used of the legion of evil spirits: *When he saw Jesus, he cried out and fell down before him and said with a loud voice, "What have you to do with me, Jesus, Son of the Most High God? I beg* [entreat] *you, do not torment me"* (Lk. 8:28). It is also used of prayer, which is simply talking to the Father and trusting that He hears us through Christ. *The harvest is plentiful, but the laborers are few. Therefore pray earnestly* [entreat, beg] *to the Lord of the harvest to send out laborers into his harvest* (Lk. 10:2).

This is a personal appeal by Paul to be like him, to live free in the Gospel as He does. Though he had been circumcised and grew up under Jewish law, Christ and the coming of faith changed everything. He willingly conformed himself to their type of living, so the Gospel would not be hindered unnecessarily. This sounds strange, but pastors, even today, are to live out their lives in accord with the Scriptures and as an example for the flock. Paul states that a pastor's outward behavior and reputation is also important:

> *The saying is trustworthy: If anyone aspires to the office of overseer, he desires a noble task. Therefore an overseer must be above reproach, the husband of one wife, sober-minded, self-controlled, respectable, hospitable, able to teach, not a drunkard, not violent but gentle, not quarrelsome, not a lover of money. He must manage his own household well, with all dignity keeping his children submissive, for if someone does not know how to manage his own household, how will he care for God's church? He must not be a recent convert, or he may become puffed up with conceit and fall into the condemnation of the devil. Moreover, he must be well thought of by outsiders, so that he may not fall into disgrace, into a snare of the devil* (1 Tim. 3:1–7).

He can un-preach with his life and family all that he preaches with his mouth.

Paul does not claim any mistreatment during his work in Galatia. He is not mad at them personally—he is fighting against Satan's falsehood, which is attacking their hearts. His passion is for the freedom of the Gospel that he personally enjoys.

Next, we get a bit of personal information from Paul. [**v13**] See how God uses all things for His good? We cannot see, and likely will never figure out, how God works good in suffering and horrible diseases. These things can, though, drive us to Christ and His Gospel. All earthly tribulations are small potatoes compared to knowing God and being righteous in His eyes. Paul is not complaining or feeling sorry for himself. He speaks like Christ, who explained why a particular man was born blind: *It was not that this man sinned, or his parents, but that the works of God might be displayed in him. We must work the works of him who sent me while it is day; night is coming, when no one can work. As long as I am in the world, I am the light of the world* (Jn. 9:3–5). We are not to ask "why me?" when we suffer, but to trust in Christ, who forgives sins and bestows an eternal inheritance in Baptism and the Word.

Paul starts v13 with "you know." He recounts the plain facts that they already know. *Bodily ailment* is not a literal translation. The Greek actually says "weakness of the flesh." "Flesh" carries the overtone of that which is natural in sinners and opposed to the Spirit. This phrase is also used in Rom. 6:19 to speak of our mental and spiritual limitations in understanding God's truth:

> But thanks be to God, that you who were once slaves of
> sin have become obedient from the heart to the standard of
> teaching to which you were committed, and, having been
> set free from sin, have become slaves of righteousness. I am
> speaking in human terms, because of your natural limitations
> [in Greek: "the weakness of your flesh"]. For just as you
> once presented your members as slaves to impurity and to
> lawlessness leading to more lawlessness, so now present your
> members as slaves to righteousness leading to sanctification
> (6:17-19).

This interesting phrase also recalls the thorn in Paul's own flesh, given
to him by God: *So to keep me from becoming conceited because of the
surpassing greatness of the revelations, a thorn was given me in the
flesh, a messenger of Satan to harass me, to keep me from becoming
conceited* (2 Cor. 12:7). Though a weakness caused Paul to come to
the Galatians, it was God's will, not an accident. After he preached,
his teaching was received. All Gospel preaching and faith is ultimately
Christ's work.

Rather than speculating on what the text does not say, it is better
to focus on what it does say. Paul had some weakness—maybe not
a physical illness—that forced him to stay in the area. **[v14]** Rather
than "do him wrong," the Galatians received Paul as an angel, even
as Christ Himself. This is an outstanding phrase on which we should
all meditate. Paul, because of the Gospel he relayed, was Christ to
them. This illustrates the proper respect a faithful minister of the Word
deserves. It is not a lowly task to forgive sinners in Christ' name, thereby
bestowing the Spirit and taking away death.

The word translated "condition" actually means "flesh." But here
it refers to the body or the effects of sin, not strictly the power of sin
within man. This is different than Paul's normal usage of this word:
it indirectly refers to the effects of sin, since sickness, injury, mental
suffering, and all weakness are effects of Adam's first sin. Everything
was cursed in that first sin. Christ redeemed our bodies in His body, so
we look forward to the Resurrection, the redemption of our bodies.

The Greek word translated "trial" is the common one for temptation
and testing. Is Paul saying his condition might have impeded his words
if the Galatians had judged only by appearances? The Word he preached
was of the Spirit, opposed to the flesh and sin. However, they disregarded
the weakness and outward form of Paul and listened to him as an angel.

They paid attention to the message.

We know from elsewhere that Paul was not a bold, impressive speaker, as his writing might otherwise indicate. *For they say, "His letters are weighty and strong, but his bodily presence is weak, and his speech of no account"* (1 Cor. 10:10). He says in the next chapter of 1 Cor.: *Even if I am unskilled in speaking, I am not so in knowledge; indeed, in every way we have made this plain to you in all things* (11:6). One of the great sins of Christians is to be impressed only by the sound of the words and vigor of the one preaching, ignoring the content. But anyone who speaks the one Gospel, even the worst preacher, should be regarded as God's mouth. The Galatians heard the Gospel, and it made them righteous. They saw Paul as Christ. This would be blasphemous if not done in faith. Christ comes in His Word. Whether we like a pastor personally or not, we are bound to listen if he speaks the truth, lest we deny the truth of God's Word. It is not just the cross that is offensive to our flesh, it is also those whom Christ chooses to bring the message of the cross. Recall that "angel" means, simply, "messenger."

If Christ is in His Word, we dare not think that it is weak and useless, even if it sounds so by human standards. God does not work like we think He should. *For the word of the cross is folly to those who are perishing, but to us who are being saved it is the power of God. For it is written, "I will destroy the wisdom of the wise, and the discernment of the discerning I will thwart"* (1 Cor. 1:18–19). Hearing the Gospel from a sinner always brings temptation to the flesh, but that is the only way we can count on hearing it. Christ instituted the ministry of public preaching as the place He should be sought.

You can see why Paul was heartbroken over this situation. The Galatians received the Gospel so gladly, but once Paul left, they forget how they received the Spirit. When he was there in person, they did not despise, reject, or "scorn" [ESV] him. The second verb listed in this verse most basically means "to spit." As in our culture, it was unspeakably rude to spit at someone. After relaying his warm reception on account of his message, Paul highlights the reversal in behavior.

[v15] In Greek it reads like this: "Where then [is] your blessedness?" It was there initially, Paul witnessed it. They received the one, true Gospel. This "blessedness" is specific. It is not found in earthly blessings, such as wealth, health, or a happy family. It refers to the Gospel promise

applied and received in the joy of faith. The only other two times this word occurs in the New Testament is in Rom. 4:6–9:

> Just as David also speaks of the blessing [blessedness] of the one to whom God counts righteousness apart from works: "Blessed are those whose lawless deeds are forgiven, and whose sins are covered; blessed is the man against whom the Lord will not count his sin." Is this blessing [blessedness] then only for the circumcised, or also for the uncircumcised? For we say that faith was counted to Abraham as righteousness.

This blessing is an eternal one—the pronouncement of righteousness by the Father in Christ. The fruit of this blessing is love, joy, and the works of the Spirit, which the Galatians had shown Paul.

"To pluck out the eyes" was evidently a proverb of that time. It conveyed honor and respect. It would be a great price indeed to dig out one's eyes to give to another. The same word for "gouging out" is used in Mk. 2:4 for digging through a roof: And when they could not get near him because of the crowd, they removed the roof above him, and when they had made [dug; gouged] an opening, they let down the bed on which the paralytic lay.

Jesus' statement in the Gospel is not encouraging us to physically gouge out our eyes: And if your eye causes you to sin, tear it out and throw it away. It is better for you to enter life with one eye than with two eyes to be thrown into the hell of fire (Mt. 18:9). Avoiding sins against the Law should be desired very greatly, but doing that kind of surgery does not get rid of sin or its curse. We should still hate sin in ourselves and desire to be remade in Christ's image by the Spirit, though. For those whom He foreknew he also predestined to be conformed to the image of his Son, in order that he might be the firstborn among many brothers (Rom. 8:29). This happens by the Gospel: you have put off the old self with its practices and have put on the new self, which is being renewed in knowledge after the image of its creator. Here there is not Greek and Jew, circumcised and uncircumcised, barbarian, Scythian, slave, free; but Christ is all, and in all (Col. 3:9–11). It is evident that the Galatians had a great affection for Paul, since he first brought Christ to them, in spite of the weakness of his flesh.

The reference to eyes does not necessarily refer to the problem that caused Paul to reside in Galatia at first, though he did have poor eyes, it seems. At the end of this letter, in 6:11, he writes: See with what large *letters I am writing to you with my own hand.*

As with his thorn in the flesh, which was possibly of a spiritual nature, Paul shows no interest in the particular details of his personal struggles. They are a curiosity the Spirit does not want to tell us about. However, malaria happens to be a favorite explanation of modern interpreters. Either way, the particular weakness does not affect the content of Paul's letter expounding the glory of the Gospel.

Satan often attacks godly men and the proclaimers of the Gospel, just as he tried to drag Job away from the promised Christ. *In all circumstances take up the shield of faith, with which you can extinguish all the flaming darts of the evil one* (Eph. 6:16). Satan would seem to have more success attacking minds and hearts than hands and feet. Luther, who suffered great spiritual turmoil, describes Paul in terms of his own experience in taking a stand against the whole world alone: "for the Galatians and others with whom Paul had contact often saw him moved by great sadness, trembling, terrified, and crushed by an unspeakable sorrow and grief" [*Galatians*, 420].

A great spiritual despair would have affected Paul's body and possibly his ability to travel as well. The important thing is that Paul was strong in doctrine. His sins were forgiven in Christ's name, even though he was weak in the flesh. The Galatians overlooked the weak flesh of Paul in order to hear God speaking to them. As an apostle of Christ, he said in the strongest possible language: *We have become, and are still, like the scum of the world, the refuse of all things* (1 Cor. 4:13).

There are some odd translations of v15: "Where, then, is your blessing of me now?" [NIV]. This makes the blessing something the Galatians give to Paul, as if he needed something from them. The KJV has: *Where is then the blessedness ye spake of?* The word "spake," meaning "have spoken," is not in the text at all. The RSV reads: *What has become of the satisfaction you felt?* That makes the blessedness a subjective emotion, not the Gospel verdict that makes us blessed in Christ. This shows the challenge of translating. Every translation also requires some interpretation.

The later betrayal of this warm reception is unexpected. **[v16]** The same conjunction is used in Jn. 3:16: *for God so loved the world, **so that** He gave his only begotten Son.* What an odd response to the precious promise. Paul has become their enemy and he must oppose them. While "enemy" is a noun, "telling the truth" is a verb, the action of witnessing to God's truth. The only other place it is used is in Eph. 4:15: *speaking the truth in love, we are to grow up in every way into him who is the head, into Christ.* This truth is hard to hear, especially when the Lord's angel preaches against our personal sin. It must be done, however, to highlight the glory of Christ's death for the forgiveness of sins. As long as we have the flesh, this is a never-ending process. The true Gospel brings on persecution and rejection.

Evidently, Paul's authority and former testimony did not carry enough weight to combat the false teachers. Paul deals with them here slightly, and then also in chapter 6, the last one.

[**v17**] The verb starting out this verse is "zealous" or "jealous." The false teachers, the Judaizers, tried to win the Galatians over by flattery and praise—not Christ's Gospel. Paul demonstrated the opposite approach in this letter. He did not tell them what they wanted to hear or promote human wisdom. Instead, he proclaims the truth, even though they would be disturbed to hear it. No sinner wants to hear that he is a slave, that he can do no good thing, but before God, it is true. In contrast, teachers who are jealous for attention and followers will teach false doctrine. It will be more readily accepted than the truth, but it does not offer righteousness, peace, or freedom.

It says they are "jealous of you," meaning "it is not well, fitting, or appropriate." It is out of place. The emotional appeal made to win their hearts has compromised the message. The Judaizers tried to enslave the Galatians to the flesh and childish, weak, and beggarly elements. But they are so nice, Paul intimates. A nice murder of souls is still murder. It is easier to take away salvation by words and human tactics than by force. Paul is not condoning the approach of "how to win friends and influence people." He who speaks for God must be ruled by God's Word, even if persecution and hatred result. Consider how much rejection and hatred Christ faced. He spoke even His harshest words in complete love, but sinners, by their nature, do not want God's love or truth.

The same word for "jealous," or "zealous," is used in a positive way too: *But earnestly desire* [be jealous for] *the higher gifts* (1 Cor. 12:31). Paul says to the Corinthians that he is jealous for them: *For I feel a divine jealousy for you, since I betrothed you to one husband, to present you as a pure virgin to Christ* (2 Cor. 11:2). The object and aim are what make this human passion right or wrong. Outside of the Spirit, our zeal is always misguided.

The false teachers the Galatians are tolerating want to exclude them, to make them withdraw from Christ's fellowship or association. The only other New Testament reference containing this verb, "shut out," is in Rom. 3:27: *Then what becomes of our boasting? It is excluded* [shut out]. *By what kind of law? By a law of works? No, but by the law of faith.* So by seeking to include them in a human way, these teachers really seek to shut them out from God's truth and fellowship in Christ's body.

Paul notes the deceptive appearance of the teachers who claim to speak the Gospel with only the one addition of circumcision. In reality, they are excluding the Galatians from Christ by their inclusion of the Law. That sounds like our times, does it not? "Inclusive" and "diversity" are modern slogans. We are told to accept everything—that is called the highest good. It has become the god of our culture. Yet, truth does not admit error or untruth. It does not believe everything. It must confess and stand against the wrong. But the world hears only hate. It cannot fathom how we can condemn a sin and say it deserves hell, but love the person enough to also forgive the sin in the name of Christ. They only hear that we are hurting their self-esteem and damaging their psyche. "Love the sinner, hate the sin" is quite accurate, but the world does not know sin, forgiveness, or Christ.

We feel pressure to fit in and accept abhorrent practices and harmful morality. The world claims currently that love is always accepting, but love is also decisive and absolute. If a small child wanders out onto a busy highway, you would snatch that child quickly, even if he found it uncomfortable and harsh. The child was happy to be near fast-moving cars, but love requires action and a stern warning to never to do that again. God does nothing different to adults, it is just that we consider ourselves so wise that we do not want to hear we are dead wrong. The unrepentant person, though, is actually dead in his sins.

Paul warns about false teachers in Rom. 16:17–18: *I appeal to you, brothers, to watch out for those who cause divisions and create obstacles contrary to the doctrine that you have been taught; avoid them. For such persons do not serve our Lord Christ, but their own appetites, and by smooth talk and flattery they deceive the hearts of the naive.* Christ does not want us to judge a teacher by his personality or what others think of him, but by his doctrine. We live by the doctrine Christ gives us in Scripture.

The last phrase in v17 says "in order to make you jealous of them." The teachers of laws seek their own glory. "They want the Galatians completely for themselves" [Lenski, 225]. No sinner is perfect, but one's sin should not affect the substance of what is taught. God allows various trials and difficulties to temper the expectations of preachers, so that they are jealous of God's praise, not the attention of sinful men.

From the words and tone of this verse, we can conclude that Paul was under attack. Paul did seek to win the Galatians, but only to deliver them from their sins in Christ's name. Once he was far away, his teaching was all but forgotten. The people were really in danger of losing Christ, who Paul had portrayed before them. After Paul had laid the theological foundation—that embracing the Law is a return to slavery—he addresses the human side. They were in real danger of being shutout from fellowship with Christ, because they were listening to the teachers of works.

Luther magnificently summarizes the smallness of the human emotion of love when compared to the divine truth that saves: "A curse upon any love and harmony whose preservation would make it necessary to jeopardize the Word of God" [*Galatians*, 424–25]. The false teachers evidently were successful in using their charisma and human appeal to win over the Galatians Paul had carefully instructed. But the Word of God cuts much deeper than what meets the eye. That is why Paul is so careful to show the purpose and limitations of the Law in contrast to the righteousness of the Gospel. There is no true power for salvation other than the one, true Gospel.

[v18] The same root for "good" here is also the one used in v17 for "no good purpose." "Good" is used in a general sense, not in regards to righteousness or a divine goodness, though in other contexts it can mean that. It means here what is proper and fitting. We might say "fine" today. Paul means the same when it says in 1 Cor. 7:1: *It is good for a man not to have sexual relations with a woman*. It is good, meaning not a sin. However, refraining from knowing the opposite sex is fairly impractical for most, due to lust. We were made for marriage, and, while it is unavoidable for the majority, celibacy is also good for those

so gifted. Neither prevents true righteousness.

"To be made much of" is the same word in Greek for "zealous" and "jealous." Paul stings them by first praising them for his reception, despite the weakness of his flesh, then saying it is also good he is absent. The key is that it must be "for some good (purpose)." We are not to forget who first taught us the truth. New faces do not undo God's truth. It is not subject to the whims of man or culture. Paul painted clearly that he was called by God. He did not choose to be a public figure just to get praised by men. He had a holy calling. Woe to those who want to preach, but do not *have* to preach. The seriousness of the office is inculcated and emphasized by Paul. We should be wary of fly-by-night preachers and teachers who claim to be called, but draw attention to themselves without a public call.

If Paul was received as Christ when he was with them, what has changed? Not the Word of God, certainly. "Not only when I am with you"—by praising them, he has also highlighted their immaturity and instability. But he does not dismiss them, but gently and carefully wins them back.

[v19] The Galatians are, according to this verse, Paul's children. He shows his fatherly concern and jealousy for their souls. After all, he gave birth to them, in a way, by the Gospel that he first preached. He was their first nurse and doctor, who welcomed them into God's kingdom. How could he be so quickly forgotten? St. John also uses this language: *I have no greater joy than to hear that my children are walking in the truth* (3 Jn. 1:4). A pastor is more a father than a therapist, who is not allowed to correct and rebuke. We see that zeal and enthusiasm are good, if they are used according to God's will and Word.

Paul is in "anguish." This verb means "to suffer birth pains." It is used in Rev. 12:2 this way: *She was pregnant and was crying out in birth pains and the agony of giving birth.* Birth is a horrific thing, if one were just to witness the pain as an outsider. But because this pain allows parents to receive a child into their arms, it is a joyous occasion. *When a woman is giving birth, she has sorrow because her hour has come, but when she has delivered the baby, she no longer remembers the anguish, for joy that a human being has been born into the world* (Jn. 16:21). The most difficult birth does not diminish the value of a human being made in the image of God.

We have written for us the incredible phrase: "until Christ is formed in you." The Galatians are immature, but Christ will be formed and shaped in them by patient instruction in His truth. They have not been fully formed by the Gospel, since they are so quickly enticed by the slavery of the Law. Paul is suffering birth pains until Christ takes shape within them. The Spirit must create and strengthen the new man and make us strong enough to resist the false doctrine of flattering teachers. Paul implies here that the Galatian Christians are unformed. They are Paul's "children," but not yet formed or born. They exist and have faith, but are not ready for the harsher conditions outside the protection of the womb. Paul is personally suffering great anguish until this happens, as if he were having labor pains. He not saying they need to be more zealous or do more, but that Christ is formed when He comes to us in the promise. We cannot give birth to ourselves. We are born of water and the Spirit in Baptism. All spirituality comes by returning to what we were already given by the Spirit. We are fully formed by patiently enduring suffering. so that we can remain steadfast upon the Gospel.

Two other references in Paul use the same Greek root translated "formed." They speak of being be co-formed with Christ: *conformed to the image of his Son* (Rom. 8:29). Also: *who will transform our lowly body to be like* [co-formed with] *his glorious body* (Phil. 3:21). The Gospel causes us to look forward to when our bodies will be formed gloriously without sin.

[v20] Paul does not relish this upbraiding and rebuke he must administer. In our words, he is saying, like a parent, "this hurts me more than it hurts you." So that there can be peace in Christ, he must be forceful and stern with them, lest they lose the Spirit and Christ entirely. Paul wants to be with them, to let them know that they are not lost, but this letter must suffice. Without their separation, we would not have this letter today to read and help form Christ more perfectly within us.

The external elements of the ceremonial law (and all the Law) cannot change the heart. Only the promise can deliver us and form a new heart within us. Scripture is full of admonishments to not be immature children, but to learn to eat the solid meat of God's Word. We are to handle the Word as an adult, not a child. Young children often pretend to read a book, even though it might even be upside-down. Yet, they are very pleased with themselves because they are holding it and look like they are reading—to those who cannot read. How many Christians do the same: pretending to be mature and spiritual, while they are ignorant of God's Word about sin and grace?

> *We have much to say, and it is hard to explain, since you have become dull of hearing. For though by this time you ought to be teachers, you need someone to teach you again the basic principles of the oracles of God. You need milk, not solid food, for everyone who lives on milk is unskilled in the word of righteousness, since he is a child. But solid food is for the mature, for those who have their powers of discernment trained by constant practice to distinguish good from evil* (Heb. 5:11–14).

Paul wants to be with them now, as a mother, and guide them personally. He has to be the one to warn them, so they do not go off the cliff of righteousness by the Law, which looks attractive, but ends in death. He does not want to be so stern and harsh, but love demands it. He shows that his devotion is pure. Someone who only tells you the positive and refuses to address the negative is not a friend, but a sycophant or bootlicker. A true friend is willing to tell the truth, even when it hurts, as Paul is doing.

We know that it is more difficult to convey emotion in writing. Email and texts can be easily misunderstood, because they do not convey much in the way of tone or context. Letters are better, which is why some courting a husband or wife send handwritten letters to convey serious and meaningful thoughts. But care must be taken, because the recipient cannot see the author's face or hear his voice in writing.

The word for "tone" is just "voice" or "sound" in Greek. The English words "phonetics" and "phonograph" derive from the same Greek root. Paul is raising his voice figuratively by his words. He would rather comfort them, but he is perplexed and at a loss. He cannot just assume the best and encourage them. That would be to hate their souls. Paul is not confused in himself, though he expects better for them. This word for "perplexed" is also used of Paul's legal situation: *Festus said to King Agrippa concerning the case of Paul: Being at a loss* [perplexed about] *how to investigate these questions, I asked whether he wanted to go to Jerusalem and be tried there regarding them* (Acts 25:20).

Paul is at a loss from an emotional standpoint, but certainly not in doctrine. He gives no hint of wavering in the divine words revealed here, which testify to the righteousness of faith. Here is a nice quote: Paul "knew how to adapt himself [by the Spirit's inspiration] to every mood of his readers without any sacrifice of principle. It was no a trick, but love for the souls of men that made him become all things to all men" [Lenski, 231]. Despite their apparent rejection of Paul and his first message, he does not abandon them when they most need their spiritual father. He remains like a mother suffering during childbirth, willing to suffer all to see his children formed. This foray into the personal and subjective shows that Paul's feelings are genuine and no less intense than the false teachers.

Next, Paul offers an illustration. [v21] This verse can be confusing due to the nuances of the word "law." To review, the first "law" is the power that enslaves. The Galatians seek to be "under" it by not relying on the Gospel. It is the guardian and tutor that restricts. The second use of the word "law" refers to the written Scriptures: "the law and the prophets." It refers to the Old Testament, especially the first five books, which detail the giving of the Law to Israel.

"You tell me," Paul starts out. He confronts the Galatians directly with a question. He asks if they hear the Law, that is, God's written Word. Here begins a section where Paul uses "the law" (the Scriptures) against "the Law" (as a way to righteousness). *Do you not listen to the law?* He will go on to show they do not, despite the fact they are listening to Law-preachers who demand works. He returns to the distinction between the promise, which gives freedom, and the commands, which enslave. He also again uses Abraham, the man of faith, as proof that the Gospel should have priority over the Law.

[v22] Abraham had two sons. One was of the slave-woman, Hagar, the female servant of his wife Sarah. Abraham did not trust God to fulfill the promise of a son, so he took matters into his own hands. This account is in Gen. 16:1–4:

> *Now Sarai, Abram's wife, had borne him no children. She had a female Egyptian servant whose name was Hagar. And Sarai said to Abram, "Behold now, the Lord has prevented me from bearing children. Go in to my servant; it may be that I shall obtain children by her." And Abram listened to the voice of Sarai. So, after Abram had lived ten years in the land of Canaan, Sarai, Abram's wife, took Hagar the*

211

> *Egyptian, her servant, and gave her to Abram her husband*
> *as a wife. And he went in to Hagar, and she conceived.*

This history is part of the scriptural "law," the second "law" of v21. The Greek word for "it is written" is often used in the New Testament to refer back to and quote the Old Testament. It means that it has been written and still stands—it is God's Word, which does not change, even after Christ has come into the flesh.

[**v23**] The other son, Isaac, through whom the promised seed would come, came by faith. Abraham had little to do with it. It was entirely God's work. It was physically improbable for Sarah to have a child at such an old age, so Abraham could not take credit for it.

The child of the slave-women, Ishmael, was born according to the flesh. *That which is born of the flesh is flesh, and that which is born of the Spirit is Spirit* (Jn. 3:6). Hagar was Egyptian and under the control of Abraham's wife, Sarah. At this point Sarah was called Sarai. Hagar did not have a choice in the matter, because she was a slave. The son of the free woman, however, is not a slave. Isaac is born free, of faith. He was born of the promise, not by human works. Abraham trusted that God would do it, so it was by faith. He was passive—it was all God's work.

Paul is being vague by not mentioning names, but his point is not the history (though the Galatians must have known the basics of Scripture). He is making a big-picture illustration.

[**v24**] Paul is applying this true history allegorically. Allegory uses one basic truth to show another truth. In this case, Paul has established from the clear words of Genesis that Abraham believed the promise and was counted righteous by faith. Now, Paul gives an illustration, not a proof. It is almost a parable, but he in no way implies the history is not true. He is teaching in a different way: by allegory.

The Greek word used in this verse is where we derive our word "allegory" from. Its root means "speaking another way," that is, non-literally. This method has been quite popular in various points of church history. During periods of the Early and Middle Ages, some Christians used allegory quite excessively. At times, the literal meaning of the words was lost and ignored.

Here Paul is merely making an application of what he has already proved. Many modern interpreters of Scripture treat it as myth or fiction, either ignoring the historical nature of the accounts or out-right denying it. That is not using Scripture correctly, since that makes it mere powerless stories. Without a factual basis, the Word of God is denied and its power is taken away. It then becomes a children's fairy tale that we do not allow to invade our lives. But God's Word is truth and cannot be broken. While preachers can apply the Scriptures in different ways, the literal meaning must always be upheld and made prominent, for it is what establishes doctrine. Paul is not playing with God's Word, he is writing under the inspiration of the Spirit. After his personal appeal and declaration that he is in the anguish of child-birth, he paints a picture from the record of the Law, about the Law.

Hagar is of Mt. Sinai, where the Law was given to Israel on two tablets (mediated by angels). The one of the Law bears for slavery—"into slavery"—it says. The Greek original does not mention children, but a state of slavery. A slave cannot deliver into freedom.

[v25] Here, Paul makes a new connection. Mt. Sinai was a holy mountain because the Law was given there. This event occurred after God led His people out of Egypt, bringing them across the Red Sea on dry ground. Mt. Sinai was glorious, though not comforting at all. Hagar is Mt. Sinai, corresponding to the Law.

Paul uses an interesting word to say that Hagar is Mt. Sinai and corresponds to physical Jerusalem. It means "to be in series with." It is the only time it is used in the New Testament. The root, meaning "to walk in a line," is used here in Galatians: *If we live by the Spirit, let us also keep in step* [walk] *with the Spirit* (5:5). The full word here was originally used of soldiers standing in line. Paul does not make a one-to-one correspondence, but, within this allegory, Hagar represents the place the Law was given, which now stands for Jerusalem. This would have been somewhat shocking to Jews, though maybe not so much to the Galatian Gentiles. Even today, we have many Christian Zionists who attach importance to the physical state of Israel and its holy city, Jerusalem. Now that Christ has come, worship is in the Spirit and truth and no longer at a specific place or time, or in a certain manner. The external things, the elementary principles, are hard for sinners to let go of. Jesus very clearly prophesied the destruction of the temple: *And as he came out of the temple, one of his disciples said to him, "Look, Teacher, what wonderful stones and what wonderful buildings!" And Jesus said to him, "Do you see these great buildings? There will not be left here one stone upon another that will not be thrown down"* (Mk. 13:1–2). Conservative Jews today long to rebuild it. Some have even fashioned many of the temple furnishings according to Old Testament specifications, hoping to restart the temple sacrifices and services. Muslims have thwarted that wish, which ignores the temple of Christ's crucified body. The glory of the Law is nothing compared to the freedom of Christ's Gospel. Only one truly helps sinners and grants divine freedom.

The Law, the whole Old Testament code (including its rules for ceremonial worship), specifies Jerusalem as the place to be in God's gracious presence. It was truly the holy city, Zion, for Jews. There are well over 100 references to it in the New Testament. Speaking of Israel's physical captivity by Babylon, Scripture says: *If I forget you, O Jerusalem, let my right hand forget its skill! Let my tongue stick to the roof of my mouth, if I do not remember you, if I do not set Jerusalem above my highest joy!* (Ps. 137:5–6). *Blessed be the Lord from Zion, he who dwells in Jerusalem! Praise the Lord!* (Ps. 135:21). The temple is where God promised to be for them. The promise was why the city of Jerusalem was valued, not the real estate itself. Since Christ died for the world's sins, God is with us everywhere. Christ said: *I am with you always, to the end of the age* (Mt. 28:20). Christ is had by His Word, not at any particular physical location. There is a reason the temple curtain tore at Jesus' death. The old code was done away with, and the Law was fulfilled in Jesus, our God. We are no longer under the tutelage of the Law, but free by the promise.

The KJV translation for this verse reads: *For this Agar is mount Sinai in Arabia, and answereth to Jerusalem which now is, and is in bondage with her children.* An archaic definition of "answer" is: "to be or act as an equivalent to." "Answer" does not mean that in modern English. One problem with using the KJV today is that language changes. For someone raised with it, it might not be a problem, but many words have shifted or completely altered their meaning during the last 400 years.

A good way of understanding Paul's metaphor is that Hagar is in line with, or aligned with, Jerusalem. The connection is made to Jerusalem, which like Hagar and her children, is enslaved. They are of the flesh. Read this in light of the slavery of the Law versus the freedom of the promise received in faith, which Paul laid out so carefully in chapter 3.

There are two systems or ways of salvation. Only one has the Son of God as the mediator, punished in our place for all sin. "For this is my blood of the new testament, which is shed for many for the remission of sins," according to the words of the Lord's Supper's institution (Mt. 26:28; KJV). The Gospel promise is not newer in origin, but in prominence and priority. The Law enslaves. Its children are born in slavery, while the promise of Christ makes us new to the Father.

[v26] The Jerusalem above is our mother. Paul says "our," meaning those of the promise. It includes us—all believers. It is free, because we are free in the Gospel from the curse, since Jesus became our curse. We are born of the heavenly Jerusalem. A true child of Abraham is free by faith in the promise.

[v27] Again, Paul introduces Scripture with "it has been written." He cites Is. 54:1. "Rejoice" here means "to celebrate and be cheerful; to have a party." The barren—"sterile" in the Greek—who cannot have children are to rejoice.

This language of "barren" is odd to our ears, because, as a society, we do not universally see children as a blessing. The world makes the value of children dependent on the parents' wishes. Today we have the category of "unwanted" child, "the mistake [child]," and so forth. But every child is a unique creation of the Holy God Himself. Life is always a gift and treasure, but those who trust the Gospel and the promise of Baptism have all the more reason to welcome children. Without new life, there is no one to hear the great promise of the freedom that Christ won with His own blood. The parents' will and desire have nothing to do with the value or sanctity of a human life. God alone creates life. He just happens to use men and women to do His work of creation. We think we do the work, but it is all the Lord's.

Paul says what is cursed, barrenness, is now blessed. As strange as it may sound to our ears, not having children was the greatest curse for godly women in the Old Testament. It says they are to burst out wildly. The same word is used for "tear," as in "tear to pieces." True joy is spontaneous, not formulaic and according to custom. Think of little children hearing news they like. They do not worry about how they look. They do not practice their routine ahead of time. They are free to express their joy without inhibitions. So do the barren women, not because they lack children, but because of the promise of God. The ones not in the pain of childbirth shall "cry out," which means they will voice their joy forcefully and loudly. Remember that Paul is in the anguish of childbirth while Christ is being formed in the Galatians. It is the same Greek word for "labor" here that is used in v19 for "anguish."

Many are the children of the "deserted" or "desolate" one. Children are not simply a biological process isolated from the Lord. God gives and withholds children, according to Scripture. We do not choose them or make them by our will—conception is the Lord's work. The word for "desolate" is used of the desert or wilderness—a place with no people. The greatest blessing is not physical children, but to be a child of God and in His family, the Church, the true Israel. *God settles the solitary in a home; he leads out the prisoners to prosperity, but the rebellious dwell in a parched land* (Ps. 68:6).

The one without children has more children than the one who is married with a family. Specifically, this applies to Sarah, who could not naturally have children. Hagar could, but Abraham, through the promise given to him and his barren wife, is the father of many nations. This is about the spiritual promise, not the physical elements or objects of this earth. We are not enslaved by the Law.

[v28] Paul applies this allegory to our status in Christ, and to that of the Galatians. We are not in slavery anymore, but have been born of the promise. We are like Isaac, born of faith, not according to the flesh, that is, from deeds of the Law. By God's grace, we have been given the promised seed, Christ. Out of barrenness, God has brought many, including us, into the heavenly Jerusalem of the promise. We live above, by faith, in the Lord's full favor.

The inverse of "above," being born of God by the promise, is "below" or "under." That is the preposition used of spiritual slavery—to be "under the Law." Before faith, we were under the Law's authority as slaves, subject to the curse of death. We are under the Law, according to the flesh, until we are freed from the guilt of our sins by Christ. This is how we partake of Jerusalem, the heavenly Zion, the Church of Christ. This is a fellowship of the Holy Spirit, not a man-made or denominational one. It consists of all born of the Spirit who live by the promise. They are born from above. *Our citizenship is in heaven, and from it we await a Savior, the Lord Jesus Christ* (Phil. 3:20). We are to live as we were born, of the promise, trusting that the Lord does what He says.

The Gospel makes new children to the Father. To hear the Gospel is the greatest worship, since it creates the Church. Luther explains: "this allegory teaches in a beautiful way that the church should not do anything but preach the Gospel correctly and purely and thus give birth to children. In this way we are all father and children to one another, for we are born of one another [by the Gospel]" [*Galatians*, 441].

[**v29**] The result of this distinction between children of the flesh and children of the promise is explained. Paul goes back to the two children of Abraham: one born in slavery of the Law to Hagar and one born of Sarah by the promise of the Gospel into freedom. We live together now, according to our bodies and flesh. We are not to escape the world or try to avoid unbelievers, but to live above in faith. Unfortunately, we are treated like Isaac was treated by Ishmael.

> *And the child grew and was weaned. And Abraham made a great feast on the day that Isaac was weaned. But Sarah saw the son of Hagar the Egyptian, whom she had borne to Abraham, laughing. So she said to Abraham, "Cast out this slave woman with her son, for the son of this slave woman shall not be heir with my son Isaac." And the thing was very displeasing to Abraham on account of his son* (Gen. 21:8–11).

There can be no peace between those who live by the Law and those who live by the Gospel.

The one of the flesh, in slavery, persecutes the one of the Spirit, who is free. This happened to the faithful believers in the Old Testament, to Jesus, and still happens to believers today. *Therefore I send you prophets and wise men and scribes, some of whom you will kill and crucify, and some you will flog in your synagogues and persecute from town to town, so that on you may come all the righteous blood shed on earth, from the blood of righteous Abel to the blood of Zechariah the son of Barachiah, whom you murdered between the sanctuary and the altar* (Mt. 23:24–35). If we live according to the promise, we do not live in this world: we live above it. That drives those of the Law crazy. The Gospel is the one thing that pagans hate most about Christians, not their morality. Those who are enslaved want others enslaved, as it says.

217

We are not to expect things to be better today.

[**v30**] Again Paul returns to the Scriptures, which reveal the purpose of the Law and the content of the Gospel. The word "scripture" just means "writing." The citation from Gen. 21:10 speaks of Abraham sending Hagar away on account of the true son, born of the promise. *The slave does not remain in the house forever; the son remains forever* (Jn. 8:35). Paul detailed this earlier in v7: *So you are no longer a slave, but a son, and if a son, then an heir through God.* The key is to know who lives forever: only the one who receives the inheritance. A slave and heir do not look different now, but only one is owner of all. The sons of the free woman—that is, we who live by faith—are free and have eternal life. Those enslaved by the Law do not inherit anything. They reside outside of God's favor in Christ.

Paul sums up his allegory with a promise to us. [**v31**] He concludes that we should see ourselves as heirs through the promise. Why would we want to be slaves, born of Hagar, under the Law? We are free, born of Jerusalem above by the promise of Christ.

Chapter 5

After the personal appeal and the allegory of the children of Hagar and Sarah in chapter 4, Paul expounds upon the meaning of the Gospel, the freedom Christ won for us.

[v1] This is an astounding verse. It seems redundant, but it is not. Freedom is a state we live in continuously. Freedom is not submitting to the Law at any point in time, which is slavery. We are to use our freedom freely.

Freedom is not just an idea. Liberty is living the Christian life. For freedom, we were freed. "We" means that the Gospel offers freedom to all. Christ did it. His victory over sin and the Devil is our freedom. The promise delivers it and creates faith.

Our world defines freedom very differently than Scripture does. Here in this world, liberty is doing as one pleases. It means having no restrictions or responsibilities, but to think and say and do what we want is actually slavery, since we can only sin, according to the flesh. Worldly freedom is misused so that it leads to death and hell. We have seen a long struggle for civil liberties and rights in our society, but these are enacted by government laws and judicial decisions. They do not free, but use force to enact and promote a worldly sort of freedom for some. No law can give the freedom to know and love the Father.

How many celebrities have all the worldly and financial freedom one could want? But in trying to be free, some fall into the slavery of addiction and even kill themselves, because their supposed freedom is not freeing at all. Worldly freedom is a powerful illusion, but it does not lead to God. The elementary principles of this world cannot give the freedom that Christ earned by His stripes and death.

God works much differently than man expects Him to. He frees the conscience by the forgiveness of sins. We are free to love Him and not hate Him, though sinning is all the flesh can do. As His children, we have the Spirit. This is a spiritual freedom, not of laws and worldly government, but of the Spirit within us. This Satan hates above all things, so he works to bring us back again into slavery. *Be sober-minded; be watchful. Your adversary the devil prowls around like a roaring lion, seeking someone to devour. Resist him, firm in your faith, knowing that the same kinds of suffering are being experienced by your brotherhood throughout the world* (1 Pet. 5:8–9). Satan works to turn our attention away from the eternal Gospel, like he did with Job.

In 2:4 Paul said that false doctrine denied the pure freedom bestowed by the Gospel: *false brothers slipped in to spy out our freedom that we have in Christ Jesus, so that they might bring us into slavery.* The Gospel is not a pit stop on the road to more laws, demands, and slavery.

The verb form of "freedom" means "to set or make free from slavery." It is being a son before God, an heir by the promise. Christ frees us "to make our conscience free and joyful and unafraid of the wrath to come," as Luther says [*Galatians*, 4]. Faith is freedom to know and love God.

How we use our freedom is a controversial topic. We are free, but freedom never hurts another person. We are not free to sin, but, in the Spirit, we want to fulfill the Law spiritually. Love is the fulfillment of the Law. *Now the Lord is the Spirit, and where the Spirit of the Lord is, there is freedom* (2 Cor. 3:17). The new man uses freedom in love to serve others and do what is God-pleasing. God chose us, redeemed us, and takes care of us, all because of His generous will. This not something to just be talked about, but to live and enjoy—to actually be free. The Gospel leads to this blessed state we live in before our Father in heaven. Freedom is now, as we live by faith. We access this freedom by the glorious Gospel.

Freedom is not doing whatever feels good—that is the world's definition of freedom. Paul says the opposite in this verse. We must stand still, resisting the false freedom to do works in slavery. The verb for "stand firm" can mean just "to stand," but here it speaks of a fixed position. We are to resist the allure of returning to the Law. Like political freedom, spiritual freedom requires constant preservation. The Word of God can be lost so quickly, as the Galatians sadly demonstrated. *Be watchful, stand firm in the faith, act like men, be strong* (1 Cor. 16:13).

"Stand firm" is an imperative. It is not a legalistic command, as though we could create freedom. It speaks of retaining the true freedom found only in our Lord Jesus. The Gospel is not a matter of grammar, but of being in Christ, free from our many sins and dead to the flesh. Not everything that sounds free and evangelical is actually freeing, making one an heir by God's promise. Outside of the righteousness in the promise, there is no freedom. There is no moving beyond faith.

Paul often exhorts his parishioners to stand firm. There are lots of ways to fall away and lose salvation, but only in Christ do we live to God. It is not easy, and entails suffering and a struggle. There is always a need to stand firm against Satan, false doctrine, and sin. *Therefore, my brothers, whom I love and long for, my joy and crown, stand firm thus in the Lord, my beloved* (Phil. 4:1).

As it says in 1 Pet. 2:16, *Live as people who are free, not using your freedom as a cover-up for evil, but living as servants of God.* We are not free to use our freedom to sin, but only to love God. Neither is freedom inactive, doing nothing; it serves the neighbor in love, as the Spirit impels us by God's pure love. This a magnificent teaching, which Paul discusses more in some of his other books, especially Rom. and 1 Cor.

The "again" highlights their former yoke of slavery, before the Gospel came to free them. It reminds them of when they were enemies of God and slaves to sin. Why would they want to return? This puts the enticement and purpose of the Law in the right perspective. We think we must do something for God, to show Him we have changed or deserve His love. But whoever *has* to do those things is not really free. God's love is not dependent on us—it has nothing to do with the Law. We did not free ourselves, but Christ set us free.

We are not to be under a yoke of slavery. While Paul does not use the "under" preposition here, it certainly fits. We are not to be under the control of the Law—subject to the yoke of slavery again. A "yoke" is a physical restraint laid on animals. Jesus did not come to harshly control us as beasts of burden, but to give life: *For my yoke is easy, and my burden is light* (Mt. 11:30). He came to bear our sins, not force those already under the Law into further submission.

After Paul has carefully said that submitting to the Law is slavery, he tells us not to be slaves again. To be a slave is to fear the wrath of God—the opposite of faith. Slavery brings wrath, because it is opposed to the freedom of Christ. Under the Law, in slavery, we are condemned for our sin. There is no forgiveness in the Law. It says: "do it, or else you will die." If the Law is relied upon for freedom, then one does not have Christ or His forgiveness. The Law can only enslave sinners. The yoke of the Law is not to be tolerated—to do so is to reject Christ. He sacrificed His own body for us. Only in this promise that God died for us is there freedom and life. Freedom is the result of our justification by God. He grants it. It is not something that we take by force.

Paul does not ask a rhetorical question here to express his disbelief over their actions, as he does earlier in the letter. He directly commands them, and us, who now have this freedom. We are to guard it and stay in it, because it is so precious.

Paul is even more direct in v2. [**v2**] It starts with "look" or "see," meaning we are to pay attention. Paul puts all his authority behind it: "I myself, Paul." Remember that Paul is speaking as Christ's called emissary, which is laid out at the very beginning of chapter 1. All these words of Paul are the Lord's words. He speaks to "you"—signifying the Galatians—but also to any who are tempted by the Law—truly all of us.

Here Paul finally makes circumcision, which is the beginning of outward obedience to the Law, an explicit issue. Circumcision was initiation into the Mosaic Law. It was to be done on the eighth day, not right after birth. Paul has not mentioned it as an issue among the Galatians thus far. He first dealt with the bigger issue of the Law itself. Of course, the moral law is still in effect. Then, he speaks of the elementary principles of the world and the outward laws that deal only with physical matter, not the heart. Circumcision falls under that category.

The text has "accept circumcision," but "accept" is not in the text; it is an interpretation. "If you are circumcised, Christ is of no value to you, he cannot help you." This seems too drastic. How can it literally be true? Many newborn males are still circumcised today at hospitals. Can Christ not help over 50% of the male population in the U.S. who are circumcised? Paul is addressing a specific situation, one that exists today, but not regarding circumcision. When the Gospel is being exterminated by legalistic commands, one can by no means submit. To do so is to give up Christ and faith. This kind of earthly freedom is actually slavery.

The issue is the freedom of Christ, which only comes in the one, true Gospel. The ESV translation has "accept." For the Galatians to be circumcised would mean an acceptance of the whole Jewish Law. This is the same religious understanding a Jew would have of the act of circumcision today. Under this pressure to keep the Law, circumcision was a denial of Christ. It would be submitting to slavery. Remember that this letter is written to Christians, those who heard the Gospel and believed it. The false teaching present among the Galatians made circumcision no longer a neutral, free work. The act of circumcision was itself a denial of Christ and the loss of freedom for the Galatians.

It speaks of a "benefit," which means "an advantage, help, or that which does something." Christ died for all, but, outside of faith, we are under the Law in slavery. Christ's salvation, won for all, does not help without faith. The same word is used in 1 Cor. 14:6: *Now, brothers, if I come to you speaking in tongues, how will I benefit you unless I bring you some revelation or knowledge or prophecy or teaching?* A Word of God in an unknown language cannot help us, even if we hear it many times. So, also, if a man submits to the Law and its works, Christ does not profit him. Salvation still stands, but he personally does not have freedom. He does not possess it, even though it is offered. This application of the Gospel, God's justification of us, happens in time, through faith in the promise.

The teaching of universalism, that all are saved, regardless of faith, is false. Christ did die for all, saving the world, objectively. However, faith is the personal appropriation of this salvation. The promise is given to a person, so he is transferred into God's kingdom and truly puts on Christ in faith. This happens through the Word, and Baptism also has the command and Word of God with it, through which the Spirit creates faith. One *under* the Law is not *in* Christ, so He is of no benefit to that person.

Because no one's faith is strong or whole, we do not enjoy the fullness of our freedom. However, freedom is something God grants. It is more than a feeling or realization, but since we are by nature of the Law, we are tempted to rely on our deeds before God. Paul's forceful statement here should be kept in the heart, so that we rely on the promise of help from Christ, as it says in v1. This is the faith in which we are to live.

From the first verse of this letter, Paul laid claim to being an apostle of God. He is speaking from his position as one called by God to speak His word. That authority is over every Christian and preacher today, since through these words God speaks to us.

In v3, Paul clarifies what circumcision means. **[v3]** Paul testifies to the obligation of circumcision as a command of God. Today, most non-Jews who circumcise do so for reasons of tradition or hygiene. It is not a specifically religious rite for non-Jews today. The principle remains true, though; Paul is addressing the Galatians, who have Judaizers in their midst. To accept any aspect of the Law as part of justification is to restrict the freedom of the Gospel and rob of the Spirit.

Again, "accept" is an interpolation—it is not in the text. "Every" excepts no one. Because the Gospel was so threatened by this Jewish legalism, there could be no circumcision done in freedom. In different circumstances it is certainly possible. Paul had his understudy, Timothy, circumcised in a completely different context: *Paul wanted Timothy to accompany him, and he took him and circumcised him because of the Jews who were in those places, for they all knew that his father was a Greek* (Acts 16:3). This was done in freedom, since the Gospel was not under attack at this point. Timothy was circumcised in freedom to remove a human obstacle that might have prevented the Gospel from being heard. It was not an act of submission to the Law, but an act of love. It was a very generous one, considering the invasive nature of the physical act of circumcision.

The Greek word for "obligated" can also mean "debtor," one who owes a debt. To submit as a slave to the Law is to lose freedom. In other words, there is no choice. A slave must obey. If justification is based on circumcision, then it requires observance of all the Law's ceremonies and works. Then, no grace remains, for one under the Law is outside of Christ. The Law only produces slavery.

But, even for non-Jewish laws, the Law cannot be used piecemeal. It demands holiness, perfection, and complete submission to God's will. Paul uses "debtor" positively of himself in regards to other people, but not to God. *I am under obligation* [a debtor] *both to Greeks and to barbarians, both to the wise and to the foolish* (Rom. 1:14). There is no debt to God. He forgives us our debts as we forgive our debtors, which is a different version of the Lord's Prayer found in Mt. 6:12.

One detail that is not obvious in English is that the word for "debtor" or "obligation" in Greek is derived from the word for "advantage" or "help." They look similar and evidently have a common root. This wordplay from Paul contrasts the benefit of Christ, which is freedom, with slavery, the inability of the Law to save.

The command of the Law is displayed in the verb "do." The Law requires full obedience, not just a little. It condemns any incompleteness in regards to God's will. The one who is under the Law is required to fulfill the whole thing. To become Ishmael, after being Isaac, is the worst way to become a slave. It gives "backsliding" a whole new meaning.

In v4, Paul connects the Law and the Gospel. They are both ways to be justified, but only in the Gospel did Christ do the Law for us all. [v4] The basic meaning of the word translated "severed" is "idle" or "useless." It is used as "separation" in Rom. 7:2: *For a married woman is bound by law to her husband while he lives, but if her husband dies she is released* [freed, severed] *from the law of marriage.* Or, again: *When I became a man, I gave up* [ceased] *childish ways* (1 Cor. 13:11). Those who insist on circumcision, who thereby obligate themselves to keep the whole Law, are separated from Christ. They have put our Lord, who rose from the dead, aside. He is useless to them. While the Bible contains much Law, it is not commands that bring anyone to God. Demands of the Law must be kept separate from the Gospel, the promise which gives the Spirit.

We are not to read the Scriptures as Jews, hearing the Law and reasoning to ourselves that this is what we must do to be saved and make God happy. Instead, we read the Law in light of Jesus' fulfillment of it and His blessed taking of the curse upon Himself. We are free from the burden and curse, but not from God's will. Christians in the Spirit see the Law from the standpoint of freedom, unlike all other natural people, who do not know the Gospel.

The second person is used in this verse: "you." You cannot have Christ and seek to do the Law, because you cannot be justified in two ways. A person is either free or a slave. Our justification, the righteousness given by God, is whole. We are either forgiven in Christ or guilty outside of Him. There is no partial freedom.

225

"Fallen" implies a downward, negative descent. After faith in the Gospel, going back to the Law is most shameful. No one under the Law has God's favor or grace. They are not justified. This is a state before God. It does not help that they once had the Spirit—they are now lost, outside of Christ. This is a warning to us not to rest on our achievements, especially in religion. If we do so, we are relying on works and risk being severed from Christ. This is not God's will. We are to remain firm in the Gospel. It is possible to deny Christ and be damned after having true faith. We are to never find security in ourselves. There is no salvation apart from what Christ has done and continues to do for us. Only in grace is there freedom.

This is why Paul said one could not be circumcised: they would have done it to be justified by the Law, to submit to *doing*, which is opposed to *believing* in Christ. "Pick Christ or the Law," Paul is saying. These are the only two options. He dashes all attempts to add legal demands to the Gospel of freedom.

In contrast to the previous verse, here we find out how to live in grace. [**v5**] The verb translated "eagerly wait" means "to expect or look for." It is used twice in this Rom. 8:23–25 passage: *And not only the creation, but we ourselves, who have the firstfruits of the Spirit, groan inwardly as we wait eagerly for* [expect] *adoption as sons, the redemption of our bodies. For in this hope we were saved. Now hope that is seen is not hope. For who hopes for what he sees? But if we hope for what we do not see, we wait for* [expect] *it with patience.* We *expect* nothing but righteousness. That could be taken to mean that we are not righteous now, but, in God's sight, we are fully justified in Christ. The Gospel conveys this heavenly action to us, but we are not yet free of sin in mind and body. We possess as a child heir—we do not fully enjoy our inheritance, yet, it is real and will be completely realized at the Resurrection of the dead. Col. 1:5 speaks of *the hope laid up for you in heaven.*

Verse 5 describes the opposite of v4. Grace is in the Spirit, *by* faith or *of* faith. This faith is worked by the Spirit of Christ, and there is no faith without Him. We have hope because Christ has saved us and will complete our redemption from sin. This trust looks forward to eternal life. It is not simply an intellectual process. It is being filled with true, certain hope that God's love for us is true and will be fulfilled. God's promise delivers and creates this hope. Faith is not a work, but the passive reception of Christ and His declaration of righteousness. With it comes freedom, which the Spirit allows us to enjoy. Then we can know God and call Him Father, Abba.

In "the faith" we have the Spirit and all of God's favor. Faith exercises itself in difficulties, which are called "tribulations" in Scripture. We do not presently look like God's children and are certainly not treated like righteous people, yet He says that we are blameless. We live by His promise, not how things seem to us. Rom. 5:2–5 speaks clearly to this:

> *Through him we have also obtained access by faith into this grace in which we stand, and we rejoice in hope of the glory of God. Not only that, but we rejoice in our sufferings, knowing that suffering produces endurance, and endurance produces character, and character produces hope, and hope does not put us to shame, because God's love has been poured into our hearts through the Holy Spirit who has been given to us.*

We are not to depend on anything else in the world other than the hope we have in Christ. We eagerly expect what He promises.

Now Paul goes back to his original statement in v2. [v6] It is not avoiding circumcision that helps, either, but *in* Christ nothing counts for or can add to our righteousness.

This verse says that both states are powerless. Both circumcision and uncircumcision can do nothing by themselves. But if one is *in* Christ, he is righteous, lacking nothing before God. The outward act means nothing in Christ, but as a way to *be* in Christ, to seek to be justified, circumcision is death, as are all deeds of the Law.

Here we see the result of faith: it works in love. Faith is how we have Christ. In Christ, by faith, we love others, but in our flesh, which cannot believe, we do not love—we only sin. *And if I have prophetic powers, and understand all mysteries and all knowledge, and if I have all faith, so as to remove mountains, but have not love, I am nothing* (1 Cor. 13:2). There is no true love without the Spirit of God, who is love.

The danger is to think that love can create faith or be a reliable indicator of it, but love, as a burden we must fulfill, is simply a work of the Law that brings into slavery. Love, which is the true fulfillment of the Law, is the fruit of being justified. A faith that has no love is not faith at all.

This love is not directed towards God as an appeasing work; it is rather the completely normal fruit of faith. Phil. 1:15 describes the orientation of faith and love: *I have heard of your faith in the Lord Jesus and your love toward all the saints.* Faith is toward God, but love, because of God's love, is toward our fellow man, our neighbor. Only the freed man can love freely.

These two, faith and love, are often mentioned together in Scripture. The Spirit works love in us, and if we have faith, we have the Spirit. Love is not the cause of salvation, rather, it is faith which receives Christ. Love, though, is always present where there is faith. This is not a manufactured love, a fake passion, but genuine love, a product of the Spirit. *Let love be genuine. Abhor what is evil; hold fast to what is good. Love one another with brotherly affection. Outdo one another in showing honor. Do not be slothful in zeal, be fervent in spirit, serve the Lord* (Rom. 12:9–11). The Father does not need our love. It is the Gospel that establishes our relationship as sons to Him and delivers our inheritance in full. Yet, this faith is never apart from good works, done in love for those Christ places around us. The Spirit cannot be inactive, though the flesh always resists what pleases the Father. Whoever walks in the Spirit does the deeds of the Spirit.

The Spirit, who is present in believers, expresses Himself through love. This agape, self-sacrificing love we know nothing about in our flesh. The Spirit renews us and creates a new, spiritual man in us, so we can love in faith, but never apart from faith. We cannot show our faith, but we can show our love to those in need around us.

Luther says it very well:

> Faith is a divine work in us. It changes us and makes us to be born anew of God. It kills the old Adam and makes altogether different people, in heart and spirit and mind and powers, and it brings with it the Holy Spirit. Oh, it is a living, busy, active, mighty thing, this faith. And so it is impossible for it not to do good works incessantly. It does not ask whether there are good works to do, but before the question rises, it has already done them, and is always at the doing of them ["Preface to Romans"].

A free person does not seek to remain in slavery to sin. Instead, he seeks to do the Father's will. A Christian free in the Gospel does not become God-like, deciding what is right and wrong. The Law remains God's will, but it is viewed in the Spirit, from the vantage point of Christ, who is our righteousness. So the Law has nothing to do with righteousness, yet much to do with Christians who are not entirely renewed. Due to the battle of the old and new man within the individual Christian, this division of faith and works is not easily made within us. Without the comfort of the full Gospel, the Law curses and will be used against the freedom Christ earned.

[v7] Paul uses the running analogy several times, including here. The Galatians began well. They started by receiving the Gospel with joy. There are no awards in the Olympics for leading the first one-fourth or one-third of a race. Only the order at the finish line counts. If a runner leads the whole race and gets passed right at the end by a runner with a great kick, he is not the winner. *Do you not know that in a race all the runners run, but only one receives the prize? So run that you may obtain it* (1 Cor. 9:24). Paul says that nothing was wrong at the beginning, but someone is now pulling them off-track. They are not running well right now, but the race has not yet ended.

Paul applied the running analogy to the Christian life and to himself earlier in this very letter: *I went up because of a revelation and set before them (though privately before those who seemed influential) the gospel that I proclaim among the Gentiles, in order to make sure I was not running or had not run in vain* (2:2). The race is not over until the finish line is reached, that is, until we fall sleep in Christ. At that point there is no more need to struggle with doubt or against Satan's temptations. The victory is ours—there is no more hope, because, at the Last Day, our hope will be given to us. We will see Christ as He is and receive our glorious inheritance.

Notice it asks "who," not "what," hindered them. "Hinder" could also be rendered "impede" or "thwart." It can also mean "to cut into." One commentator translates it with the literal meaning: "You were running well. Who cut in on you . . . ?" [Lenski, 263]. This fits perfectly with the running analogy. A runner is cut off when another runner goes right in front of him, forcing him to slow down, lest their legs get tangled and both go down. In heavy traffic, the same situation can occur, when one car cuts in on another. To avoid a certain accident one must slow down or get out of the way. Whether Paul meant that exactly or not, it does fit well with the situation he is describing. You have not yet reached the finish line, or you would not be reading this. So do not let up—the end is still ahead. We can lose Christ, while the goal is still ahead of us.

The truth is the Gospel. The Galatians had heard the basics, but they were listening to teachers who made the Law into a partial power of God, replacing the Gospel.

"Obeying" is a word to us which denotes outward conformity. It is not a good fit here. The Greek word means "to be convinced or persuaded to believe something." In this context, "to follow" would fit better, since a runner follows a path. He does not "obey" a running course. The New American Bible translates it exactly this way: *You were running well; who hindered you from following* [the] *truth?* But "obey" has a long tradition in this verse and is pretty much universal in English translations. "Obey" can also mean "to follow directions," but, when applied to the Gospel, it is not the best translation. It can be understood correctly as referring to the doctrine which preserves Christ, not just bare commands.

The same verb for "obey" is used in Mt. 27:43 to describe an insult against Jesus. When He was on the cross, it was said: *He trusts in* [obeys] *God.* This persuasion or conviction in the truth leads naturally to the next verse. [**v8**] The Greek word for "persuasion" is related to the verb translated "hinder" in the previous verse: "Who hindered you from being persuaded of the truth. This persuasion is not from the one who calls you." If it is not of God, it is of the Devil, who is an active, evil force in this world. This is the only time the Greek noun for "persuasion" is used in the New Testament. It is derived from the verb in v7. One expert claims that this is the first known use of this word in Greek literature. This means that Paul, in the Spirit, might have coined it fresh for this letter. How were the Galatians persuaded? By being made much of—by flattery. *They make much of you, but for no good purpose. They want to shut you out, that you may make much of them. It is always good to be made much of for a good purpose, and not only when I am present with you* (4:17–18). He calls them back to the race Christ laid out for all of us.

Although we like to think of ourselves as independent thinkers, we are weak and shallow sheep. Without the Spirit and Christ's Word, we would wander off the cliff and cling to the Law as our savior. Christ is the good shepherd: *When he has brought out all his own, he goes before them, and the sheep follow him, for they know his voice. A stranger they will not follow, but they will flee from him, for they do not know the voice of strangers* (Jn. 10:4–5). We are not beyond simple correction which calls us back to the Lord's race.

Paul states a general truth. [v9] Leaven is yeast, an organism that multiplies very rapidly, allowing for exponential growth. We discussed this phrase previously in 1:2 on page 9. Here it refers to false doctrine and false persuasion. It cannot be tolerated. It is like saying you have a little gangrene: because it spreads, it must be dealt with, perhaps even by amputation, to save the rest of the body. Sometimes a congregation must amputate itself, so that not all are infected with false doctrine. Error due to weakness is one thing, if correction is accepted, but false teachers are by no means to be tolerated. If it can happen in Paul's church, it can certainly happen in yours. We must stand firm in the truth, being sure of what we have learned.

The word "leaven," here, alludes to dough kept aside, containing the desired yeast. It was reserved for the next batch. Because yeast multiples so quickly, a bread yeast can be used indefinitely, but here, the evil teaching infects everything. The Law seems harmless enough, but if it is mixed in with the Gospel, as a cause of justification, then Christ is of no benefit to us.

The "lump" is that which is mixed and kneaded together. When referring to bread, it means dough without yeast. In Rom. 9:21, the same word is used for a lump of clay: *Has the potter no right over the clay, to make out of the same lump one vessel for honorable use and another for dishonorable use?*

"Leavens" describes the multiplying activity of yeast. Yeast cells divide rapidly, causing exponential growth. In fermentation, the cells make carbon dioxide, which forms bubbles in beer and homemade soda. It also causes bread to rise. Yeast naturally do this, just as false doctrine naturally endangers faith.

False teaching, here, is said to have a real power. It draws away from Christ. It infects and multiplies rapidly throughout the whole batch. Nowhere does it say that the Gospel leavens the whole batch. It is resisted by our flesh, and faith encounters numerous difficulties in this world, so it seems that no one believes. False teaching is like a wildfire, threatening to overtake the world. The whole history of Christian theology shows this. It always looks like the Church is about to collapse, due to one heresy or another, but Christ sustains His Church. There is always a remnant, so that the Gospel is never completely extinguished.

Before this letter was read, it must have seemed like circumcision was a small matter. "All we need is Jesus," we hear in our day. The problem is that this attitude often leaves one with nothing, not even Jesus. Any error in doctrine eventually leads back to our relationship with Christ, our justification in Him. Fundamentalism is usually correct insofar as it goes, but, by only defending particular "fundamental" articles of the truth, the rest of Christ's truth is left open to attack on many fronts. It is not enough to defend just the front door. The back door and windows must also be secured. Satan is no a fool, he knows he can best attack us in the areas we perceive to be minor points.

Doctrinal indifference is a great danger for Christians. Paul uses all sorts of illustrations and analogies to prove this exact point to us. Yeast is a great analogy because it works rapidly, even though we cannot see it without a microscope. Billions of yeast cells multiply out of sight, even though it looks like nothing is happening. So it is with unchecked false doctrine.

[v10] Despite Paul's anxiety about the Galatians being unformed, he expresses confidence here. The same verb for "persuaded" or "confident" is also used, though in a different voice, in v7. He can be so confident only in the Lord, not in himself or in the Galatians.

Paul is convinced that they will think no other way. The false teachers are not called out by name, but their condemnation is assured. Those who lead away from Christ in God's name are worse than all the criminals in the world. They deserve swift judgment. Teachers of God are held to a stricter account: *Not many of you should become teachers, my brothers, for you know that we who teach will be judged with greater strictness* (Jam. 3:1).

The false teachers seem to be flattering, but, in reality, they are harassing and troubling the Galatians. They should not be tolerated, but judged. It is likely that some did not agree and wanted a diversity of gospels. Division must occur, if the truth is to stand. It does no good to play Mr. Nice Guy and think offense over the Gospel can be avoided. The false teacher will bear condemnation. It does not ensure his damnation, but for the sake of others his false teaching cannot be tolerated. This is why Paul corrected Peter publicly, as he relates in chapter 2.

We also should be wary of those who say that any point of doctrine is small or insignificant. All doctrine supports the truth of Christ and faith. Luther understood this very well:

> doctrine must be distinguished from life. Doctrine is heaven, life is earth. In life there is sin, error, uncleanness, and misery, mixed, as the saying goes, "with vinegar." Here we should condone, tolerate, be deceived, trust, hope, and endure all things (1 Cor. 13:7); here the forgiveness of sins should have complete sway, provided sin and error are not defended. But just as there is no error in doctrine, so there is no need for the forgiveness of sins. Therefore there is no comparison at all between doctrine and life, "One dot" of doctrine is worth more than "heaven and earth" (Mt. 5:18), therefore we do not permit the slightest offense against it [*Galatians*, 41].

It is never loving to cut one off from the source of God's love: Christ, who comes in the teaching of the Gospel.

Paul turns to himself, explaining that his mistreatment is proof of the correctness of his position. [**v11**] He contrasts his situation to that of the false teachers. They are well-received and lauded, but Paul is persecuted, as we have detailed previously. Paul formerly persecuted the truth: *They only were hearing it said, "He who used to persecute us is now preaching the faith he once tried to destroy"* (Gal. 1:23). As an apostle of Christ, Paul suffered much persecution—the exact same kind he dished out when he lived under the Law. Right after Paul's conversion on the road, the Lord spoke to Ananias: *Go, for he is a chosen instrument of mine to carry my name before the Gentiles and kings and the children of Israel. For I will show him how much he must suffer for the sake of my name* (Acts 9:15–16). Paul boasts of his suffering and weakness, to magnify his Gospel. *If I must boast, I will boast of the things that show my weakness. The God and Father of the Lord Jesus, he who is blessed forever, knows that I am not lying. At Damascus, the governor under King Aretas was guarding the city of Damascus in order to seize me, but I was let down in a basket through a window in the wall and escaped his hands* (2 Cor. 11:30–33). And again in 2 Cor. 12:9–10: *But he said to me, "My grace is sufficient for you, for my power is made perfect in weakness." Therefore I will boast all the more gladly of my weaknesses, so that the power of Christ may rest* *upon me. For the sake of Christ, then, I am content with weaknesses, insults, hardships, persecutions, and calamities. For when I am weak, then I am strong.*

The incredible truth is that suffering is a sign of God's favor and the possession of the true Gospel. Being treated poorly in the world is a sign you are on God's side, if you suffer for His name and doctrine. The world is at odds with Christ, it cannot stand Him. It must hate Him. In faith, suffering becomes holy to God, a sign of His love, given in Christ. We are privileged to suffer with Him.

If Paul had preached circumcision, he would have been accepted by the Judaizers, but his reputation would have suffered. The ESV seems to indicate that Paul at one point preached circumcision. As a Jew, he no doubt trusted in it as a work of the Law, but to proclaim or preach is a Christian thing. The word translated "still" should be understood as "in addition," not a continuation of the same proclamation. This is not the normal meaning of this Greek adverb, but Heb. 11:36 uses it in a similar way: *Others suffered mocking and flogging, and even* [furthermore; still] *chains and imprisonment.* The "still" in the two clauses shows a contrast, not a similarity.

Paul asks a simple question: "Why am I being persecuted?" This is his proof, his divine evidence, so, we are not to fear extreme suffering or unfair treatment by the world. It becomes a holy sign that we possess the true Gospel. There must be divisions, offense, and false teachers. Christ did not come to bring peace between men, but a sword.

Paul makes this statement in his second letter to Timothy:

> *You, however, have followed my teaching, my conduct, my aim in life, my faith, my patience, my love, my steadfastness, my persecutions and sufferings that happened to me at Antioch, at Iconium, and at Lystra—which persecutions I endured; yet from them all the Lord rescued me. Indeed, all who desire to live a godly life in Christ Jesus will be persecuted, while evil people and impostors will go on from bad to worse, deceiving and being deceived* (3:10–13).

It is no coincidence that the three cities mentioned—Antioch (the lessor), Iconium, and Lystra—were in Galatia, which is also the birthplace of Timothy.

Persecution can be physical, such as imprisonment, beating, the taking of possessions, and even death. Some around the world face this now. We are starting to see persecution of a different kind here in America. Christians are mocked as ignorant simpletons. Our biblical positions and morals are ridiculed and legislated against. The world pressures us to compromise, to not hold the full truth, but, as it states in this verse, the point at which we are tempted to compromise is the very one on which we need to stand most firm. If Paul had caved on this one little issue of the ceremonial law, all would have been lost. Christ would not have benefited them.

The next phrase explains what would have happened if Paul had compromised the truth. The scandal of the cross would be removed. But his persecution showed he had stood firm. "Offense," in Greek, is "scandal." It can mean "a trap or ensnarement." Paul, in Rom. 11:9–10, quotes the Old Testament: *Let their table become a snare and a trap, a stumbling block* [scandal] *and a retribution for them; let their eyes be darkened so that they cannot see, and bend their backs forever.* In 1 Cor. 1:22–23, Paul names the Gospel as a scandal to the Jews: *For Jews demand signs and Greeks seek wisdom, but we preach Christ crucified, a stumbling block* [scandal] *to Jews and folly to Gentiles, but to those who are called, both Jews and Greeks, Christ the power of God and the wisdom of God.* That God would suffer and die for them, to redeem them, was offensive to the Jews, but take away that and nothing is left—there is no Gospel to save.

We should not expect the Gospel to be loved by those perishing, whose minds are blinded. The goal is to suffer what we must, united with Christ by Baptism, trusting that we are justified and have a heavenly inheritance. If the Gospel is rejected and we suffer personally for it, we are blessed before God in heaven—great is the eternal reward. This goes for all Christians who suffer for the Word, but doubly for preachers of the offense of the cross. Christ says that this persecution is a reason to "rejoice and be glad" (Mt. 5:12).

The word for "removed" is the same one Paul used previously in this chapter. In v4, it is used to indicate separation from Christ. Paul keeps the offense before the world, which cannot love God, so that some will be saved. He does not preach circumcision, a work of the Law, but Christ. He can only preach the truth. The Spirit must turn hearts to the truth by faith. What causes others to fall into the trap of death—rejecting the Gospel—is also what saves us. Paul says in 2 Cor.

2:15–17 that the Gospel of Christ is viewed in one of two ways: *For we are the aroma of Christ to God among those who are being saved and among those who are perishing, to one a fragrance from death to death, to the other a fragrance from life to life. Who is sufficient for these things? For we are not, like so many, peddlers of God's word, but as men of sincerity, as commissioned by God, in the sight of God we speak in Christ.* Not just the Gospel smells like the aroma of death, but the ministers of it are a fragrance of death to death.

Paul then turns to the enemies of the Gospel. [**v12**] How strong are these words. He sees the true nature of their error and intentions. They are creating a disturbance. This word is also used in Scripture of political rebellion and revolt (Acts 21:38).

The first word, translated "I wish," is related to the word translated "debt" or "obligation" in v3. It is an interjection used to refer to an unobtainable wish. It could be translated "would that" or "if only."

The false teachers in Galatia based their teaching on cutting a member of the body—a purely outward work. Paul highlights the futility of this focus on material things. The elementary principles of the world deal only with the edges of the Law. Circumcision cannot help them, so they might as well go the whole way. It is an offensive statement, but it shows the passion and righteous anger of Paul, who cannot be misunderstood. He does not placate this false teaching, but rejects it with the harshest words.

The Greek word for "emasculate" means "to physically make a eunuch; to castrate." He is not advocating violence, but shows where the power of their teaching lies. The Greek word for circumcise alludes to cutting around (the foreskin). Cutting a little does not bring righteousness, and neither does cutting off everything—that is their religion of works. If these words had not come by the Holy Spirit, it would be difficult to imagine a Christian teacher saying this. Yet, this extreme phrase shows how little they understand the Scriptures or the Gospel. He adopts their simplistic, flawed way of thinking: "if a little bit is good, a lot is better." Paul says: "go all the way!" He wishes these false teachers would show their true colors. Christ bids us to care for His Word with the same earnestness.

Paul has made his point quite forcefully, so now he transitions to instruction and pastoral guidance. [**v13**] Freedom is not an opportunity for the flesh. The freedom Christ calls us to results in love for others. The word for "opportunity" in Greek can mean "the starting point or base of operations." It is used in 1 Tim. 5:14 as well: *So I would have younger widows marry, bear children, manage their households, and give the adversary no occasion* [opportunity] *for slander.* The Lord directs the spiritually renewed to the normal, biological tasks we were designed for, even though they seem completely limiting and unspiritual to the world.

The flesh misuses freedom. The body does not need freedom of movement. It should be restrained by responsibilities in this world, such as a job and family. Since the sinful flesh can only sin, physical freedom is not healthy. True freedom is in Christ, knowing that we are acceptable to the Father through the promise. We are free before God in our conscience. In v1 of this chapter, Paul contrasted the freedom of Christ to the slavery of the Law. Now he tells us how to use our freedom. We are not to disobey the Law. Sinning is not freedom, since it can only lead to slavery. As stated earlier in this letter: *Is the law then contrary to the promises of God? Certainly not! For if a law had been given that could give life, then righteousness would indeed be by the law* (3:21–22).

The world is full of this false freedom, which is really an opportunity for the flesh to sin against God. Remember that all sin is really against God. The joy we have in Christ—being free from the guilt of sins—results in love, not further sin. *Therefore I tell you, her sins, which are many, are forgiven—for she loved much. But he who is forgiven little, loves little* (Lk. 7:47). God the Son is the one who calls to this freedom. In freedom—by the Spirit, in faith—we give thanks to God by showing our love to others in need. *For God has not called us for impurity, but in holiness* (1 Thess. 4:7). So, while the Law defines holiness for us, it has no power to get us there. Yet to go against the Law, in lawlessness, is sin—a real rejection of Christ's will. There is no true contradiction between the Law and the Gospel. Jesus said to the woman caught in adultery: *Neither do I condemn you; go, and from now on sin no more* (Jn. 8:11).

The way to show off worldly freedom is to offend and shock others. But spiritual freedom—that is, love—sacrifices oneself to serve others, just like Christ did. The word for "serve" is the based on the root for "slave." In love, we volunteer ourselves to be slaves. We become slaves willingly in the freedom of Christ. Why? Because it is Christ's will, and He gives us neighbors to love. That sounds unappealing to the flesh, but this is what it means to be a living sacrifice (Rom. 12:1). True good works are done in joy and contentment by one free from sins and reconciled to God. False freedom is doing what the flesh wants and hurting others. True spiritual freedom for God's adopted sons is serving without regard for one's own pain or pleasure. It sees only the needs of others.

Luther said it very well in his treatise, titled "The Freedom of a Christian." Here is a taste of it:

> A Christian man is the most free lord of all, and subject to none [in faith before God]; a Christian man is the most dutiful servant of all, and subject to every one [in body, love, and the fruits of faith]. Although these statements appear contradictory, yet, when they are found to agree together, they will be highly serviceable to my purpose. They are both the statements of Paul himself, who says: "Though I be free from all men, yet have I made myself servant unto all" and: "Owe no man anything, but to love one another." Now love is by its own nature dutiful and obedient to the beloved object. Thus even Christ, though Lord of all things, was yet made of a woman; made under the law; at once free and a servant; at once in the form of God and in the form of a servant.

This end of this verse could be rendered: "through love be slaves to one another." The Law has nothing to do with gaining freedom, yet true freedom is never against the Law or the biological body Christ made. We were made to serve.

[v14] The Law cannot be fulfilled by those under it. It is holy, but we are not. Only in Christ can the Law even begin to be fulfilled. It happens through faith, in complete freedom from the burden of the Law. Without the freedom of Christ, there is no love, and therefore no fulfillment of the Law. However, this love always remains incomplete, and we never cease needing Christ's righteousness. The Law and our deeds are never something to be relied upon, for then we would no longer be free in the Spirit. Only the spiritual can understand this rightly: "all the law is comprehended in this."

For the whole law is fulfilled in one word—"word" meaning "saying" or "statement." This is not a new idea. This verse references Lev. 19:18, the summary of the second table of the Law: "you shall love your neighbor as yourself." While man thinks of the Law as individual divine rules, it is spiritual and unified. It demands the singular love of God in all the commands. If we love God, we will love others and not do the things which hurt our neighbor.

Only in the Spirit can we truly love and do any good works out of love for God. True good works, done in faith and according to the Law, are pleasing to our Father. Only the spiritually free can actually love their neighbors out of love for God, not for personal gain or attention. We see what true good works are here: not punishing ourselves or being slaves, but living to God in Christ and joyfully offering ourselves in freedom to those around us. Circumcision and the rest of the ceremonial law help no one. True service looks to the basic needs of others. Some examples of good works are: "teaching the erring; comforting the afflicted; encouraging the weak; . . . [bearing with your] neighbor's rude manners and impoliteness; putting up with annoyances, labors . . . ; obeying the [government]; treating one's parents with respect; being patient in the home with a cranky wife" and loud children [Luther, *Galatians*, 56]. This is simply doing what God has given you to do, no longer as a slave, but in the freedom of Christ.

This true agape love is not like worldly love, which is always performed under the Law and expects something in return. Paul describes this heavenly love that only the Spirit can bring us into: *Love is patient and kind; love does not envy or boast; it is not arrogant or rude. It does not insist on its own way; it is not irritable or resentful; it does not rejoice at wrongdoing, but rejoices with the truth. Love bears all things, believes all things, hopes all things, endures all things. Love never ends* (1 Cor. 13:4–8). This love cannot be weighed or measured, since it is of the Spirit. Our actions may not look any different to the neutral observer than selfish acts done in the spirit of slavery, but faith allows for true love and fear of the Father.

In a way, the Law actually requires Gospel freedom. Doing the Law by submitting to its demands is not the way to fulfill it. The Law, by itself, only has the power to expose sin and bring punishment. Instead, in Christ, we see the Law for what it is, without the curse, punishment, and fear of death into which we were born. So the Law is not a power here, which can only be negative, but God's simple will, which is to love others. We should teach and meditate upon the commandments, the true Law, not just to harass consciences, but to instruct Christians impelled by the Gospel. Christ did not come to destroy the Law. The Spirit is not given for us to do nothing or cast the Law aside. We are to teach the spiritual nature of the Law. This is using the Law lawfully, according to God's will—not as a yoke, but as the Father's will for His children. This is not a matter of being coerced by punishment. The Spirit, who is always active in faith, moves our conscience to exercise our bodies in love. To resist such works of love—by appeasing the flesh—is to resist the Spirit and His freedom, which is to reject Christ Himself. This struggle against the flesh remains as long as we live in the world. Yet, love that is not free in faith is no love at all. A freed man has nothing preventing him from being a willing slave to others.

True love is not a matter of talk, but action. *Little children, let us not love in word or talk but in deed and in truth* (1 Jn. 3:18). Paul proves again his point that the Law is not about material things, but love—true, divine love, which we do not have of ourselves in our flesh. This love we only know in Christ, who comes in the promise. The Gospel promise brings the Spirit and true spiritual freedom, which allows us to freely serve our neighbor as a slave. We are truly free, because God needs nothing from us, leaving us free to serve others. This true love is not manufactured, but from the Spirit, in those who are spiritual. No one can exhaust these words.

Next, Paul gives a practical warning to the Galatians. [v15] If they do not serve one another in love, in true freedom, they will consume one another. They are "biting" or "snapping," we might say, like a crocodile. Where the Gospel does not reign, there love will not reign either. This is the only time this Greek word for "bite" is used in the New Testament. It is used in classical Greek of a dog's bite.

The word for "devour" denotes consuming thoroughly. It is also used for fire, which consumes its fuel. The Galatians were not loving one another as brothers and sisters in Christ. This is no doubt because the Gospel was unclear in their minds. We must also be careful in our words and actions; while we cannot prevent offense, it is unloving to be an offense, scandal, or stumbling block. *So, whether you eat or drink, or whatever you do, do all to the glory of God. Give no offense to Jews or to Greeks or to the church of God, just as I try to please everyone in everything I do, not seeking my own advantage, but that of many, that they may be saved* (1 Cor. 10:31–33). We are freed by the Spirit to serve in love, not to indulge our sinful flesh.

The result of this biting and consuming is destruction and annihilation—that is, defeat. This treatment will expend them, so there can be no unity in the Spirit. Doctrinal problems manifest themselves visibly. How many practical problems are due to a doctrinal deficiency, a lack of true Christian freedom?

[v16] This is a clear statement that must be kept in the forefront our minds, if we are to understand God's Word. "Walk" refers to the Christian life. We are to be guided by the Spirit. We cannot complete that process, since we are fleshly, but we can fight against the Spirit, and even reject Him, by following the flesh into sin. Walking in the Spirit means being led by the Spirit in love toward others, not in a selfish, Law-based measurement of ourselves. The righteous in Christ are free from thinking of themselves and even their welfare.

"Desires" is actually singular in the Greek original. The singular desire or impulse of the flesh is to sin, which is the opposite of true love. *Therefore God gave them up in the lusts* [desires] *of their hearts to impurity, to the dishonoring of their bodies among themselves* (Rom. 1:24). Even our most sincere passions and thoughts are sinful and need to be repented of. There is nothing of the flesh for which Christ did not die. *We all once lived in the passions of our flesh, carrying out the desires of the body and the mind, and were by nature children of wrath, like the rest of mankind* (Eph. 2:3). We still have the flesh as a part of us, but in Christ the old is gone and the new is come, which is freedom in the Spirit. We are to walk in this new man of the Spirit, doing the works of God.

The word for "gratify" means "to complete or perfect." This is helpful, because we cannot stop lusting or desiring evil. We cannot change our fleshly hearts or make them spiritual by ourselves. Freedom in Christ, however, is not an opportunity to sin or to indulge the flesh, which is opposed to the Spirit. *For at one time you were darkness, but now you are light in the Lord. Walk as children of light* (Eph. 5:8). The Christian is no less tempted than the unbeliever, though the promise is given to use against, and live above, such passions of our flesh. We are called to walk in the Spirit, fighting against our flesh and its deadly passions.

What does the flesh desire? [**v17**] The verb "desire" is related to the "desire" noun in the previous verse, as it reads in English. It is nice when translations work out like that. However, flesh is the subject of the verb "desire." This speaks of the cravings of the flesh, its actions, which are always against the Spirit. We cannot say "the flesh desires against the Spirit," which is a literal rendering, but bad English. It could be rendered "the flesh sets its heart against the Spirit." The KJV has: *For the flesh lusteth against the Spirit.* The Wycliffe Bible from the 1300's has a very interesting translation: *For the flesh coveteth against the Spirit, and the Spirit against the flesh.* "Covet" is also used in the commandments: "you shall not *covet* your neighbor's house."

Regardless of the exact translation, this verse means that the flesh is in conflict with the Spirit. We are not to be surprised that we cannot stop our flesh. We must have sinful thoughts and actions, because we are still fleshly. Our flesh struggles against the Spirit. There is a battle in every Christian. See Rom. 7, where this "war" is described. Just as the flesh struggles against the Spirit, so the Spirit wars against the flesh. There is no verb in this second clause in Greek, but the same verb is understood to be repeated.

Though the flesh and the Spirit are powers within the believer, they are spoken of as two separate things. They are hostile, as natural enemies. In the Christian, both the Spirit and the flesh coexist, waging war against each other. This explains why God's children can sin so much—they are still fleshly. But they also are to do good works by the Spirit, for the Spirit cannot do otherwise. We are never philosophically free to do neutral things, as if we can freely choose good or evil, like picking food off a menu. We serve the flesh or the Spirit. One must be our master. Luther called this slavery "the bondage of the will," because we cannot will good or righteousness without the Spirit. It also recalls 3:13: *Are you so foolish? Having begun by the Spirit, are you now being perfected by the flesh?*

The result is that you cannot do the things that you desire or will. As Christians with the Spirit, having the mind of Christ, we want to please the Spirit—that is, to do good works, but we cannot accomplish this aim completely. We can double down and really try to do good, but we are hindered by the flesh. The answer is never to try to be good apart from the Spirit, as this would be only fleshly slavery to the Law. The only solution is to rely on the Gospel, through which the Spirit comes and strengthens us.

[**v18**] Our victory is not inside us yet, but in Christ who has promised us a glorious hope. *Little children, you are from God and have overcome them, for he who is in you is greater than he who is in the world* (1 Jn. 4:4).

We are in Christ, led by the Spirit. Though we are still fleshly, our sin is not counted against us. So sin is not our concern. We are to be dead to it, returning to our Baptism, which is simply returning to Christ's righteousness. We do not walk in sin, but in the freedom of the Spirit, not agonizing over every past sin, because we are righteous by Christ. The Law is not over us, threatening us with the curse of death, because Christ became our curse. We are to live by faith, not works. *For God has done what the law, weakened by the flesh, could not do. By sending his own Son in the likeness of sinful flesh and for sin, he condemned sin in the flesh, in order that the righteous requirement of the law might be fulfilled in us, who walk not according to the flesh but according to the Spirit* (Rom. 8:3–5).

We are not under any demands, but are free before God. This is our joy and peace. In faith, we ignore all sin in us, living by the Spirit. Only in the Spirit can love result, which is the fulfillment of the Law. *For if you live according to the flesh you will die, but if by the Spirit you put to death the deeds of the body, you will live* (Rom. 8:13). The more spiritual we are, the more sin rages against the Spirit, and the more helpless and dependent on the Spirit we become. We despair of ever being good and holy in our flesh, but since Christ is our holiness, we have been brought out from under the Law. We have nothing but thanks and love to give. The Law has nothing to do with our status, so long as we walk by the Spirit.

We constantly fail to walk by the Spirit. We fall into sin and gratify the flesh. But forget it—that sin has been crucified in Christ. We always have comfort in our Lord, who died for sins and rose to give us life in the Spirit. The Christian life is not about improving or growing according to the standard of the Law, it is about living in the Spirit, free from all laws, sins, flesh, and death. This is what putting the flesh to death means. The flesh does not get better, but we are not to be controlled or mastered by it. No, in the Spirit we resist temptation and seek Christ's good will.

Paul lists some examples of what the flesh does, which are seen in those not led by the Spirit. [**v19**] These fleshly works are visible, manifest, and evident—we can see them. We cannot see the flesh and the Spirit, but we can see their works, at times. These are the things by which we are to judge people. Many church constitutions use this passage to show who cannot be considered a member of the congregation. Because they are observable, we have a duty to warn, discipline, and possibly excommunicate, if repentance is not shown. Whoever does not resist sin and repent does not know Christ.

Those who continue in these works are condemned already. They cannot inherit the kingdom of God. Not because there is no forgiveness for them, but because the Spirit cannot rule where the flesh dominates. The Holy Spirit does not play second fiddle. The Spirit and the flesh are in conflict within the Christian, so we must assume that one sinning in these ways does not have the Spirit. They are advertising to the world that their flesh rules, not the Holy Spirit.

However, Christ's promises are still true. If anyone stops sinning, so that the flesh is not completely ruling, they should be forgiven and welcomed back into the Church. The goal of all Christian discipline, including excommunication, is repentance. There is a parallel passage in 1 Cor. 6:

> *Or do you not know that the unrighteous will not inherit the kingdom of God? Do not be deceived: neither the sexually immoral, nor idolaters, nor adulterers, nor men who practice homosexuality, nor thieves, nor the greedy, nor drunkards, nor revilers, nor swindlers will inherit the kingdom of God. And such were some of you. But you were washed, you were sanctified, you were justified in the name of the Lord Jesus Christ and by the Spirit of our God.*

As long as these works of the flesh continue, there can be no life in the Spirit. That fleshly person has been severed from Christ. This speaks of public sins, not those hidden in the heart, of which all Christians are guilty. Those who advertise their hard, unturning hearts must not receive the Gospel. The Law must accuse them until they turn from their sinful ways and seek life in the promise. We too have sinned, but, in Christ's freedom, we do not continue in slavery to sin. Yet, the Law must serve its accusing function for our entire lives—as long as the flesh is still active and sinning.

What kinds of sins are these? They are public, visible sins. The first one, sexual immorality, is from the same Greek root we get the word "pornography." It denotes adultery and fornication. God made our bodies for holiness, not to be dishonored with someone we are not joined to in marriage. Divorce for an unbiblical reason is a great sin. Society's laws do not change God's holy Law. Jesus said exactly this: *But I say to you that everyone who divorces his wife, except on the ground of sexual immorality, makes her commit adultery, and whoever marries a divorced woman commits adultery* (Mt. 5:32). Only an unbeliever breaks the holy bond God Himself creates between male and female. *But if the unbelieving partner separates, let it be so. In such cases the brother or sister is not enslaved. God has called you to peace* (1 Cor. 7:15). A Christian, by definition, does not want this fleshly action of divorce, which results in adultery. It violently rips apart both husband and wife. It is always a sin against the holy God. So, the Spirit can never lead one to sin against marriage, which Christ calls holy.

While all people lust and are dissatisfied with their spouse at times, this speaks of the bodily act which breaks marriage. But even the unmarried do not escape. God calls them to be chaste. They are not to pretend to be married or indulge in sexual pleasure without the lifelong commitment of marriage. Our culture despises celibacy, virginity, and marriage, but God created these divine estates for our good. The Spirit leads us not to walk according to the world, but His holy will.

The same word in Greek for "sexuality immorality" is used in this passage for incest:

> It is actually reported that there is sexual immorality among you, and of a kind that is not tolerated even among pagans, for a man has his father's wife. And you are arrogant! Ought you not rather to mourn? Let him who has done this be removed from among you. For though absent in body, I am present in spirit; and as if present, I have already pronounced judgment on the one who did such a thing. When you are assembled in the name of the Lord Jesus and my spirit is present, with the power of our Lord Jesus, you are to deliver this man to Satan for the destruction of the flesh, so that his spirit may be saved in the day of the Lord (1 Cor. 5:1–5).

Paul is clear that people who do such things and refuse to stop have no fellowship with Christ, despite whatever Christian facade they put up.

Impurity and sensuality are next on the list. We are not to treat our bodies as objects of sexual power for mass distribution. The world tells women that sexuality is their power over men, so some use their body as a weapon, in an immodest fashion. Homosexuality falls in this group of sins, too, because that is plainly not how God made our bodies to fit together. Those who practice such sin must use parts as they were not intended to be used—in an unnatural way, which is punishment in itself.

> *For this reason God gave them up to dishonorable passions. For their women exchanged natural relations for those that are contrary to nature; and the men likewise gave up natural relations with women and were consumed with passion for one another, men committing shameless acts with men and receiving in themselves the due penalty for their error. And since they did not see fit to acknowledge God, God gave them up to a debased mind to do what ought not to be done* (Rom. 1:26–28).

God confirms, as punishment, such people in their sin. They will by no means escape judgment.

We live in sensual times. Nearly-nude figures are everywhere. "Sex sells" is the mantra, and we are sold a lot. But we are to be satisfied where God has placed us, whether married or unmarried. If those single cannot control their lust, they should seek to be married. The married should not treat their spouses as objects of lust, although there is always sin, even in the valid marital act. We live in Christ, not by our works.

We are to live self-controlled lives, not following our passion and lusts—that is not why we were given the Spirit. It is not good to avoid marriage, if we burn with lust and are led to behave as the sexually immoral. This is not a work of the Spirit, but of the flesh. This is why marriage is unavoidable for most. Modesty, however, is demanded of our less presentable parts. What we look like does matter. Ham was cursed because he saw his father Noah's nakedness (Gen. 9:22–25).

After the three words for sexual sins, which are some of the strongest works of the flesh in the young, Paul lists other sins that relate to the visible, social realm. [v20] These are all around us in the world.

Idolatry is clear. We are not to worship anything man-made as God, who is spirit. Whether idols or art, God is not found in bare, earthly material, but in the Gospel of Christ. However, we do not have to fear even three-dimensional art. The Gospel gives true knowledge of God and dispels idolatry, which is always a matter of the heart. The material, elementary principles are free to one free in Christ.

Sorcery, or witchcraft, refers to accessing a supernatural power apart from the Spirit and God's Word. Black magic, astrology, and Ouija boards are not of God, nor are we to seek Him there. To go outside preaching and His Word for spiritual power is satanic. It cannot lead to faith, since there is no promise outside of God's Word.

The next word, "enmity," can mean today an internal hatred, but here it means "public hostilities and feuds." Think of the Hatfields and McCoys. Their war started over something very small, but devolved into many murders. We are not to pour gas on conflicts and escalate them. No one is truly loving, so we can never completely overlook wrongdoing, but to bring on this sort of enmity publicly is completely of the flesh. The Spirit moves us to die to such outbursts and unloving words. We should seek to get along with everyone, since Christ loved them enough to die for them, too, even if they do not act likewise.

"Strife" can "mean debate, discord, or quarrels." We are not to use our mouths to inflame each other or to bite and consume as in v15. Division has a place, when it is over the truth of Christ's doctrine, but it should not be over human controversies and battles over words. *Charge them before God not to quarrel about words, which does no good, but only ruins the hearers* (2 Tim. 2:14). This word "strife" can be understood also as self-centeredness or ambition, which naturally divides.

"Jealously" is practically a virtue today. We are told to want what others have and are programmed by advertising to covet the latest and greatest products. *Keep your life free from love of money, and be content with what you have, for he has said, "I will never leave you nor forsake you"* (Heb. 13:5).

"Rage" is in our flesh. It is visible in little children who must be taught not to throw themselves on the floor or hit others when they do not get their way. The heart does not change, but we are not to give free range to our fleshly, base emotions

"Rivalries, dissensions, and divisions" fit together. Taking sides over what Christ does not demand is not loving in freedom. The Spirit unites in Christ. He does not divide into political parties that pit Christians against each other. Christ's body cannot be divided. The Greek word for "rivalries" can also indicate "selfishness."

Verse 21 continues the thought from v20. [**v21**] "Envy"—or actually "envies," since it is plural—fits better with the previous grouping. When the crowd before Pilate chose to free Barabbas over Jesus, *he knew that it was out of envy that they had delivered him up* (Mt. 27:18). "Envy" is close to "jealousy." The focus of this word is on the negative emotion of jealousy over the success of another, like our English word "envy." The dictionary definition of the English word is: "a feeling of discontent or covetousness with regard to another's advantages, success, possessions, etc." [Dictionary.com].

"Drunkenness" is a plural noun in Greek, indicating ongoing occurrences. Alcohol is a gift of God, but any good thing can be abused. People can use it to escape problems and suffering, making it a false god offering a false deliverance. *But watch yourselves lest your hearts be weighed down with dissipation and drunkenness* [singular] *and cares of this life, and that day come upon you suddenly like a trap* (Lk. 21:34). *Let us walk properly as in the daytime, not in orgies and drunkenness* ["drunkennesses," plural], *not in sexual immorality and sensuality, not in quarreling and jealousy* (Rom. 13:13). Drunkenness is a sin because intoxication gives almost complete reign to the flesh. The drunk do things they would not normally do. It entails a loss of self-control. Overindulging in alcohol is often used as a pretense for doing what the flesh desires, those things described by all the other fleshly works listed in this chapter.

"Orgies," in our context, refers to sexual acts involving multiple people. But this word is not in the grouping of sexual sins that occurred first in the list. It more generally means reveling, carousing, and merry-making. Originally, this word described a religious festival honoring the wine god Dionysus. These ancient rites were "celebrated with extravagant dancing, singing, drinking," and all that go along with those things [dictionary.com]. This is the opposite of self-control. The flesh is quite creative, so it should not be given free reign to pull the believer into slavery.

This verse is not exhaustive by any means. The flesh is limited only by man's evil imagination. This list is very general in nature. These works of the flesh are contrasted with the fruits of the Spirit, which are more narrowly defined.

Those who *practice*—a critical word—these things and those like them, will not inherit the kingdom of God. This verse speaks not of Judgment Day, but of our state before God, whether we are justified in Christ or not. The fleshly, external practice of sin must cease, if the Spirit is leading someone. But the temptation to sin will not subside. An alcoholic is said to always be an alcoholic, even without drinking alcohol for decades. That makes it clear that the problem is not alcohol itself, but the sinner who cannot use it in a godly way. It is better to avoid the temptation completely, if a person has such a weakness. The flesh always remains active by fighting against the Spirit, but the important thing is that one is not ruled by the flesh. The one whose flesh controls him does not have the Spirit, and without the Spirit there is no faith, no inheritance, no Christ, and no life. So continuing in public sin is a visible witness to the flesh, which is not controlled. Where there is no Spirit, there is no forgiveness or freedom.

[v22] The Spirit produces fruit according to God's will—which is expressed in the Law—but this fruit is of love, not of slavery. It is no surprise that love is the first fruit mentioned, for it encompasses all the others. It is the motivation for all good works in the Spirit. *God's love has been poured into our hearts through the Holy Spirit who has been given to us* (Rom. 5:5). We are not to think of love as an emotion that does nothing—that is the world's idea of love. Love leads to action, specifically, in sacrifice for our neighbor. Love for the Christian is a motion, or action, shown in deeds, not merely an internal, inactive emotion. It is a doing for others, not just a passive, subjective feeling. The heart is never pure, but in faith, people are free from the curse of the Law and acceptable to the Father. No true good work or love is possible without first being freed to be a son of God.

Works of the flesh are opposed to the fruit of the Spirit. A healthy tree produces good fruit. The Christian who has been given the Spirit cannot help but do these things. They are not called works, but inevitable fruit. There is something wrong with a fruit tree that never produces fruit. The fruits of the Spirit are not outward shows of the flesh, but manifestations of the Spirit. Also, "work," instead of fruit, would signify the Law. So these fruits are simply natural products of the Spirit, who worked faith in us.

"Joy" is not something we create—it is the fruit of faith, the result of being adopted by God and receiving the inheritance. Even in suffering, we have much to be thankful for in Christ. *As for what was sown on rocky ground, this is the one who hears the word and immediately receives it with joy* (Mt. 13:20). This joy is from the Spirit, which is why it is called a fruit. *May the God of hope fill you with all joy and peace in believing, so that by the power of the Holy Spirit you may abound in hope* (Rom. 15:13). This joy and peace, safe in Christ, helps us to patiently endure suffering and trials, knowing that we have a better hope and world to wait for and expect.

Joy and peace often stand together in Scripture. We have joy, a living hope, on account of our peace with God. It is right to sing and praise God, no matter how miserable we feel about things or how the flesh suffers. The Spirit is undaunted, so He will cause us to look to the Resurrection. The gift of God in Christ does not change one bit, no matter what happens in this world. *Rejoice in the Lord always; again I will say, rejoice* (Phil. 4:4). We rejoice in the Lord, always, because there is always a solid reason for rejoicing: our salvation has already been procured, and we rest in God's gracious hand.

Because we have peace with God, we lack nothing, even if we seem pitiful by worldly standards. The Gospel of Christ is called the "good news of peace" in Acts 10:36. Paul addressed the Galatians in v3 of the first chapter with God's peace: *Grace to you and peace from God our Father and the Lord Jesus Christ.* This gift is a fruit of the Gospel.

Patience is not something that is given all at once. At times, we must endure painful suffering for years on end, but we trust that God will deliver us. He is patient with us, forgiving us continually in Christ. We learn to show patience when we are disciplined. Patience is not a quick fix—it endures and suffers in living hope. It is never apart from the sure promise of Christ. "Longsuffering" in the KJV is a great translation for this word, now often rendered "patience." It does not mean getting what the flesh wants, but pleasing the Spirit at the cost of what the flesh desires.

"Goodness" is a gracious attitude, or simply kindness. "Generosity" is also a possible translation. The Spirit, in this fruit, moves us to treat all people, even enemies, as God's beloved creatures. Christ Jesus died and rose so that the Father *might show the immeasurable riches of his grace in kindness toward us in Him* (Eph. 2:7). Paul said to the Romans, in 15:14: *I myself am satisfied about you, my brothers, that you yourselves are full of goodness, filled with all knowledge and able to instruct one another.* Filled with the Spirit, we are able to teach and guide by Christ's Word. Showing goodness is an action, not a passive selfishness. *You shall not harden your heart or shut your hand against your poor brother, but you shall open your hand to him and lend him sufficient for his need, whatever it may be* (Dt. 15:7–8).

The Greek word for "faithfulness" can also just mean "faith," depending on the context (see the discussion on page 129, describing the translation difficulties of 3:9). There is no faith without the Spirit. Here "faithfulness"—as in trustworthiness, honesty, and reliability—fits better as a fruit of the Spirit in us. *Bondservants* [slaves] *are to be submissive to their own masters in everything; they are to be well-pleasing, not argumentative, not pilfering, but showing all good faith* [faithfulness], *so that in everything they may adorn the doctrine of God our Savior* (Tit. 2:9–10). All those entrusted with a trust should aim to be faithful, not to get an earthly reward, but to please the Father, who saved us. Jesus calls this fruit the weightier part of the Law: *Woe to you, scribes and Pharisees, hypocrites! For you tithe mint and dill and cumin, and have neglected the weightier matters of the law: justice and mercy and faithfulness. These you ought to have done, without neglecting the others* (Mt. 23:23). We are called to integrity in whatever we do. This pleases the Spirit. It is better to be deceived by assuming the best about someone than think evil of someone unjustly. Love is often deceived, which is good, since true love is not about getting something in return.

Paul continues the list of the spiritual fruits. **[v23]** "Gentleness," here, signifies "meekness" and "friendliness" in our consideration of others. Even in speaking the truth, mildness is called for, so as not to offend or shun people by our tone or language. *I, Paul, myself entreat you, by the meekness and gentleness of Christ—I who am humble when face to face with you, but bold toward you when I am away!* (2 Cor. 10:1). *Correct opponents with gentleness. God may perhaps grant them repentance leading to a knowledge of the truth* (2 Tim. 2:25). We are to give people no unbiblical reason to reject God's Word.

"Self-control" refers to power over one's self—that is, the sinful nature. Only the Spirit can give us this control in freedom and love. This word is used of sexual matters, but it applies to all things. "Moderation" would be another way to understand it.

> *Make every effort to supplement your faith with virtue, and virtue with knowledge, and knowledge with self-control, and self-control with steadfastness, and steadfastness with godliness, and godliness with brotherly affection, and brotherly affection with love. For if these qualities are yours and are increasing, they keep you from being ineffective or unfruitful in the knowledge of our Lord Jesus Christ* (2 Pet. 1:5–8).

We are not to react in an unloving way to what we dislike and hate. A quick, unthinking reaction is usually a work of the flesh, not a fruit of the Spirit.

These fruits of the Spirit offer us more than enough to think about. We can find them in high or low places, whether we are strong or physically weak, whether we work constantly or are confined to a bed. It is excellent to consider them and think of them as the most blessed fruit, though they are despised by the world. They do no look important or very good to sinners. These, however, are the fruit which the Holy Spirit produces, so they are holy and are to be highly sought after. They, like the manifest works of the flesh, also manifest themselves. Perhaps they are overlooked by the world, but they are precious works of the Spirit nonetheless.

"And things like these" parallels the phrase in v21, but Paul does not say that those who do them will inherit the Kingdom of God. That is only through the promise of Christ, not works in us. Only one sure of his inheritance produces such fruit of the Spirit. Instead, we are to see this fruit as fulfillment of the holy Law of God, the Law of love. These fruits are not against the Law, but pleasing to God when done out of love for Him. The Law does play a role for the Christian who has the Spirit. We are not to be against the Law, but not under it or outside it, either. In Christ's freedom, it becomes something we are free to do in love. We are free to have all of the fruits the Spirit produces in us. None of them go against the holy Law.

Paul returns to the flesh after listing its works and the Spirit's fruit. [v24] This is a statement of pure Gospel. In Christ, the flesh is dead and killed. It is crucified, because Christ was crucified with our sin on

Him. This is a great comfort when the flesh rears its head and wars against the Spirit.

Paul explicitly mentions the passions and desires of the flesh. "Passions" are the inward emotions and impulses of the flesh. These we must live with, like a recovering addict, but never are we to indulge in them and drive out the Spirit. We are to see ourselves righteous in Christ, because we are righteous in God's sight. We feel and see our sins constantly, but, in Christ, our sin is crucified. Even the active flesh in us is dead and not held against us.

The word for "desires" is the same one Paul has used already in this chapter when he said: *Walk by the Spirit, and you will not gratify the desires of the flesh* (5:16). The fruit of the Spirit comes from faith in this promise, from believing it is true, even through the flesh does not decrease in strength. Our holiness is in Christ, not in the flesh.

The verb "belongs" is not in the original. It says "of Christ" or just "Christ's." This is by faith, as Paul has laid out many times in this epistle. If we are in Christ, the flesh is dead to us; it cannot condemn us according to the Law. We are to be dead to the Law as the accusing authority and revelation of God's anger. *I have been crucified with Christ. It is no longer I who live, but Christ who lives in me* (2:20).

While we are already dead to the flesh in God's sight, we actively suffer in controlling and restraining the flesh in us. *If anyone would come after me, let him deny himself and take up his cross and follow me* (Mt. 16:24). The cross is good for one thing: killing. This crucifixion happens daily, and it is God's work. Paul knew this well, since he was persecuted for not removing the scandal of the cross.

[v25] We live by the Spirit, in faith, by the promise. The Spirit gives life. The Greek word for "walking in step" means to "follow in line" or "imitate." It is more precise than the simple verb "to walk." We are conformed to the image of Christ by our crosses. In this death to the flesh, the Spirit is given room to lead us. Since the Spirit does it, there is no room for boasting, except in Christ, who made us alive. The only thing we do, according to the flesh, is to die. This is the only possible godly action for our flesh. This is not glamorous at all, but it is a most holy work of the Spirit.

[v26] The word "conceited" means most literally "false" or "vainglo-

rious." Pride goes before a fall. Many evils happen because we think more of ourselves than we should. A related word is used in Phil. 2:3: *Do nothing from selfish ambition or conceit, but in humility count others more significant than yourselves.* Our flesh thinks that love is something others deserve or do not deserve.

Since we are flesh, and anything good is a fruit of the Spirit, there is no reason for conceit. In English, this word is defined as "an excessively favorable opinion of one's own ability, importance, wit, etc." [dictionary.com]. Understanding the role of the Spirit is essential to not overestimating ourselves. For we are born of flesh, but are reborn of the Spirit. *For if Abraham was justified by works, he has something to boast about, but not before God* (Rom. 4:2). We merely follow the Spirit's leading, careful to avoid being ruled by our flesh.

By the end of this chapter, Paul has completely left the thought of the false teachers and the defense of the Gospel. He applies and lays out the basic Spirit/flesh distinction. He names the works of the flesh and the fruit of the Spirit in a general manner, so they may be obvious to us.

Chapter 6

Paul has already taught the Gospel and rebuked the Galatians for listening to false teachers who were trying to bring them under the Law. Chapter 5 dealt with the works of the flesh and the fruit of the Spirit and how the flesh and Spirit are opposed.

Now Paul shows how to deal with one in the congregation who shows himself to be momentarily overtaken by the flesh. [v1] Love, the primary fruit of the Spirit, also corrects and hates evil. It is not weak, flabby, and accepting of everything. Christian love emboldens and moves to action, in order to truly help the neighbor. This love includes correction and rebuke, which is exactly what Paul has done with this letter. Yet, it was all in love, even when he called them foolish, immature, and even unformed children.

Where Christ is not endangered by false doctrine and there is no public, ongoing work of the flesh, we are to endure sin as weakness. We all say things we do not really mean and would not defend. Foot-in-mouth disease, this is called. We do not expect perfection from sinners forgiven in Christ. We bear with these brothers in love, not expecting public repentance for every sin of weakness, though the Christian does repent of all sins, even those he is not aware of.

Verse 1 starts out with "brothers," indicating their unity in Christ. While it says, "if also a man is overtaken in a certain transgression," we are not to search for defects. Though, if someone is overtaken by weakness, then the flesh is ruling or trying to rule them. Then the Spirit is in real danger of being lost. We know exactly what kind of sins the flesh leads to, thanks to 5:19–21. Hidden sins can lead to those more visible sins.

When the flesh controls a person, the Spirit is not leading. A man cannot have two masters, so we are to restore him with the Law and the Gospel. The Spirit does not cause us to break God's Law, so any willful disobedience—that is manifest in deed—we must address. The spirit of the world, however, is timidness. We do not want to bring up the sensitive topics of sin and error, because the world approves of everything, but we are called to believe in Christ and follow His Word, not the world. We should fear God's wrath and the transgressor's future judgment more than our own personal discomfort. Rebuking is to be an act of love.

Who should do it? "You, the spiritual ones." This is not referring to outward holiness of living, because someone without the Spirit can look holy. This refers to one who has the Spirit and is able to instruct others—those who are convicted by God's Word are willing to stand against the flesh, so the Gospel can reign. They are not blown around like a reed in the world's hot air, but know that the truth does not change. Scripture continually warns against novices who may be moved by pride and worldly ambition. What does the previous verse say?

The word for "caught" denotes surprise. Christians with the Spirit cannot plan to sin, but we are tempted and can fall away from the truth by walking according to the flesh.

The English word "artisan," meaning "a skilled craftsman," comes from the same root of the word Paul uses here for "restore." "Restore" can also mean "repair" or "mend." It is the common word for "fashion" or "form." The same word in Greek is used of repairing fishing nets: *And going on from there he saw two other brothers, James the son of Zebedee and John his brother, in the boat with Zebedee their father, mending [repairing] their nets, and he called them* (Mt. 4:21).

How does one restore gently? Gentleness is mentioned in 5:23 as a fruit of the Spirit. It is done out of love for the whole person, not a supposed superiority. Christians are not above sin, since they have the same flesh as everyone else, even though they walk by the Spirit. *I [Paul] therefore, a prisoner for the Lord, urge you to walk in a manner worthy of the calling to which you have been called, with all humility and gentleness, with patience, bearing with one another in love, eager to maintain the unity of the Spirit in the bond of peace* (Eph. 4:1–3). We are all in the same boat, needing the righteousness of Christ as much as anyone else, but some sins are incompatible with the Spirit, or, rather, some sins show that the flesh is pushing aside the Spirit. It is not the sins, in themselves, that condemn, but the loss of the Spirit, which entails a loss of faith and salvation. The person without the Spirit is outside of Christ, under God's wrath.

This church discipline should not be done to embarrass or publicly shame, but in meekness. If a private conversation does not work or is not possible, public rebuke is acceptable for public sin. Only if correction is not received should the final step of excommunication, described in Mt. 18:15–20, be pursued. That is a different situation than what Paul is discussing right here. But, eventually, the congregation as a whole must treat the unrepentant as "a pagan or tax collector." But Paul speaks not of a hypocrite here, but one caught by surprise—one who had the Spirit, but was overcome temporarily. This is unlike Mt. 18. There, we are told how to deal with private sin against another Christian, but a public sin is against everyone, since anyone can be harmed by it. Regardless of the method, those who are spiritual should have the wisdom to gently correct and call to repentance.

We are not to watch for others to fall so much that we fail to notice how we are walking. Examining ourselves is a healthy part of the Christian life. This self-examination is also necessary for receiving the Lord's Supper, according to Christ's Word (1 Cor. 11:28). We are not to tolerate sin, but we should not be slow to forgive, either.

"Be watchful, observe yourself" implies watching attentively. That seems strange, since we are normally preoccupied with ourselves. But consider how you are walking, not just what you covet or how your feel. Ignore the chapter divisions and focus on the content. Read from 5:25. How are you walking: in the Spirit or in the flesh? We cannot know this important distinction without being taught and constantly reminded. We are after all, only flesh, unless we are given the Spirit through the promise. We can, without forethought, give into the flesh and be thrown off course.

We should observe where we are and see whether we are preventing God's Spirit from working in us. *Therefore, my beloved, as you have always obeyed, so now, not only as in my presence but much more in my absence, work out your own salvation with fear and trembling, for it is God who works in you, both to will and to work for his good pleasure* (Phil. 2:12–13). The Christian life is not an upward journey of improvement. Rather, we can be in danger at any moment, because the flesh is firmly with us and does not want to die. We must take care not to be misled or caught by flesh-strengthening sins. We are also tempted to sin by the Devil, who is called the "tempter" in Mt. 4:3.

The word for "watch" is used to form a longer word in Greek which is translated "bishop" or "overseer." The pastor, or shepherd, is always to do this by correcting, teaching, and even rebuking, but always in gentleness. *Pay careful attention to yourselves and to all the flock, in which the Holy Spirit has made you overseers, to care for the church of God, which he obtained with his own blood* (Acts 20:28). But this is not just the pastor's responsibility. Do you know the Gospel? Do you consider yourself spiritual? Then do not sit in judgment on the sidelines, but love your brother enough to restore him.

This spiritual restoration is the opposite of provoking out of conceit (5:26). Spiritual judging is good when it helps in love, but worldly judging uses the Law selectively to lift oneself up above the neighbor. In Christ, there is no first or last, but only forgiven sinners. We too also might need to be restored by the skill of someone spiritual. In this way, the Spirit works through others. We are not to be too proud to be corrected by another sinner, for it is really God the Holy Spirit doing it.

To use an illustration, I usually knew when my 18-month-old son was going to trip, when we were out on a walk. He would see something that caught his attention, perhaps a big truck, but as he focused on that, his head and body would turn. That alone did not make him fall, but any slight misstep and or rough place then would, because he was not paying attention. This is similar to the Christian and his relationship to the Gospel promise. *Therefore let anyone who thinks that he stands take heed lest he fall* (1 Cor. 10:12). Paul is instructing on how to love and how the Spirit manifests Himself in us for the sake of others. Love is always directed outward.

[v2] After all the harsh words against the Law of Moses and its inability to save, we have here the phrase: "the Law of Christ." This is the Law starting to be fulfilled in love, for those in Christ. Those outside of Christ, not knowing God's love, must see the Law as a burden and master, because they are slaves to sin. But one who is spiritually free in Christ sees the Law in a new light. The Law is not a tedious, disconnected list of regulations we are forced to do, but in the Spirit

we desire to love others as God wills. All flows from the love of God, poured into our hearts by the Spirit. We are not to consider ourselves, since we are already holy in Christ. Without Christ, there is no "Law of Christ" to live in.

"Bear" means "to carry." We are to make the burdens of others our own. We can help carry them. This is done out of love. Here, Paul gives more instruction on what love actually looks like. The world says that "it's the thought that counts." But love cannot be merely a thought. True Christian love acts in service to the neighbor. The same phrase is used in the parable of the workers: *These last worked only one hour, and you have made them equal to us who have borne* [carried] *the burden of the day and the scorching heat* (Mt. 20:12). This bearing in love means putting up with other sinners. Without this love, there can be no unity, no congregation, and no bond of peace. Love sacrifices itself, not because it has to, but because the Spirit moves us to. The opposite—not bearing burdens—leads to *enmity, strife, jealousy, fits of anger, rivalries, dissensions,* [and] *divisions* (5:20).

"Burdens" is plural. The word, in Greek, means "weight or hardship." It is something that is not easy or fun to carry. It is work to the flesh, but an act of love and free to one in the Spirit. This is not a burden God lays on us, as a demand, but something we willingly pick up. It is to be like Christ, since we are given Christ's Spirit. This love fulfills the Law. *For the whole law is fulfilled in one word "You shall love your neighbor as yourself"* (5:14). Love does not consider itself, but sees others' burdens and makes them its own.

There are all sorts of burdens. This is the Law of Christ for the spiritual, those with the Spirit. The motive is to be like Christ, who is in us and has already justified us. You are free to see and pick up the burdens of those around you in Christ. Freedom is not doing nothing, for Christ took our curse upon Himself, making it His own. He did it in love, choosing humility. Insofar as we are new, the Law of Moses is not the Law over us. We are in the Law of Christ. We have plenty of opportunities for service in the Spirit, right where God has placed us. Paul uses "law" in an entirely different way, here. It is fulfilled only in true love by God's Spirit in the Christian. In Christ, the Law is opportunity, not slavery.

[v3] Of ourselves, we are flesh. Whatever is good is from the Spirit.

So, Paul's admonition is for humility. We are really nothing. Paul calls himself the chief of sinners, in whom nothing good dwells (Rom. 7:18). Are we better than him? No, we all are Law-breakers, according to the legal code.

This is not the normal word for "deceive." It is the only time this Greek word is used in the New Testament. The noun form of the same root is used by Paul in Tit. 1:10: *For there are many who are insubordinate, empty talkers and deceivers, especially those of the circumcision party.* It means here "to deceive one's own mind." "He deludes himself," we might say. It is not the Spirit's work, in other words.

We are not to have a high opinion of ourselves, since everything we have is a gift of God. We deserve—a Law word—nothing but punishment, but Christ loved us. Of ourselves we are "nothing," as Paul says here, but precisely where we are nothing in ourselves, we are everything in Christ. He is our righteousness, our status before the Father. This verse speaks of what we are in the flesh, outside of Christ.

[v4] While boasting seems out of place, we are able to boast in Christ. We are to examine, test, and prove our own work. If we do so, we will not think of ourselves more than we ought. No one is without sin. Even works that seem great are done by people with sinful hearts. No one is completely spiritual. This word for "test" was originally used to describe weighing and proofing metals.

"Reason" is not in the Greek text. It says: "then he will have only a boast in himself, and not for another." "Boast" can mean the boast itself or the justification for a boast, the basis for it.

We are not to boast in comparison to others, which would be to submit ourselves to the Law. But if our boast is in Christ, it is because we have the Spirit. Then we will not think more of ourselves than we ought. We are doing *our* works in freedom, not the works of others. The word "boast" can be positive or negative. One translation renders it: "But let each one examine his own work and then he will have reason for boasting in himself alone, and not in comparison with someone else" [MRINT]. Some have translated it as "not in regard to the other person" [YLT; Lenski, 300]. That fits the context. In love, there are no comparisons under the Law, because we are led by the Spirit, not our own covetous flesh. In the Gospel, we answer to Christ alone who forgives all our sin.

There is a parallel passage in Rom. 14:4–6:

Who are you to pass judgment on the servant of another? It is before his own master that he stands or falls. And he will be upheld, for the Lord is able to make him stand. One person esteems one day as better than another, while another esteems all days alike. Each one should be fully convinced in his own mind. The one who observes the day, observes it in honor of the Lord. The one who eats, eats in honor of the Lord, since he gives thanks to God, while the one who abstains, abstains in honor of the Lord and gives thanks to God.

We who have the truth in Christ need not compare ourselves to others. That is not loving or helpful to anyone. We bear burdens, putting others above ourselves. Our boast is in the Spirit, not with respect to other sinners. In the Gospel, we do not need to have any reference, or comparison, to others—Christ is everything for us in faith.

[v5] A "load" is not a burden. We are to bear one another's burdens, as it says in v2. But the word for "load" here in v5 is different. It is used of cargo in Acts 27:10: *Sirs, I perceive that the voyage will be with injury and much loss, not only of the cargo* [load] *and the ship, but also of our lives.* Jesus also used this word: *For my yoke is easy, and my burden* [load] *is light* (Mt. 11:30). It has a more neutral meaning than "burden."

We all have our own responsibilities, duties, and crosses to bear. We cannot share what the Lord has given specifically to us. It is our own, and we must answer to Christ, not others. So our reason to boast is only in comparison to ourselves, not others. This is a judgment in the Spirit, not with reference to laws or others who demand something of us. In freedom, we care only about what God our Father wills.

In the words of Luther: "One who carries out his office correctly and faithfully does not care what the world says about him; he does not care whether it praises him or blames him. He has his boast within himself, which is the testimony of his conscience and a boasting in God" [*Galatians*, 117]. There is no room for opinion polls or popularity contests in determining a good work. We should have a holy confidence in what we do—a boast in ourselves, knowing that we possess the Spirit of truth and walk according to Him. But, because we are weak and fleshly, we care what people think. We think that if everyone hates us, then we have failed and do not please God, but He calls us out of the

261

world by giving us a new Spirit. True love, born of the Spirit, will make us hated by the world.

We know what God has given us to do, and to do it faithfully is enough. We do not live by others' standards, but free in the Law of Christ. We *do* have works to do, planned beforehand by our Father. They have nothing to do with our status in Christ, but, in the world, we have been entrusted with duties. We are to do them in freedom, not as slaves, but as sons of God and heirs of the kingdom.

[**v6**] Teachers of God's Word should be supported. Is Paul being greedy because it obviously also includes himself? It is for our sake that the Spirit gave these words. Christians expect the Word of God to be free and often take the preaching of the truth lightly. The "word" is the Word of God. It brings Christ's righteousness without money, but teachers are real people, with bodily needs and, often, families. We should exalt the office of preaching as much as companies glorify CEOs. Pastors bring us God's Word, and, therefore, Christ's righteousness. We magnify the office, not the person, because of the Word. It is shameful for pastors to be treated like hirelings, to pay them little for delivering the Gospel of peace. It is even worse to dismiss them and deny their call when they are speaking the truth of God. Paul, here, makes it a Christian work to support the teaching office and those in it. This, of course, includes not only material things, but "all good things." They also need our encouragement, for pastors retain the flesh, even while they wield the sword of the Word against Satan. This is a praiseworthy calling, but one that is quite burdensome to the pastor's flesh.

This word translated "share" in the ESV speaks of a common participation, a communal sharing. This word is used of sins that we are not to participate in, but also of hardships we are not to avoid: *But rejoice insofar as you share* [have in common] *Christ's sufferings, that you may also rejoice and be glad when his glory is revealed* (1 Pet. 4:13). Here the meaning of "all good things" is clear; nothing is to be withheld that is good. This is rarely done, because so many take the Gospel for granted, expecting it to always be there when they might want to hear it. But the pastoral office is a great weight. Carrying and forgiving sins and putting up with hypocrites and people seeking false glory is burdensome. The one who is being taught or "catechized" (as it reads in Greek) should do this. We are to learn and not be too stuffed with the Spirit to hear God's Word.

Do you not know that those who are employed in the temple service get their food from the temple, and those who serve at the altar share in the sacrificial offerings? In the same way, the Lord commanded that those who proclaim the gospel should get their living by the gospel (1 Cor. 9:13–14). Those who preach the Gospel are to be devoted to the task of studying the Scriptures and applying God's Word. Although this does not seem like real work to the world, it is for the sake of Christ's ministry. It is our Lord's will to have overseers over us.

The preceding verses are strengthened with a threat. **[v7]** We have here a different Greek word for "deceive" than we had in v3. This verb denotes being led astray, something that causes one to wander off course or be mistaken. The gardener knows this truth: if he plants no seeds, he will not harvest the produce he wants. In Christ, we are not eternally condemned for our sin, but there are consequences to our actions here on earth. The Lord does not promise to shield us from the result of every poor decision. God is not mocked. We cannot treat Him or His Law with contempt and expect blessings because of it.

What we plant and sow is what we reap and gather. This fits with the fruit of the Spirit in chapter 5. On the subject of giving, Paul uses the same analogy: *The point is this: whoever sows sparingly will also reap sparingly, and whoever sows bountifully will also reap bountifully. Each one must give as he has decided in his heart, not reluctantly or under compulsion, for God loves a cheerful giver* (2 Cor. 9:6–7). Our spiritual planting yields a harvest of spiritual fruit pleasing to Christ.

The sowing analogy is broadened. **[v8]** To sow "the flesh," or, "with regard to the flesh," reaps destruction. The verse says "his flesh," since we all have the flesh. But we are not to be led by it. That leads to destruction, ruin, and decay. This is not eternal punishment, but the fruit of the flesh, the works of our natural sinful nature. The work of the flesh actually leads to the fire of hell. *God has granted to us his precious and very great promises, so that through them you may become partakers of the divine nature, having escaped from the corruption that is in the world because of sinful desire* (2 Pet. 1:4).

The result, or harvest, of walking in line with the Spirit is eternal life. We do not sow into the Spirit or for the Spirit, but by the Spirit's leading. There are different amounts of good fruit produced in the parable of the seed: *But those that were sown on the good soil are the ones who hear the word and accept it and bear fruit, thirtyfold and sixtyfold and a hundredfold* (Mk. 4:20). But when the Word takes root and faith endures, fruit will result.

Corruption and eternal life are not polar opposites. Even the one who has reaped according to the flesh can have life in Christ, if there is repentance. There are no preconditions for Christ's righteousness. It is apart from the Law. But the destruction of the flesh *does* lead to eternal punishment. The goats, the unbelievers, *will go away into eternal punishment, but the righteous* [the sheep] *into eternal life* (Mt. 25:46).

Those who sow according to their own flesh in order to reap earthly riches, acclaim, or pleasure will only find the poverty of hell. But those patient in enduring their loads, by the guiding of the Spirit, will reap eternal life. We can have confidence that we do not follow the Spirit in vain. This applies to supporting the preaching office, and all other works of the Spirit. Just because we are saved by grace, apart from works, does not mean that works are optional. The world is in a dire famine of good works. The Spirit does not lead us away from works, but *to* true works, done in love, which fulfill the Law of Christ.

We do not reap according to our own spirit or soul, but the Holy Spirit. This means we must deny ourselves, so that our flesh does not get what it wants. We are to do so by the Spirit—meaning how we live, our walk (5:25). A similar thought is expressed in Rom. 8:12–13: *So then, brothers, we are debtors, not to the flesh, to live according to the flesh. For if you live according to the flesh you will die, but if by the Spirit you put to death the deeds of the body, you will live.* The Spirit, not the flesh, must be our leader. We cannot trick or mock God. Sowing leads to reaping more of the same. The farmer plants the same kind of seed he hopes to get. But he expects to get much more back in order to compensate him for the trouble of sowing and harvesting. We can count on getting much more back in the Spirit. We do not struggle to walk in the Spirit without the hope of a greater reward.

[v9] Doing good—what is right according to the Spirit—speaks of tangible acts. The fruit of the Spirit is manifested visibly. Love is an action for the Christian. There is much to discourage us. Satan works to make us despair, not just do bad things. He wants us to think there is no

point, that we are rowing up a waterfall. The parable of the persistent widow also shows that we should not give up, be discouraged, or lose heart. *And he told them a parable to the effect that they ought always to pray and not lose heart* (Lk. 18:1). Jesus likewise tells his frightened disciples many times to take heart, that is, to rest in the promise that He is bigger than our restless, fleshly hearts. Paul reiterates this truth in other epistles, too. *As for you, brothers, do not grow weary in doing good* (2 Thess. 3:13). *Therefore, having this ministry by the mercy of God, we do not lose heart* [become wearied] (2 Cor. 4:1).

The day of harvest will come in due time and at the proper season, that is, when it has been set. Only the Father knows the time of the final judgment, but we are promised that it will be our vindication. We do not suffer for nothing. We will be justified before all people who have ever lived. We wait in the hope of expectation, knowing we will reap at the right time. Our Lord has not forgotten us as we live by faith.

Paul encourages us to *not give up*. The Greek phrase for "give up" is used of physical and mental exhaustion in Mt. 15:32: *Then Jesus called his disciples to him and said, "I have compassion on the crowd because they have been with me now three days and have nothing to eat. And I am unwilling to send them away hungry, lest they faint* [give up] *on the way."* Here it is used in the context of faith and sowing by the Spirit. We are not saved by works, but, if we frustrate the Spirit, we put ourselves in grave danger of losing faith. So, Paul exhorts those in Christ to do works of love in the Spirit.

[v10] "Therefore" marks the end and summation of the exhortation to works. Good works are not a burden for the Christian, but an opportunity to love. The Greek word for "opportunity" is the same as that for "due season" in the previous verse. The Spirit is not inactive, but moves us to love others. We do not need to look for a higher purpose in this life, something great and grand that people will notice. Simply bringing children to Christ, taking food to the neighbor, or visiting the sick is enough for us to do. Every work in the Spirit is great and noble, because, in faith, we are doing God's work, or, rather, God the Spirit is the one working through us.

Knowing our future is secure, that we are free from all laws, makes us free in the Spirit. We do not have to worry about tomorrow or make everything about us. *See then that you walk circumspectly, not as fools but as wise, redeeming the time* [opportunity], *because the days are evil* (Eph. 5:16; NKJV). We are free to be humble like Christ, who did not consider His own welfare in loving us. This is spiritual love, which the world cannot understand.

We have a different Greek word for "doing" here, which is not used in v9. It means "to be active, work out, or accomplish." It is even used of earning one's living. Our world thinks of life energy in terms of money, but the Spirit is limitless. We do not need to conserve our love, because it cannot be exhausted in the Spirit. Once we are free in Christ and partake of forgiveness, we see works in the right light—not as Law-measured burdens, but as fruits of the Spirit, who is deposited within us.

We do not need to divine God's precise will in what we should do in every activity of daily life. We are free in the Spirit to help and love others according to our good judgment. That is true freedom, motivated by love, not "musts."

No one is omitted from this excellence, but it should be directed especially to those in Christ, who live by faith. The "house of faith," speaks of a family, the physical closeness of God's saints. We are related to family and friends in a human way, but it is the one Spirit who unites us most closely. *So then you are no longer strangers and aliens, but you are fellow citizens with the saints and members of the household of God* (Eph. 2:19). Again, the fruit of the Spirit is tangible; it is directed toward specific people. The text says "to," indicating its referents. We have two groups: all (the living) and the household of faith, which is primary. What is spiritual is actually manifested physically—to our neighbor.

[**v11**] Paul refers to the original written manuscript, which we do not have before us. In fact, no one has it, as it has not survived. We must be careful not to say what we cannot prove. Thankfully, we do have many old copies to compare and know with surety the letters and words Paul wrote. He witnesses that this epistle is genuine by his very hand. "Letters" here means individual letters of the alphabet. It is plural in the original Greek. Yet, the KJV translation gives it an entirely different meaning: *Ye see how large a letter I have written unto you with mine own hand.* "Letters" in the plural does not allow this interpretation, so we must say it is a bad translation of this verse.

Why did Paul write in large letters? Put aside practical and historical speculations that do not address the content of this letter, such as bad eyesight or a physical difficulty. Large letters also draw attention. We must suppose this fact carries some meaning. He tells us, so we do not need the original writing of Paul to deduce it. Writing large is like typing in all caps or bolding letters on a computer to emphasize them. Apart from reading into the words things we cannot prove or disprove, we know for sure that Paul himself establishes the authenticity of these words. He draws all eyes to them. We can read in the same way the Galatians did, even without the original writing of Paul, because he describes in words how he wrote. In 2 Tim. 3:15, Paul refers to the Scriptures, our Old Testament, as "letters:" *from childhood you have been acquainted with the sacred writings* [letters], *which are able to make you wise for salvation through faith in Christ Jesus.*

The very end of 1 Cor. says: *I, Paul, write this greeting with my own hand. If anyone has no love for the Lord, let him be accursed. Our Lord, come! The grace of the Lord Jesus be with you. My love be with you all in Christ Jesus. Amen.* Here in Galatians he also mentions not just the final greeting, but the letters themselves, which he wrote himself. Regardless of how much of Galatians he wrote down personally, the content and words are his, but, more than that, they are also God's own words.

"See" invites the Galatians to look at his letters like little children. It reminds us of Jesus inviting Thomas to explore the wounds in His glorified body. In other letters, Paul wrote with another's hand. In Colossians he writes merely one final line: *I, Paul, write this greeting with my own hand. Remember my chains. Grace be with you* (4:18). Rom. 16:22 even indicates the writer of the epistle: *I Tertius, who wrote this letter, greet you in the Lord.* At the end of 2 Thess. we have another reference to the distinctiveness of his handwriting: *I, Paul, write this greeting with my own hand. This is the sign of genuineness in every letter of mine; it is the way I write. The grace of our Lord Jesus Christ be with you all* (4:17–18).

Some letters, both long (2 Cor.) and short (Philemon), have a greeting with no reference to the writing of the letter, so drawing attention to his handwriting was not formulaic for Paul. This was no ordinary letter. We see his fire and zeal for the Gospel and his deep, motherly concern for the addressees in this letter. Think of this final greeting as both a signature and a final message and summary.

The appeal to his own writing leads into a final word against the Galatian heresy. [**v12**] This is like a closing summary by a lawyer. He states the truth plainly and succinctly. Those who put forth a good "face," or "showing," in the flesh are dealing with the material, outward things of the Law. They desire to look good before others. This is in contrast to the v4 statement that one's boast should be in oneself, not others. The false teachers care only about appearances, not Christ. They are making their "showing," their case, only about the flesh. In fact, they are ashamed to be treated as Christ was, to be persecuted. That is why they are forcing circumcision upon the Galatians as the end and fulfillment of the Gospel and the essential ingredient to justification, but in doing this they nullified all Christ did, making another gospel.

Paul does not say they are especially evil, just that the false teachers want to avoid persecution. Paul is not making a judgment of their hearts, but stating what is plain to see. So, even they are not firm in their convictions, since the basic idea of a Christian returning to the Mosaic Law does not fit the Gospel at all. They are not dealing with or acting by the Spirit, but only the flesh.

There is always pressure to fit in, especially in our culture. In the name of diversity and getting along with everyone, we are tempted to deny Christ, rather than face persecution. We do not want to be thought of as backwards and simple. But there is no Christ without the cross. Let the text teach. The only reason for this forcing of circumcision is to not be persecuted for the cross of Christ. "Persecute" means "to oppose, pursue, seek after, or harass." It can be used positively, but here it definitely refers to hostile persecution.

The false teachers were compelling and forcing circumcision, which meant an acceptance of the whole Law. In other words, they denied the Gospel. Ceremonial works, including circumcision, cannot be free under such circumstances. *To accept circumcision is to reject Christ. Look: I, Paul, say to you that if you accept circumcision, Christ will be of no advantage to you* (5:2). While circumcision is kept free in Christian churches today, we can be sure that other optional, material matters will be falsely forced upon Christians. Christ's freedom cannot reign unopposed in this world.

While we must be compelled by rules and authority, even in churches, we do not submit to man-made laws for salvation. When those who preach the Gospel introduce the Law as a helper or means of empowerment, in addition to Christ's righteousness, they create another gospel. *I am astonished that you are so quickly deserting him who called you in the grace of Christ and are turning to a different gospel—not that there is another one, but there are some who trouble you and want to distort the gospel of Christ* (1:6–7).

Accepting circumcision would have seemed like an easy fix in the face of persecution, which was physical and real. Paul himself was such a persecutor at one time, before he was called to be an apostle. Yet, at this controversial point hangs the Gospel. Paul makes this clear, in big letters, for all to see and hear. We should expect real persecution as well. Our aim cannot be merely to keep up appearances. Our God wants us to hold and confess the truth with a sincere conscience. The cross of Christ saves us, but also brings a real cross to us. Persecution is still a sign of faithfulness to God's Word.

[v13] To be circumcised under this pressure and false understanding of justification necessitates that one keep the Law—to try to please God outside of Christ. But those who are circumcised into the Law do not keep the Law—it is impossible. Christ would not have come if the Law could do what the false teachers said it could. Even in them, the Law shows no power. Paul is saying nothing new here, but summarizes the matter and draws their mind to the points he made earlier.

If their boast is in the flesh, it is not in Christ, but before the world, the very ones who persecute Christ. If they submit to circumcision for righteousness, then they have turned from Christ and do not seek Him by faith. Paul utterly destroys his opponents' arguments. The whole letter, from different angles and approaches, buttresses the truth and shatters this falsehood. This is done so that Christ's Gospel is uplifted.

[v14] "May it not be for me to boast, except in the cross." Paul uses this phrase, "May it never happen," often, including twice in this letter. *But if, in our endeavor to be justified in Christ, we too were found to be sinners, is Christ then a servant of sin? Certainly not* [May it never happen]*!* (2:17). *Is the law then contrary to the promises of God? Certainly not!* [May it never happen] *For if a law had been given that could give life, then righteousness would indeed be by the law* (3:21).

The cross of Christ is the place where our redemption was procured. It stands for Christ's suffering, punishment, and death for our sin. But the cross also stands for the persecution we will face. The cross is not an abstract idea or philosophy. It becomes living and real for those who live in Christ by faith. We will suffer if we have Christ's cross as our righteousness, but it is truly a small yoke to bear, since we know God and possess eternal life. Paul died to the world by crucifixion. It happened objectively by Christ's cross, but a personal crucifixion was still ongoing in his flesh, through suffering and persecution. The world has been killed to him. He will only boast in Christ's suffering and his own. Both testify to the Gospel. Everything outside of Christ—the Devil, the opponents in Galatia, and all evil—is crucified to Paul. There is nothing except Christ. To know God is to know Christ crucified and partake of His sufferings. We are crucified—what a great promise to hold dear. Nothing in the world, or in us, can harm us. Christ is everything, through His cross.

It is through Christ that we are delivered from the world. This is the promise upon which faith relies. It is already accomplished, although we do not see the final result yet. In Christ, there is no world and there is no flesh. All is restored in faith, even if this hope is only a hope for now. Though we face great temptation, and the world does possess the power of Satan, we are to believe all is dead, outside of Christ. We live to God and have His Spirit. In Christ, the world is dead, and, conversely, we are dead to the world. It can have no influence over a dead person. *And those who belong to Christ Jesus have crucified the flesh with its passions and desires* (5:24).

[v15] Circumcision itself is not the main concern. *For in Christ Jesus neither circumcision nor uncircumcision counts for anything, but only faith working through love* (5:6). But because it is the point at which the Gospel is being unraveled, Paul spares no effort in this letter in addressing it. He displays the full range of emotions, from the bitter anger against the Judaizers to motherly concern for his congregations, his unformed babies.

Neither having a bit of skin, nor removing a bit of skin, has anything to do with true righteousness. It was only won by the cross of Christ. It is delivered in the message of the cross. *For I decided to know nothing among you except Jesus Christ and him crucified* (1 Cor. 2:2). This

Gospel gives the Spirit, and, apart from Him, there is only flesh and worldly concerns. Now you are dead to the world, completely free from it. In Christ, this world has nothing to offer—He supplies everything. He is our righteousness.

In Christ, we are new. Outside of Christ, there is no Spirit or newness for us. Creation stands for the created world. The world is now new to us, because we are new, forgiven, free, adopted, and heirs in Christ. The same phrase for "new creation" is used in 2 Cor. 5:17: *Therefore, if anyone is in Christ, he is a new creation. The old has passed away; behold, the new has come.* This is a promise to grasp, not an observable reality yet.

[v16] Paul again refers to "walking," which can only be done in the Spirit. "Rule" is "canon" in Greek, a norm or measurement. The canon of Scripture measures all teaching. We are to measure all things by Christ and the new creations we are in Him. A rule generally suggests obedience to a law to our ears, but this is more of a principle or "just standard"—by which to judge all things, including ourselves. We are to walk in this principle, just as we live in Christ. This is not an idea to be treated as a new toy—to be played with a bit and then thrown aside. *If we live by the Spirit, let us also keep in step [walk] with the Spirit* (5:25). In both verses, the stronger form of "walk" is used, meaning "to follow in line with" or "to imitate." To walk by this rule is nothing more than to live by faith. This is not about only outward doing, but having a new hope and life. This very promise is our life. We live in Christ, and all things are made new in His righteousness.

The true Israel is all those in Christ who partake of salvation. Israel proper is God's people, those justified by faith. It is not based on a physical trait or certain genetic code. It is being new to God in Christ. Many of physical Israel, starting with Abraham, were also of the Israel of God, but most were only of Israel according to the flesh, not by faith. *For not all who are descended from Israel belong to Israel* (Rom. 9:6). Romans deals extensively with this teaching. In Christ, we are new, chosen to be God's holy people. Therefore, we have peace with God, but not the world.

This verse recalls the start of this great letter to the Galatians: *Grace to you and peace from God our Father and the Lord Jesus Christ* (1:3). Here we have "mercy" instead of "grace," but these two terms are

271

theologically related. In Christ, we have them both. These are spiritual things. They are ours, no matter what we have in this world or how much we suffer. They are the prime things that Paul wants delivered. They undergird the entire letter. It is correct to say that the Gospel is simple, but false teaching is not, since it is perverts the truth of God. So, Paul used logic, spiritual reasoning, and the Scriptures to demolish these arguments against Christ. Sophisticated heresies deserve sophisticated responses.

In the second to last verse, Paul appeals to his suffering in Christ one last time. [**v17**] The Greek word for "trouble" means "toil," "hardship," and (most literally) "beating." Paul needs no more troubles—he has suffered for Christ. He bids no one bring him any more such suffering as he has encountered in Galatia. One can sense a weariness of dealing with this issue. It has weighed on him heavily, since he so desires to have Christ formed in them, but they are not even infants yet.

He refers to "the remaining," or "the rest." He considers the matter closed. He refers not to marks on Jesus, because we do not have access to His glorified body, to inspect it as Thomas could have. Instead, he refers to his own body and calls its marks Christ's. He bears them as tokens of God's love and a sign of his holy calling.

Paul bears the marks, literally, the "stigmas," of Christ. He bears, or carries, them in pride. They mark Paul as Christ's chosen apostle. They indicate the cross he boasts in and by which he has been freed (vv14–15). In 2 Cor. 11:23, Paul begins a list of his credentials with the same Greek word we have here as "trouble": *Are they servants of Christ? I am a better one—I am talking like a madman—with far greater labors* [troubles]*, far more imprisonments, with countless beatings, and often near death.*

He refers not to his flesh, the source of sin, but his physical body. These were not just general ailments or scars, but signs of Christ's cross, received in this world for preaching the cross. His persecution and chains mark him as Christ's own, and faithful to Him. No other proof is necessary. The matter is settled.

Verse 16 does not have "grace," but "mercy." Here in v18, the last one of this letter, we have "grace" given in a blessing. [**v18**] This is a benediction. It is by grace we enter into Christ's righteousness. It is through Christ's crucified body and exists because of His accomplished redemption for the world. But Paul especially refers to their "spirit." This grace is not for the flesh, which cannot be redeemed. It is for the new man, the one created by the Spirit.

With "brothers" Paul signifies that their fellowship is unbroken. He is still one with them in Christ, under this grace of Christ, freed from the Law and its dealings with the beggarly elements.

"Amen" is the Hebrew word which confirms that this is a statement of truth and faith. We can rest in the Gospel God delivered through Paul. Christ is our Lord, who was crucified, through whom grace comes to us today, just as it did for the Galatians through Paul's words. Amen.

Works Cited

Das, A. Andrew. *Galatians.* In *Concordia Commentary Series.* St. Louis: CPH, 2014.

Dictionary.com Unabridged. Random House. http://dictionaryreference.com.

Chrysostom. *Homilies on Galatians.* Trans. Gross Alexander. *Nicene and Post-Nicene Fathers.* First Series. Vol. 13. Ed. Philip Schaff. Buffalo, NY: Christian Literature Publishing Co., 1889. Rev. and ed. for New Advent by Kevin Knight. http://www.newadvent.org/fathers/2310.htm.

Lenski, R.C.H. Lenski. *The Interpretation of St. Paul's Epistle to the Galatians, Ephesians and Philippians.* Lutheran Book Concern, 1937; Minneapolis: Augsburg, 1961.

Lindberg, Conrad Emil. *Christian Dogmatics and Notes on the History of Dogma.* Trans. C. E. Hoffsten. Rock Island, IL: Augustana Book Concern, 1922.

Luther, Martin. *Complete Sermons of Martin Luther.* 7 vol. Eds. John Nicholas Lenker and Eugene F. A. Klug. Grand Rapids: Baker Books, 2000; Vol. 1–4 published as *Sermons of Martin Luther: The Church Postils.* 8 vol. in 4 vol. 1995; Vol. 5–7 published as *Sermons of Martin Luther: The House Postils.* 3 vol. 1996.

Luther, Martin. *Lectures on Galatians* (1535). *Luther's Works.* Eds. Jaroslav Pelikan and Helmut Lehmann. Vol. 26–27. St. Louis: Concordia Publishing House; Philadelphia: Fortress Press, 1955–86.

Maurer, Wilhelm. *Historical Commentary on the Augsburg Confession.* Trans. H. George Anderson. Philadelphia: Fortress Press, 1986.

Pieper, Francis. *Christian Dogmatics.* 4 vols. Trans. T. Engelder, J. T. Mueller, and W. W. F. Albrecht. St. Louis: Concordia Publishing House, 1953.

www.ingramcontent.com/pod-product-compliance
Lightning Source LLC
Chambersburg PA
CBHW071953040426
42447CB00009B/1317